Queer Histories and the Politics of Policing

Despite ongoing challenges to the criminalisation and surveillance of queer lives, police leaders are now promoted as allies and defenders of LGBT rights. However, in this book, Emma K. Russell argues that the surface inclusion of select LGBT identities in the protective aspirations of the law is deeply tenuous and conditional, and that police recognition is both premised upon and reproductive of an imaginary of 'good queer citizens'—those who are respectable, responsible, and 'just like' their heterosexual counterparts.

Based on original empirical research, Russell presents a detailed analysis of the political complexities, compromises, and investments that underpin LGBT efforts to achieve sexual rights and protections. With a historical trajectory that spans the so-called 'decriminalisation' era to the present day, she shows how LGBT activists have both resisted and embraced police incursions into queer space, and how—with LGBT support—police leaders have re-crafted histories of violence as stories of institutional progress.

Queer Histories and the Politics of Policing advances broader understandings of the nature of police power and the shifting terrain of sexual citizenship. It will be of interest to students and researchers of criminology, sociology, and law engaged in studies of policing, social justice, and gender and sexuality.

Emma K. Russell is Lecturer in Crime, Justice and Legal Studies at La Trobe University, Australia. She researches in the fields of queer criminology and critical carceral studies. She is the co-author of *Resisting Carceral Violence: Women's Imprisonment and the Politics of Abolition* (2018).

Queering Criminology and Criminal Justice

Edited by
Matthew Ball, Queensland University of Technology
Angela Dwyer, University of Tasmania
Vanessa Panfil, Old Dominion University

Research into the criminal justice experiences of lesbian, gay, bisexual, transgender, and queer (LGBTQ+) people has grown significantly in recent years, particularly under the label of 'Queer Criminology'. Criminologists and criminal justice scholars are increasingly responding to the historical exclusion of LGBTQ+ people and their lack of representation in criminal justice studies and policies.

This series explores LGBTQ+ issues in relation to crime, criminology, and criminal justice, including LGBTQ+ victimisation and offending; theoretical and conceptual developments required to ensure criminology better represents LGBTQ+ people; and studies into the experiences of LGBTQ+ people in relation to criminal justice agents, institutions, and practices.

Queering Criminology and Criminal Justice serves as a focal point around which the field of queer criminology can develop and allows a diverse array of researchers globally (including those from the Global South) to discuss a variety of criminological topics. It also aims to reinforce the importance of queer and intersectional critiques to criminology more broadly and act as a point of reference for criminologists outside of queer criminology, as well as criminal justice agents/LGBTQ+ service providers seeking to develop more inclusive, representative, and diverse understandings and practices.

Queer Histories and the Politics of Policing
Emma K. Russell

For more information about this series, please visit: www.routledge.com/Queering-Criminology-and-Criminal-Justice/book-series/QCCJ

Queer Histories and the Politics of Policing

Emma K. Russell

Routledge
Taylor & Francis Group
LONDON AND NEW YORK

First published 2020 by Routledge

2 Park Square, Milton Park, Abingdon, Oxon, OX14 4RN
52 Vanderbilt Avenue, New York, NY 10017

Routledge is an imprint of the Taylor & Francis Group, an informa business

First issued in paperback 2020

British Library Cataloguing-in-Publication Data
A catalogue record for this book is available from the British Library

Library of Congress Cataloging-in-Publication Data
Names: Russell, Emma K., 1986–
Title: Queer histories and the politics of policing / Emma K. Russell.
Description: Milton Park, Abingdon, Oxon ; New York, NY : Routledge, 2020. |
Series: Queering criminology and criminal justice | Includes bibliographical references and index. |
Summary: "Based on original empirical research in Australia, this book presents a detailed analysis of the political complexities, compromises, and investments that underpin LGBT efforts to achieve sexual rights and protections"— Provided by publisher.
Identifiers: LCCN 2019018257 (print) | LCCN 2019022126 (ebook) | ISBN 9780815354901 (hardback : alk. paper)
Subjects: LCSH: Sexual minorities—Civil rights—Australia. | Discrimination in criminal justice administration—Australia. | Police—Political aspects—Australia.
Classification: LCC HQ73.3.A8 R87 2020 (print) | LCC HQ73.3.A8 (ebook) | DDC 306.760994—dc23
LC record available at https://lccn.loc.gov/2019018257
LC ebook record available at https://lccn.loc.gov/2019022126

ISBN: 978-0-8153-5490-1 (hbk)
ISBN: 978-0-367-78428-7 (pbk)

Typeset in Bembo
by codeMantra

Contents

Acknowledgements

This book was written on the unceded lands of the Wurundjeri and Wathaurong peoples of the Kulin Nation. I foremost acknowledge their elders: past, present, and emerging. I also want to honour the intellectual labour of Aboriginal and Torres Strait Islander people, many of them queer, who continue to be at the forefront of movements challenging the violence of policing and the carceral state.

I began this project in 2012, when I commenced my PhD research into LGBT–police relations at Monash University. My supervisors Bree Carlton and Jude McCulloch provided consistent support, many opportunities, and, most importantly, unwavering confidence in my capacity to complete the research. JaneMaree Maher and Danielle Tyson also provided guidance and encouragement during my candidacy. Others read early drafts of chapters and offered helpful critiques and suggestions for improvement, including Steven Angelides and Jordy Silverstein. Early conversations and political collaborations with Terri Ann Quan Sing germinated the critical seeds for this project, and I continue to benefit from her reflections and long-term friendship. Volunteers at the Australian Lesbian and Gay Archives facilitated my access to archival collections that overlapped with policing, especially Gary Jaynes and Graham Willett. Mark Pendleton alerted me to the potential connections between my research and radical queer interventions into lesbian and gay politics in the early 2000s that would have otherwise remained buried in the archives. Cara Gledhill and Liz Patterson generously reviewed the entire thesis draft prior to submission. Erica Meiners and Stephen Tomsen engaged closely with the finished thesis and provided many important insights that deeply shaped the structure of the book to follow.

The second stage of this project benefited greatly from the astute observations of those I interviewed, who generously gave up their time to contribute to the project. Their reflections on their often-long-term activism and advocacy within and for members of LGBTI/queer communities undoubtedly enriched the analysis. All of those who wished to be named are included in the following list of interviews. I am grateful for the support I received from the School of Humanities and Social Sciences at Deakin University to conduct interviews and for the expert transcription provided by Felicity Hernandez Gonzalez.

During the third and final stage of the project—writing the book—I took up a new role at La Trobe University, where I have joined an especially collegial team in the Department of Social Inquiry. Special thanks to Sue Davies for aiding this smooth transition. Funding from La Trobe allowed me to work with Mel Campbell and Alisa Dodge to improve the finished product (although any errors remain my own).

The audience at the Australian Homosexual Histories conference in Melbourne in December 2016 posed constructive questions and critiques that helped me to refine my argument for a contemporary context. The 'Queer(y)ing Justice' symposium in Sydney in July 2018—organised by Nicole Asquith, Matt Ball, Trudie Broderick, Angela Dwyer, and Justin Ellis—provided a welcome opportunity to forge connections with a wonderful network of scholars working in the area of queer criminology and I have benefited from ongoing conversations about queer research and politics with Matt Mitchell, Shaez Mortimer, and Curtis Redd.

Many additional people contributed to my ability to complete this project. Deep gratitude goes to Arlene Alzona for sustaining me always with food, encouragement, and welcome breaks while finishing up the book. Many friends, including Zoe Birkinshaw, Cara Gledhill, Felicity Hernandez Gonzalez, Liz Patterson, Tess Sellar, Lorena Solin, Lara Spalinger and Alex Turnbull, have supported me in ways big and small over these years. My parents, Cheryl and Paul, my sister Amy and brother Patrick, and their partners Chris and Ellie, have provided care and help when I needed it. Bec Smith was there to support me through the epic journey of the PhD and continues to be a stellar co-parent. Lionel Russell-Smith came into the world just one month after I submitted the PhD thesis and has made all the work since infinitely more worthwhile.

Thank you to the criminology editorial staff at Routledge: Tom Sutton, Hannah Catterall, and Jake Rainbow. Thanks also go to the series editors, Matthew Ball, Angela Dwyer, and Vanessa Panfil, for their enthusiasm for the book.

An earlier version of Chapter 3 has been published in a different form and is reprinted by permission from Taylor & Francis Ltd, www.tandfonline.com, on behalf of Australian Feminist Law Journal, Inc.: 'Revisiting the Tasty raid: Lesbian and gay respectability and police legitimacy', Emma K. Russell, *Australian Feminist Law Journal*, © 2015 Australian Feminist Law Journal, Inc. An earlier version of Chapter 5 has been published in a different form and is reprinted by permission from SAGE: 'A "fair cop": Queer histories, affect and police image work in Pride March', *Crime Media Culture*, © Emma K. Russell 2016. An earlier version of Chapter 6 has also been published in a different form. Reprinted by permission from Springer Nature: Springer Netherlands, *Critical Criminology*, 'Queer penalities: The criminal justice paradigm in lesbian and gay anti-violence politics', Emma K. Russell, © Springer Science+Business Media Dordrecht 2016.

List of acronyms

ACON	A New South Wales peak gay health organisation, formerly known as AIDS Council of NSW
ACT UP	AIDS Coalition to Unleash Power
AFP	Australian Federal Police
AIDS	Acquired immunodeficiency syndrome, caused by HIV
ALGA	Australian Lesbian and Gay Archives
ALSO	Foundation: An LGBT philanthropic organisation, formerly known as the Alternative Life Styles Organisation
AVP	Anti-Violence Project of Victoria
CAAH	Community Action Against Homophobia
CAMP	Campaign Against Moral Persecution
CCTV	Closed-circuit television, a self-contained surveillance system
DINK	Double income, no kids
GALPEN	Gay and Lesbian Police Employees Network
GBA	Gay Business Association
GLAD	Gays and Lesbians Against Discrimination
GLAM	Gays and Lesbians Against Multinationals
GLBTIQ	Gay, lesbian, bisexual, trans, intersex, and queer people; also styled as LGBTIQ
GLLO	Gay and Lesbian Liaison Officer, Victoria Police
GLRC	Gay Legal Rights Coalition, known as the HLRC from 1976 to 1981
HIV	Human immunodeficiency viruses, which can cause AIDS
HLRC	Homosexual Law Reform Coalition, from 1981 known as the GLRC
HRLC	Human Rights Law Centre
IDAHOBIT	International Day Against Homophobia, Biphobia, and Transphobia
LGBT	Lesbian, gay, bisexual and trans people
LGBTI	Lesbian, gay, bisexual, trans, and intersex people
LGCA	Lesbian and Gay Community Action
MCV	*Melbourne Community Voice*, lesbian and gay newspaper
MSO	*Melbourne Star Observer*, lesbian and gay newspaper

NSW	New South Wales
PLGLC	Police Lesbian and Gay Liaison Committee
QuACE	Queers United Against Capitalist Exploitation (pronounced 'quake')
QUEER	Queers United to Eradicate Economic Rationalism
UK	United Kingdom (of Great Britain and Northern Ireland)
USA	United States of America
VGLRL	Victorian Gay and Lesbian Rights Lobby

List of interviews

Barbara Baird, 10 January 2017, conducted via Skype
Jamie Gardiner, 19 January 2017, conducted in Fitzroy
Anonymous, 19 January 2017, conducted in Melbourne
Mark Pendleton, 24 January 2017, conducted via Skype
Sally Goldner, 6 February 2017, conducted in Carlton
Alison Thorne, 6 February 2017, conducted in Melbourne
Gary Singer, 23 February 2017, conducted in Melbourne
Jack Keenan, 24 March 2017, conducted in Toorak
Sally Gordon, 12 April 2017, conducted via telephone
Jane Green, 5 May 2017, conducted in South Yarra
Lee Carnie, 5 May 2017, conducted in Melbourne

Chapter 1

Introduction

Queer histories and the politics of policing

Introduction

On 17 May 2016, police forces in several Australian states and territories held rainbow flag-raising ceremonies to mark the International Day Against Homophobia, Biphobia, and Transphobia (IDAHOBIT). In Melbourne, the flag-raising ceremony was organised out of the newly formed 'Priority Communities Division' of Victoria Police.[1] This division is the latest iteration of a community policing and public relations agenda from an organisation often accused of over- and under-policing marginalised populations, including lesbian, gay, bisexual, and trans (LGBT) people.[2] The rainbow flag stunt took place just six months after a damning independent review found that women and gay men experienced an entrenched culture of sexual harassment in the force (Victorian Equal Opportunity & Human Rights Commission 2015). In publicity for the 2016 IDAHOBIT flag-raising ceremony, Victoria Police Chief Commissioner Graham Ashton cited increasing community confidence and trust in police as key goals of this gesture. He stated that 'for police, every day of the year is IDAHOBIT' (Akersten 2016).

This example is drawn from a growing archive of efforts made by the police to achieve a queer-friendly image. From a history marked by state violence, queer criminalisation, and conflict, police organisations across the globe appear 'increasingly visible and ceremonious in efforts to demonstrate their opposition to homophobia' (Rao 2015, p. 38). From anti-hate crime campaigns to large police contingents present at pride marches, Gay and Lesbian Liaison Officer (GLLO) promotions and recruitment stalls at LGBT festivals and events, significant police resources are being dedicated to 'rainbow makeovers' of the police image. Often explained as attempts to build trust among a marginalised group, these police initiatives also have wider-reaching effects. As I argue elsewhere, they contribute to a rebranding of police 'as protectors and defenders of gay liberties and homonormative life' (Russell 2018, p. 332). Marshalling both 'traditional' and 'new' symbols of police authority to profess support for LGBT rights, this strategic communication marks a significant departure from the prior police rhetoric of queer criminality that accompanied waves of raids on gay bars, violent repression of LGBT protest, and entrapment schemes across Australia, North America, and Western Europe, particularly in the latter half of the twentieth century. In fact, it was in 1958 that the New South Wales (NSW) Police Commissioner made the infamous declaration that homosexuality was Australia's 'greatest menace' (Wotherspoon 1989). In marked contrast, a contemporary stocktake of LGBT–police relations would suggest that limited formations of sexual and gender diversity are being brought 'into the fold of the state' (Agathangelou et al. 2008, p. 122).

My research into policing and queer histories in Australia began with questions about the new visibility of police as 'rainbow allies', much like the anecdote above, and sought to understand its local and historical conditions of emergence. Early in 2011, I attended Melbourne's Midsumma Pride March as a young queer spectator. Although this was not my first time at a pride event, this was when I really paid attention to the jarring militaristic aesthetics of the marching Victoria Police officers amid a parade of loosely assembled LGBT community groups and lively corporate-sponsored contingents handing out 'freebies' to the assembled crowds. The paradoxical celebration of uniformed police in a march that evolved, however loosely, from historical queer resistance to police oppression prompted my search for the local 'backstory'. I wanted to understand the context of this peculiar alliance and its historical trajectory. In particular, I was concerned about the political story. I had been involved in various social justice movements as a student activist, some of them explicitly queer, and I wanted to understand how this performance of 'police pride' came to align with the politics of a 'mainstream' LGBT movement.

Given their systematic role in upholding the 'acceptable' boundaries of sexuality and gender, police organisations cannot achieve a gay-friendly image alone. Institutional legitimacy has a dialogic nature, involving claims by power-holders and audience receptions (Bottoms & Tankebe 2012). Accordingly, police need active support from some of the largest and most visible LGBT organisations to project their desired image and effectively engage their constituents. They also need authorisation and cooperation from LGBT organisations to participate in anti-homophobic campaigns, to attend and recruit at gay pride events, and promote the force as pro-LGBT. For example, Melbourne's gay radio station Joy 94.9 FM hosts a regular time slot for Victoria Police GLLOs to promote police news and initiatives, including a 'crime stoppers' segment. In 2016, NSW's peak gay health organisation ACON named the Australian Federal Police (AFP) as the highest-performing public-sector organisation for LGBT inclusion as part of its national 'Pride in Diversity' initiative. The AFP came in ninth position overall, behind a number of major banks and ahead of the Department of Defence. Evidently, the renovation of police image requires queer resources and labour as well as access to queer spaces. In these contexts, police come to occupy queer spaces by invitation, rather than by force or stealth—as they have done historically. Yet many queers are intimately familiar with the coercive power of policing.

Historically, queer lives and spaces have been located distinctly outside of—and often antagonistically to—the nation state and its promise of protection. Policing and law have been central to the production of non-heteronormative sexual and gender identities as threatening 'others' epitomised by the designation and treatment of queer subjects as sick, dirty, diseased, devious, and criminal (Raj 2015; Warner 1993). Despite persistent constructions of queer threat—especially to 'the children' (Angelides 2008; Thompson 2019)—the ways in which sexual and gender diversity are articulated in relation to the state and mainstream culture have significantly shifted in recent decades. Conventional representations of LGBT subjects now frequently rely upon tropes of 'respectability' (Skeggs 1997) and 'neoliberal citizenship' (Bell & Binnie 2000), which are premised on notions of sameness: that is, appearing 'just like' our straight counterparts. These normative representations are particularly pronounced for white, middle-class, able-bodied, and cis lesbian and gay subjects (Niccol 2001). In this new paradigm of 'sexual citizenship' (Richardson 2017), sexual politics are articulated through the register of citizen rights, and LGBT people are recast as domestic couples, successful entrepreneurs, and prolific consumers (Ammaturo 2015; Duggan 2004; Harris 2006). The legitimacy that has gradually accrued to a specific class of LGBT people has partially undermined an entrenched notion of 'homocriminality' (Dalton 2007). By approaching heteronormative ideals of respectability and 'investing' in the 'institutional structures of punishment', as Lamble (2013, p. 232) describes it, more privileged members of the LGBT community have been able to accrue enough 'social, cultural and financial capital' to cross the tenuous threshold between 'criminalisation and protection'. In other words, select LGBT people are now more likely to be viewed as victimised subjects, worthy of state protection, rather than as an undeserving and inherently criminal class.

To understand these recent shifts in sexual citizenship and how they have been mediated by LGBT engagements with policing and law, we need to explore much longer histories of police preoccupation with sexual and gender deviance, and LGBT campaigns against police harassment. Indeed, sexual and gender identity-based movements have had to consistently negotiate and respond to police power.

'We Treat Homosexuals Like Any Other Criminals': local histories of policing sexuality

While certainly new and somewhat novel, the symbolic condemnation of homophobia, biphobia, and transphobia by Victoria Police described previously in this chapter did not happen spontaneously or overnight. Rather, it was a product of a number of institutional pressures and social forces. At times, anti-homophobic initiatives and LGBT visibility within police organisations have been driven by LGBT police employees themselves. In Victoria, the Gay and Lesbian Police Employees Network (GALPEN) was formed in 1995, stressing the importance of being 'out' as lesbian and gay police by not only marching in pride events and challenging homophobic workplace cultures, but also pressuring police leadership to publicly demonstrate support for LGBT rights.[3] However, this internal advocacy is significantly predated by a much broader network of LGBT activists in the community who drew public attention to police targeting and created pressure for homosexual law reform.

During the summer of 1976–1977, when male homosexuality was still formally criminalised, Victoria Police orchestrated a homophobic blitz targeting 'sexual deviants' at Melbourne's Black Rock Beach. In a page-three article titled 'Police go gay to lure homosexuals' in the *Age*, it was revealed that police officers had 'posed as homosexuals' by using a 'particular walk' to apprehend 68 men for 'soliciting with homosexual intent' (Rentsch & Carman 1977). By studying 'homosexuals through binoculars', police attempted to 'imitate their mannerisms' to entrap 'likely offenders' on the beach, and confessions were allegedly extracted with threats of imprisonment (Rentsch & Carman 1977). The surveillance and arrests at Black Rock Beach prompted activists to escalate their efforts in campaigning for homosexual law reform. The Homosexual Law Reform Coalition (HLRC), described as 'representing seven Victorian homosexual groups' (Rentsch & Carman 1977), wrote a letter to the state government, opposition party, police, and civil rights groups arguing against illegitimate police actions at Black Rock Beach. In an excerpt of the letter printed in the 'Police go gay' news article, the HLRC argues:

> These practices constitute a gross abuse of police power and resources. It is not the legitimate function of the police force to entrap people into committing an offence—albeit an 'offence' which has no victim—and it is certainly not their right to prise confessions from people by threats and intimidation.
>
> (Rentsch & Carman 1977)

The following weekend, a 'picnic rally' was organised at Black Rock Beach 'to protest against alleged police harassment and to call for law reform'. News reports suggested that 'about 50 people attended the rally' and due to the terrible weather, 'people sat huddled under black brollies, amid black and pink flags and banners' (*Age* 17, January 1977, p. 10). Three years later, homosexual law reform was passed in the Victorian Parliament.

The example of Black Rock Beach illustrates that mistreatment of LGBT people by police has been the subject of activism in Melbourne since at least the 1970s. For the past four decades, LGBT activists have consistently drawn attention to police harassment and 'over-policing', as well as the problem of 'under-policing', or the lack of accessibility of police aid to queer victims (Iveson 2007). Some of this activism took place under the banner of groups such as the Gay Legal Rights Coalition (GLRC, known as the HRLC from 1976 to 1981) and the Police Lesbian and Gay Liaison Committee (PLGLC), which operated sporadically between 1981 (when the amendments to the Victorian Crimes Act came into force) and 2000. Along with others such as the Gay Business Association (GBA), these groups were concerned to delink homosexuality from criminality and deviance. In some ways, they built upon the anti-police harassment campaigns of gay liberationists in the 1970s, who conceived of policing as a key site and a form of queer oppression. But in other aspects, they departed from radical politics and extended the legacy of earlier iterations of what David Eng (2010) terms 'gay liberalism', such as Society Five in Victoria.[4] In short, LGBT activists have often taken a liberal reformist approach to legal and institutional change, adopting a normative claim to citizenship as a basis for rights (Boucher & Reynolds 2018). Accordingly, much of this activism has not questioned the fundamental role of policing in society—to protect, for instance, settler colonial and capitalist interests—but rather has sought to improve its functioning by working with those in power to correct misplaced police focus upon the homosexual community. Despite the largely cooperative, conciliatory, and reformist approach adopted by groups such as the GLRC, the PLGLC, and later the Victorian Gay and Lesbian Rights Lobby (VGLRL), police leadership has historically been dismissive and often outrightly hostile to LGBT attempts at engagement.

A dialogue between two senior Victoria Police officers in the mid-1980s offers a useful contrast to the queer-friendly police performance with which I opened this book. An internal police memo compiled by Chief Inspector Frame to the then-Chief Commissioner of Victoria Police, Mick Miller, dated 6 November 1985, discusses a letter received from the GBA. In the letter, the GBA called for an 'effective liaison committee' with police, referring to similar requests made by the GLRC since 1981. Following the removal of explicit homosexual offences from the Victorian Crimes Act in 1981, the GLRC continued to alert senior police and government officials to ongoing issues of police harassment, the enforcement of repealed statutes, and 'the need to "educate" members' of the force. In 1982, Miller had refused GLRC's repeated requests for meetings, stating that there was 'no point in a philosophical discussion' (Gardiner 2016). The GBA's follow-up letter in 1985 reiterated concerns about 'unusual police attentions', which in the words of Chief Inspector Frame amounted to 'some sort of conspiracy theory re[garding] police activity' and 'a complete lack of knowledge of our operational procedures'. As such, Frame concluded that 'a "Gay/Police Liaison Committee"' was not justified (Gardiner 2016). In another instance, Jamie Gardiner (2016), the then-President of GLRC, recalls the police commissioner reinforcing the lack of a need for community liaison by simply stating: 'we treat homosexuals like any other criminals'. In the early to mid-1980s, then, homosexuality was still firmly wedded to criminality, at least in the eyes of police. Yet 30 years later, as the opening of this book indicates, the common-sense association of queerness with deviance has been recalibrated. This raises important questions about the nature and extent of this shift from outlaw to rights-bearing citizen. What are its preconditions and limits? And how did it come to take place? These are some of the questions that this book interrogates.

The protection of homonormative life in settler states

In Australia, the rise in mainstream visibility of queer culture and formal advancements in LGBT rights are often associated with a national 'journey towards tolerance' and 'equality' (Niccol 2001, p. 191; Willett 2013, p. 207). However, political theorist Wendy Brown (2006, p. 46) reminds us that state tolerance discourse is conditional upon the 'difference' in question being lived and practiced in a 'depoliticized or private fashion'. This rings true for queer beneficiaries of tolerance discourse. Carol Johnson (2002) argues that the dominant terms for LGBT rights encourage a form of 'passing', which involves privatising and representing our relationships as 'just like' heterosexual relationships and self-monitoring our behaviour in public spaces to avoid being read as 'too confronting' or 'threatening' to the dominant order of 'heteronormativity' (Berlant & Warner 1998). Queer inclusion into dominant citizenship structures has thus required playing 'the game of assimilation' to some extent (Gross 2005, p. 520), in part through adopting and embodying the signs and practices that connote 'respectability'. Respectability is one of the most ubiquitous signifiers of class, yet it also contains judgements of race, gender, and sexuality (Skeggs 1997). Traditionally, queer signs and practices have resulted in exclusion from the category of respectability. However, the emergence of 'good queer subjects, politics and desires' (Agathangelou et al. 2008, p. 124) has allowed some LGBT identities to ascend from the status of criminal to respectable citizen.

This queer upward mobility has been enabled, in large part, by what has been widely dubbed the politics of 'homonormativity' (Duggan 2004). The concept of homonormativity is used to refer to 'a politics of gay assimilation that does not contest dominant heteronormative assumptions and institutions, but upholds and sustains them, while promising the possibility of a demobilised gay constituency, and a gay culture anchored in domesticity and consumption' (Duggan 2004, p. 50).[5] The domesticated homonormative subject is often portrayed as married, child-rearing, taxpaying, law-abiding, and patriotic (Puar 2007). The homonormative turn is reflected in demands for recognition over and above redistribution, and the promotion of individualised consumer cultures (Fraser 2000; Rao 2015). It underpins campaigns for gay marriage, military service, and hate crime statutes (Conrad 2014), wherein calls for 'equality' become, in Lisa Duggan's (2004, p. 65) terms, 'narrow, formal access to a few conservatizing institutions'. The homonormative turn is ultimately depoliticising (Manalansan 2005): it signals a shift from coalitional politics striving for solidarity and social transformation to individualised strategies for inclusion within the existing moral, political, and economic order.

In Australia, as in other settler colonies, 'the good queer citizen gains entrance into the nation through the displacement of racial, sexual and class antagonisms and inequalities' (Agathangelou et al. 2008, p. 124; Yue 2012), including claims for Aboriginal sovereignty. For example, Damien Riggs (2006) has tracked how white sexual citizens have been historically encouraged to invest in the Australian settler state, which shapes the discourses and frameworks utilised by contemporary LGBT rights campaigns (see also Clark 2015). In order to appeal to the white, heterosexual majority, Australian campaigns for same-sex marriage or adoption rights perform 'homonormative love' through imagery of white (or properly multicultural), middle-class, nuclear families—a reflection of the 'aspirational practices' that seek to facilitate lesbian and gay access to a 'national family' (Riggs 2007, p. 114) and construct 'queer lovers' (Haritaworn 2015) as newly desirable citizens of the settler state. In turn, queer projects can naturalise colonialism (Morgensen 2011). For instance, the establishment of a discursive position of 'not criminals'—or 'worthy victims'—often involves distinguishing upstanding sexual citizens from the 'proper targets' for policing and punishment, obscuring the ways in which power and structural inequality impact who is (and who is not) targeted for criminalisation. As the visibility of 'police pride' increases, does the systemic violence of policing fade into the background?

The aims of this book

Over a period of fewer than four decades, LGBT activists have largely succeeded in cleaving apart the entrenched association between homosexuality and criminality. This does not of course occlude queers—particularly sex workers and young, gender nonconforming, racialised, and/or homeless queers—from being targeted or dismally treated by police, nor does it necessitate the incorporation of a broader critique of criminalisation into LGBT politics. However, it does indicate that the boundaries of inclusion/exclusion have been reworked. In *Queer Histories and the Politics of Policing*, I interrogate how changing conceptions of sexual and gender identities, violence, and the state have reworked the relationship between policing and LGBT rights. Using the Australian city of Melbourne as my case study, I animate a number of historic 'queer' moments in which police power converges with sexual and gender politics to produce conflicts, contradictions, and alliances that resonate far beyond this local context. From a high-profile raid of a gay bar to the presence of police, corporations, and queer dissidents at Pride March; the gradual solidification of a 'crime' paradigm in LGBT anti-violence campaigns; and, most recently, an official police apology for historic queer injustice, I attempt to map the punitive or carceral investments that scaffold the shift for select lesbian and gay lives to become 'good queer citizens' or worthy recipients of state recognition and protection. By using the term 'carceral', I intend to capture diffuse logics and practices of securitisation, governance, and containment that are readily expressed through state policing and punishment (Moran et al. 2017). While queer activists have frequently exposed and challenged the violence of policing and law, there are also ways in which LGBT rights campaigns have buttressed these systems.

Queer Histories and the Politics of Policing explores the complex reorderings of sexuality and gender in relation to state policing. I show how queerness has been—and continues to be—an evolving site for policing, how LGBT rights have been incorporated into the surface priorities of contemporary police agencies, and why these processes matter. While my approach involves mapping a localised Australian history of queer activism and policing, my analysis resonates in other contexts. I develop a conceptual framework to further understand how the mobilisation of idealised LGBT identities is reshaping the ways in which queer bodies and spaces are policed. I thereby shed light on integral changes in the conception, negotiation, reproduction, and restriction of sexual citizenship through policing and law more broadly.

Through a critical queer lens, this book illustrates the dynamic nature of policing: its ability to absorb and otherwise deflect critique, re/form, and maintain power. Legitimacy is a vital component of social institutions, practices, and arrangements because it ensures their viability and survival (Jackson et al. 2013). For police, legitimacy is the foundation of their authority and broadly refers to the likelihood that people will obey a police command because they believe that it emerges from a source of moral power and right (Tyler 2006). It therefore depends on the 'myth that police and the public share a single set of coherent and consistent norms and values', and that the police have a unique power to use force if necessary to impose them (Smith 2007, p. 280). Because of the instability and mutability of social norms and values in practice, institutional legitimacy is based on a variety of shifting factors within a given context, and the process of legitimation is often incomplete, containing internal contradictions. Rather than simply a 'surface' or symbolic issue—a superficial abstraction of the 'real work' of policing—the public presentation of the work and nature of policing is a core component of their operations (Linnemann 2017). The management of police image and the maintenance of organisational legitimacy form foundational components of policing, to the extent that policing itself can be conceived as a mediated activity (Lee & McGovern 2014). Through close examination of key instances of police 'image work' (Ericson 1982, p. 10), as 'all the activities in which police forces engage … [to] project meanings of policing'

(Mawby 2002, p. 1), *Queer Histories and the Politics of Policing* reveals new insights into the mutable nature of police power and authority, particularly as it responds to the recurrent challenges of 'minority difference' (Ferguson 2012) through evolving projects of governance and incorporation.

The discursive shift towards police as queer protectors has deep implications for the politics of queer history: who tells it? Who or what is included/excluded? And how is it constructed? The chapters of this book attempt to trace how police leaders—already authoritative voices—have become increasingly proactive in retelling queer history. Through a dominant narrative in which police lead the way from a 'bad' past to a 'better' future, police not only augment their reputation and image but also occupy important political space by positioning themselves as social change actors. By interrogating the relationship between inclusion and exclusion, *Queer Histories and the Politics of Policing* explores what is at stake in the institutionalisation of queer histories and futures. More broadly, this book aims to contribute to discussion and debate about the relationship between social movements and institutional power. It raises the fundamental question of how progressive ideas can be absorbed into violent institutions in ways that strengthen and enhance those institutions' reputation, without relinquishing any power.

While this book's critical focus rests upon dynamics of normalisation, incorporation, and legitimation, it also seeks out examples of alternative trajectories of queer resistance to 'carceral recognition' (Boyce 2017; Russell 2018). Queer critiques of the links between policing, capitalism, and 'assimilationist' lesbian and gay politics have often come to the fore during Pride March—a pivotal public space for the articulation of LGBT identities and politics (Ammaturo 2016; Lamusse 2016). An integral part of my effort to write a critical history of queer activism and police power is the recognition of a multiplicity of political positions, lived experiences, and histories that make up a social movement. The temporal and spatial diversity of sexual and gender identity-based movements renders fraught any attempt to construct a monolithic or teleological account of LGBT–police relations. Instead, the analyses developed in these chapters highlight the need to move beyond simplistic narratives of progress or diagnoses of co-option in order to deepen our understanding of the complex interplay between policing and sexual citizenship.

Unravelling queer and police histories

My approach to this research has been influenced by ideas about genealogy as a 'history of the present' (Foucault 1977, p. 31), or a kind of 'historical writing that approaches the past using the concepts and concerns of the present' (Garland 2014, p. 367). As cultural theorist Stuart Hall (2001, p. 92) reminds us, 'an archive may be largely about "the past" but it is always "re-read" in the light of the present and the future'. I therefore unearth queer and police histories with new questions about power, identity, and legitimacy. I also seek to use these historical insights to deepen understandings of contemporary discourses and trends in the policing of queer lives. My intention is not to construct a 'truer' version of recent history, because such a goal is inherently elusive. After all, the question of time is always 'simultaneous with the question of historical space and its diversity' (Dinshaw et al. 2007, p. 180). Histories cannot be viewed singularly, nor treated as if they are inert. Like archives, histories are heterogenous and 'always stand in an active, dialogic, relation to the questions which the present puts to the past; and the present always puts its questions differently from one generation to another' (Hall 2001, p. 92).

The Australian city of Melbourne serves as an important case study of how sexual citizenship has become increasingly bound up with police power. Melbourne has a rich and diverse history of LGBT activism; it also has a dynamic and troubling policing history. In addition to a well-documented pattern of queer criminalisation and police harassment of sexual and gender 'transgressors', Victoria Police was also the first police organisation in Australia to have a Chief Commissioner participate in a local pride march and to offer a formal apology to LGBT people for past policing practices. It is thus a variable and complex local context, which highlights how contemporary institutional practices and relationships emerged not through a singular linear trajectory, but out of 'specific struggles, conflicts, alliances, and exercises of power' (Garland 2014, p. 372). The focus on Melbourne provides both a specific local history and wider lessons about the nature of sexual and gender politics and institutional power that will undoubtedly be relevant in other contexts.

I began this research into LGBT–police histories at the Australian Lesbian and Gay Archives (ALGA) in Melbourne, working through various collections of ephemera—made up of news clippings, campaign materials, meeting minutes, and so forth—and bound volumes of LGBT newspapers. My initial searches at ALGA drew my attention to a number of high-profile policing events during the period following the formal 'decriminalisation' of specific homosexual acts in Victoria in 1981, such as the 1994 police raid on the Tasty nightclub and the police commissioner's participation in the 2002 Midsumma Pride March. These events were often simplistically framed as historical 'turning points' within a larger teleological narrative of progress for LGBT people, which indicated to me that they required deeper interrogation. During my time at ALGA, I also became familiar with lesser-known challenges to the dominant trajectory of the LGBT movement through conversations with ALGA volunteers and other activists. I furthered my research online and in libraries, retrieving submissions and reports on anti-queer violence prepared by LGBT organisations and traditional and new media coverage of police involvement in queer lives and issues. The availability of these texts and their circulation in the public domain provided a unique opportunity to closely examine how police and queer narratives are constructed, assigned meaning, and disseminated in specific historical and political contexts. Ultimately, during this phase of the research, I analysed conventional representations of police and LGBT people within and through select historical events, queer political formations, and LGBT campaign trajectories, which are organised into the chapters that comprise the majority of this book.

I later supplemented my archival research and analysis of publicly available documents with 11 semi-structured interviews with key informants, held in 2017. I spoke with the lead plaintiff of the civil suit against Victoria Police that followed the Tasty nightclub raid, as well as her lawyer and the barrister who worked on the case. I also interviewed founders, key members, and employees from important advocacy and activist groups and organisations based in Victoria, including the H/GLRC, Bisexual Alliance Victoria, Human Rights Law Centre, Liberty Victoria, Queers United Against Economic Rationalism, Transgender Victoria, VGLRL, and Vixen Collective (Victoria's peer-only sex worker organisation). Two of my key informants were based outside Victoria. I spoke with an activist from the former Brisbane-based group Queers United Against Capitalist Exploitation in Queensland, who had strong connections to and involvement with queer anti-capitalist activism in Melbourne during the period 1999–2002. I also interviewed a key member of Lesbian and Gay Community Action in the 1990s in Adelaide, South Australia, because of her significant role in research and advocacy with police around homophobic hate crime. I sought out individuals who had particularly public profiles in LGBT advocacy around policing issues, such as media spokespeople, police liaison officers, and those chairing government advisory boards on LGBT issues. The majority of my informants had been involved in lobbying and activism for significant periods of time—often more than a decade—and were happy to be named in the research; only one elected to remain anonymous. I decided not to pursue interviewing police, in part because of the restrictions that police organisations place upon research in which their members are subjects. I was wary of censorship and embargoes. But I was also aware that police spokespeople often have a privileged position as 'primary definers' of news stories and significant events (Lee & McGovern 2014): police perspectives are often widely available in news media and, increasingly, police social media. Alternative accounts, such as those garnered from some of my informants, provide insights into some of the challenges of waging campaigns with and against the police, as well as the day-to-day rhythms of policing for LGBT people. Pairing key informant interviews with archival research and textual analysis has allowed for a closer examination of the historically situated ways that LGBT activists have approached, navigated, and resisted the fold of the state through their engagements with police and law.

Queer Histories and the Politics of Policing constructs a history of the present that is necessarily partial and particular to my research methodology, theoretical framework, and subjective concerns—as all histories are. By drawing upon concepts from sexuality and gender studies and critical literatures on policing, I have taken an interdisciplinary approach to this research. The book brings ideas from multiple disciplines into conversation in an effort to enable new insights and 'highlight methodological or epistemological blind spots' (Meiners 2007, p. 23). Building on critical criminological traditions and the discipline's more recent offshoot of queer criminology (Ball 2016; Dwyer et al. 2016; Peterson & Panfil 2014), I seek to highlight many of the limitations of 'mainstream' criminology's conceptual tools for understanding pressing and multifaceted social issues.

The outline of the book

The book begins by sketching a brief history of police reform, using Victoria as its focal point. Rather than rehearsing the history of Australian policing again, I instead trace key components of an evolving relationship between policing, social power relations, and structural violence in a settler colonial context. The discussion in Chapter 2 suggests that policing cannot be understood in isolation from its history. Policing in Victoria was explicitly conceived and utilised in the early days of the colony as a tool of dispossession and capitalist development. Throughout its history, the institution has undergone waves of reform in response to changing social conditions. Gender and sexuality, as social categories, have both informed and been informed by police culture and operations. The chapter outlines how a range of techniques have been used to police and punish sexual and gender transgression. Through a critical reading of historical laws governing homosexuality in Australia, I emphasise the different modes of governance applied to women and men, and to Aboriginal and settler populations. While the so-called 'decriminalisation' era of the late 1970s and 1980s may have changed the political and legal terrain for LGBT challenges to policing, Chapter 2 argues that it failed to signal the end of queer criminalisation.

As perhaps the clearest illustration that queer lives and spaces continued to be over-policed following homosexual law reform, Chapter 3 provides a detailed analysis of the Tasty nightclub raid. On 7 August 1994, Victoria Police raided a gay nightclub in the centre of Melbourne, falsely imprisoning and strip-searching more than 400 patrons in the early hours of the morning. The raid prompted a mass civil suit against police, which made Tasty notorious—the raid is often referred to in Melbourne as 'our Stonewall'. This chapter complicates conventional discourses of the Tasty raid by analysing the extensive media coverage it generated using the criminological concept of the 'ideal victim' in concert with theories of homonormativity. In so doing, I trace the contours of a lesbian and gay politics of respectability that plays out through the language of ordinariness and innocence. Conventional discourses surrounding the Tasty raid therefore encapsulate many of the emergent changes in sexual citizenship claims. The case is broadly significant not only for its scale and visibility, but also because it provides insights into the conditions in which police legitimacy may be undermined and queer subjects may achieve the status of worthy victims in a heteronormative context. However, it also suggests that 'ideal' victimhood might come at the cost of a structural analysis of sexual inequality and police power.

While more conventional citizenship claims came to dominate popular representations of lesbian and gay Tasty patrons, alternative iterations of sexual and gender politics have eschewed liberal frameworks and instead advanced a radical critique of the social and economic forces that reproduce queer oppression. Chapter 4 excavates a historical example of an interstate network of grassroots queer anti-capitalist groups in the early 2000s that challenged the emergent conservatism and consumerism associated with the politics of homonormativity. After briefly outlining the development of a highly marketable gay pride movement in Melbourne, I explore queer anti-capitalist critiques of that movement, drawing on the texts and accounts of groups such as Queers United to Eradicate Economic Injustice (QUEER), active during 1999–2002. The chapter highlights the heterogeneity of sexual and gender identity-based movements. Dissenting voices, archives, and experiences produce counternarratives that complicate the conventional story of LGBT rights gains as one of linear progress. It also establishes spaces of LGBT pride as important sites for queer interventions and actions.

Extending the themes of contests over queer visibility, space, and the politics of queer history, Chapter 5 examines how police can physically and discursively occupy queer space to elevate a 'proud' institutional identity. Conventional representations of Victoria Police Chief Commissioner Christine Nixon's participation in Melbourne's Pride March in 2002—an Australian 'first'—demonstrate how histories of police violence can be used strategically to construct a modernised police force in the present. Paying attention to the ways in which individual and institutional *feelings* are represented in accounts of this event, the chapter shows how police leaders can be constructed as agents of progressive social change, despite the continuities in police power and in the excessive use of force in queer spaces. Official police participation in gay pride parades not only buttresses their reputation against the negative implications of such incidents, but also contributes to the normalisation of policing at LGBT events.

Violence, in its various forms, has been a central concern of sexual and gender identity-based movements. In Chapter 6, I track and interrogate the emergence of a 'crime paradigm' in local advocacy and law reform efforts seeking to challenge homophobic and transphobic violence, frequently through its interpretation as 'hate crime'. Reflecting larger transnational trends in sexual and gender politics, LGBT anti-violence campaigns in Victoria have utilised criminal justice theories, methodologies, and approaches in attempts to explain and remedy homophobic and transphobic 'hate'. By closely reading a series of local research and advocacy reports alongside media coverage of hate crime law reform, I draw out three interconnected themes to illustrate the permeation of criminal justice logics within LGBT advocacy: the victimisation survey method; the focus on police reform; and elements of a punitive public discourse surrounding hate crime. I argue that staking sexual citizenship claims upon victimisation within a criminal–legal framework may deepen existing inequalities by bolstering carceral logics and systems. As sections of the LGBT anti-violence movement seek protection via expanded criminalisation and harsher punishment, our capacity to forge alternative discourses and practices of queer safety is restricted. This is particularly important in a historical and contemporary context in which LGBT people are continually confronted with the failures of police and legal protection, especially for the most marginalised members of our communities. The discursive practices mapped in this chapter contribute to what I term 'queer penalities' (Russell 2017), which encapsulates the ways in which LGBT movements increasingly shape and contest the social meaning of terms such as 'crime' and 'victimisation'.

Moving away from the punitive individual remedies proposed to arrest hate crime, Chapter 7 explores how powerful institutions are reckoning with historical violence in what has been dubbed the 'Age of Apology' (Gibney et al. 2008). In 2014, Victoria Police became the first police force to apologise for its past mistreatment of LGBT people when it issued a formal apology for the Tasty raid to coincide with the event's 20-year anniversary. I analyse the apology as an attempt to cleanse and redeem the institution of the negative image of police resulting from the conventional understanding of the Tasty raid as 'overkill'. In contrast to the celebratory ritual of shedding the shameful past that was depicted in Chapter 5, the formal apology represents a more sombre performance of reflexivity that makes policing look and feel good once more. Again, it is the collective identification with regret that becomes the grounds for reclaiming institutional pride in the present. In this chapter, the police apology is conceived as a practice of 'doing history'. Police reconstruct and retell queer history in such a way that past mistreatment is evacuated of police agency. Yet the progress of the present remains a credit to police initiative and goodwill, rather than a product of the sustained efforts of queer activists calling for state agencies to take responsibility for the harms of the past. My analysis of the Tasty apology reveals new insights into how state institutions navigate queer hopes for accountability through techniques of historical *closure*, such as periodisation and the demarcation of different eras of policing, and how LGBT people are extolled to invest in the future of police.

The book closes by reflecting upon the central arguments and contributions in the Afterword. Rather than accepting at face value that the incorporation of previously excluded groups signifies historical progress and positive change, *Queer Histories and the Politics of Policing* seeks to illustrate the exclusive and regulatory effects of the politics of recognition. The stories told through these chapters show that policing is a durable institution that can adapt and expand, absorb queer critiques, and repackage and retell violent histories as stories of social advancement and institutional maturity. The legitimacy that police gain through this process complicates the task of challenging injustice, because the powerful proclaim to be on the side of the weak while maintaining or building a position of dominance. Thus, paradoxically, LGBT rights discourses may bolster the power of an institution that has long functioned to shore up the 'proper' boundaries of normative sexuality and gender. Evolving LGBT-police relations require renewed discussion about the violent role and effects of policing in society, for queers and others. I hope that this book can contribute to advancing this critical project.

Notes

1 The Priority Communities Division of Victoria Police was established following a high-profile legal settlement between police and a group of young African men who brought a racial profiling case to the Supreme Court (*Haile-Michael v Konstantinidis*). Other portfolios include 'multicultural' and 'youth'.

2 By grouping the identity categories referenced in the acronym 'LGBT' together, I do not intend to imply symmetry between them. Given my interest in the politics of representation and dominant discourse, my research has most to say about how white, able-bodied, cis lesbian and gay identities—arguably the most visible and influential in LGBT rights debates—negotiate and interact with policing and law. Trans experiences are often marginalised or invisibilised in conventional accounts (or otherwise rendered hypervisible) and I attempt to highlight this 'gap' in the archive. My research provides no insights into intersex identities or experiences in relation to policing, so I refrain from using the common acronym 'LGBTI' in an attempt to avoid misrepresentation or tokenism. I use the term 'queer' to refer to a broad range of non-normative sexual and gender identities, practices, politics, and expressions (see Warner 1993). I use 'trans' to refer to gender nonconforming subjects more specifically, yet this is still deployed in its broad sense (see Aizura 2018, pp. 11–12, on this terminology). Elsewhere, I use 'queer' to refer to political orientations that eschew the dominant liberal framework of equality that is typically pursued through incremental reform in favour of a more radical approach, such as the pursuit of social and economic transformation. By intentionally delineating between 'LGBT' and 'queer', I do not necessarily resolve their insufficiencies for capturing the spectrum of sexual and gender diversity, but I do seek to recognise the important political, cultural, geographical, and historical specificities of each of these terminologies.

3 It is certainly worthwhile to consider the role played by LGBT police officers in driving change in the police image towards LGBT recognition. Numerous studies document the particular internal struggles faced by these officers in a traditionally hyper-masculine and heteronormative organisational structure (Panter 2018; Victorian Equal Opportunity & Human Rights Commission 2015). However, I fear that this approach risks reproducing a narrow focus on the intentions and experiences of individual police, rather than reckoning with the broader power effects and functions of the institution as a whole. My concern therefore rests most squarely upon the political role of policing and how it reproduces a particular sexual and gendered social order, and maintains legitimacy as an institution.

4 Originally established in Melbourne in 1971 as a branch of the Campaign Against Moral Persecution (CAMP) in Sydney, the group was renamed 'Society Five' to distance itself from the radical politics of CAMP and adopt a more 'liberal' or 'closeted' approach to social change. While they eschewed radical politics, members of Society Five organised counselling and social events, and contributed to the campaign for law reform throughout the decade (Willett et al. 2011, pp. 109–111).

5 It is important to clarify that *homo*normativity is not the oppositional equivalent to *hetero*normativity. This is because 'homosexuality can never have the invisible, tacit, society-founding rightness that heterosexuality has' (Berlant & Warner 1998, pp. 547–566).

References

Agathangelou, AM, Bassichis, DM, & Spira, TL 2008, 'Intimate investments: Homonormativity, global lockdown, and the seductions of empire', *Radical History Review*, vol. 100, pp. 120–143.

Aizura, A 2018, *Mobile subjects: Transnational imaginaries of gender reassignment*, Duke University Press, Durham and London.

Akersten, M 2016, 'Aussie cops raise rainbow flags against homophobia and transphobia', *Same Same*, 17 May, viewed 8 June 2018, www.samesame.com.au/news/13720/Aussie-cops-raise-rainbow-flags-against-homophobia-and-transphobia.

Ammaturo, FR 2015, 'The "pink agenda": Questioning and challenging European homonationalist sexual citizenship', *Sociology*, vol. 49, no. 6, pp. 1–16.

Ammaturo, FR 2016, 'Spaces of pride: A visual ethnography of gay pride parades in Italy and the United Kingdom', *Social Movement Studies*, vol. 15, no. 1, pp. 19–40.

Angelides, S 2008, '"The continuing homosexual offensive": Sex education, gay rights and homosexual recruitment', in S Robinson (ed.), *Homophobia: An Australian history*, The Federation Press, Sydney, pp. 172–192.

Ball, M 2016, *Criminology and queer theory: Dangerous bedfellows?* Palgrave Macmillan, London.

Bell, D & Binnie, J 2000, *The sexual citizen: Queer politics and beyond*, Polity Press, Cambridge.

Berlant, L & Warner, M 1998, 'Sex in public', *Critical Inquiry*, vol. 24, no. 2, pp. 547–566.

Boucher, L & Reynolds, R 2018, 'Decriminalisation, apology and expungement: Sexual citizenship and the problem of public sex in Victoria', *Australian Historical Studies*, vol. 49, no. 4, pp. 457–474.

Boyce, M 2017, 'Carceral recognition and the colonial present at the Okimaw Ohci Healing Lodge', *Sites: A Journal of Social Anthropology and Cultural Studies*, vol. 14, no. 1, pp. 13–34.
Bottoms, A & Tankebe, J 2012, 'Beyond procedural justice: A dialogic approach to legitimacy in criminology', *Journal of Criminal Law and Criminology*, vol. 102, pp. 119–170.
Brown, W 2006, *Regulating aversion: Tolerance in the age of identity and empire*, Princeton University Press, Princeton.
Clark, M 2015, 'Are we queer? Reflections on "peopling the empty mirror" twenty years on', in D Hodge (ed.), *Colouring the rainbow: Blak queer and trans perspectives*, Wakefield Press, South Australia, pp. 238–252.
Conrad, R 2014, *Against equality: Queer revolution, not mere inclusion*, AK Press, Oakland.
Dalton, D 2007, 'Policing outlawed desire: "Homocriminality" in beat spaces in Australia', *Law Critique*, vol. 18, pp. 375–405.
Dinshaw, C, Edelman, L, Ferguson, R, & Freccero, C 2007, 'Theorizing queer temporalities: A roundtable discussion', *GLQ: A Journal of Lesbian and Gay Studies*, vol. 13, no. 2–3, pp. 177–195.
Duggan, L 2004, *The twilight of equality? Neoliberalism, cultural politics, and the attack on democracy*, Beacon Press, Boston.
Dwyer, A, Ball, M, & Crofts, T 2016, *Queering criminology*, Palgrave Macmillan, Basingstoke.
Eng, D 2010, *The feeling of kinship: Queer liberalism and the racialization of intimacy*, Duke University Press, Durham.
Ericson, R 1982, *Reproducing order: A study of police patrol work*, University of Toronto Press, Toronto.
Ferguson, RA 2012, *The reorder of things: The university and its pedagogies of minority difference*, University of Minnesota Press, Minneapolis.
Foucault, M 1977, *Discipline and punish: The birth of the prison*, trans. A Sheridan, Pantheon, New York.
Fraser, N 2000, 'Rethinking recognition', *New Left Review*, vol. 3, pp. 107–120.
Gardiner, J 2016, 'From insult to engagement', unpublished paper presented at *Australian Homosexual Histories Conference*, 25 November, Melbourne.
Garland, D 2014, 'What is a "history of the present"? On Foucault's genealogies and their critical preconditions', *Punishment & Society*, vol. 16, no. 4, pp. 365–384.
Gibney, M, Howard-Hassmann, RE, Coicaud, J-M, & Steiner, N 2008, *The age of apology: Facing up to the past*, University of Pennsylvania Press, Philadelphia.
Gross, L 2005, 'The past and the future of gay, lesbian, bisexual, and transgender studies', *Journal of Communication*, vol. 55, pp. 508–528.
Hall, S 2001, 'Constituting an archive', *Third Text*, vol. 15, no. 54, pp. 89–92.
Haritaworn, J 2015, *Queer lovers and hateful others: Regenerating violent times and places*, Pluto Press, London.
Harris, AP 2006, 'From Stonewall to the suburbs? Toward a political economy of sexuality', *William and Mary Bill of Rights Journal*, vol. 14, pp. 1539–1582.
Iveson, K 2007, *Publics and the city*, Blackwell Publishing, Malden.
Jackson, J, Bradford, B, Stanko, B, & Hohl, K 2013, *Just authority? Trust in the police in England and Wales*, Routledge, Abingdon.

Johnson, C 2002, 'Heteronormative citizenship and the politics of passing', *Sexualities*, vol. 5, no. 3, pp. 317–336.

Lamble, S 2013, 'Queer necropolitics and the expanding carceral state: Interrogating sexual investments in punishment', *Law Critique*, vol. 24, no. 3, pp. 229–253.

Lamusse, T 2016, 'Politics at pride?', *New Zealand Sociology*, vol. 31, no. 6, pp. 49–70.

Lee, M & McGovern, A 2014, *Policing and media: Public relations, simulations and communications*, Routledge, Abingdon.

Linnemann, T 2017, 'Proof of death: Police power and the visual economies of seizure, accumulation and trophy', *Theoretical Criminology*, vol. 21, no. 1, pp. 57–77.

Manalansan, MF 2005, 'Race, violence, and neoliberal spatial politics in the global city', *Social Text*, vol. 23, no. 3–4, pp. 142–155.

Mawby, RC 2002, *Policing images: Policing, communication and legitimacy*, Willan, Cullompton.

Meiners, ER 2007, *Right to be hostile: Schools, prisons, and the making of public enemies*, Routledge, New York.

Morgensen, SL 2011, *Spaces between us: Queer settler colonialism and Indigenous decolonization*, University of Minnesota Press, Minneapolis.

Moran, D, Turner, J, & Schliehe, AK 2017, 'Conceptualizing the carceral in carceral geography', *Progress in Human Geography*, vol. 42, no. 5, pp. 666–686.

Niccol, F 2001, *From diggers to drag queens: Configurations of Australian national identity*, Pluto Press, Annandale.

Panter, H 2018, *Transgender cops: The intersection of gender and sexuality expectations in police cultures*, Routledge, Abingdon.

Peterson, D & Panfil, VR 2014, *Handbook of LGBT communities, crime, and justice*, Springer, New York.

Puar, JK 2007, *Terrorist assemblages: Homonationalism in queer times*, Duke University Press, Durham.

Raj, S 2015, 'Disturbing disgust: Gesturing to the abject in queer cases', in A Dwyer, M Ball, & T Crofts (eds), *Queering criminology*, Palgrave, Basingstoke, pp. 83–101.

Rao, R 2015, 'Global homocapitalism', *Radical Philosophy*, vol. 194, pp. 38–49.

Rentsch, J & Carman, G 1977, 'Police go gay to lure homosexuals', *Age*, 12 January, p. 3.

Richardson, D 2017, 'Rethinking sexual citizenship?', *Sociology*, vol. 51, no. 2, pp. 208–224.

Riggs, DW 2006, *Priscilla, (white) queen of the desert: Queer rights/race privilege*, Peter Lang Publishing, New York.

Riggs, DW 2007, 'Possessive investments at the intersection of race, gender and sexuality: Lesbian and gay rights in a "post-colonising" nation', in M Allen & R Dhawan (eds), *Intersections: Gender, race and ethnicity in Australasian studies*, Prestige Books, New Delhi, pp. 111–125.

Russell, EK 2017, 'Queer penalities: The criminal justice paradigm in lesbian and gay anti-violence politics', *Critical Criminology*, vol. 25, no. 1, pp. 21–35.

Russell, EK 2018, 'Carceral pride: The fusion of police imagery with LGBTI rights', *Feminist Legal Studies*, vol. 26, no. 3, pp. 331–350.

Skeggs, B 1997, *Formations of class and gender: Becoming respectable*, Sage, London.

Smith, DJ 2007, 'New challenges to police legitimacy', in A Henry & DJ Smith (eds), *Transformations of policing*, Ashgate, Aldershot, pp. 273–306.

Thompson, JD 2019, 'Predatory schools and student non-lives: A discourse analysis of the Safe Schools Coalition Australia controversy', *Sex Education*, vol. 19, no. 1, pp. 41–53.
Tyler, TR 2006, *Why people obey the law*, Princeton University Press, Princeton.
Victorian Equal Opportunity & Human Rights Commission 2015, *Independent review into sex discrimination and sexual harassment, including predatory behaviour in Victoria Police: Phase One report*, State of Victoria, Carlton, Victoria, viewed 27 December 2018, http://apo.org.au/node/60436.
Warner, M 1993, *Fear of a queer planet: Queer politics and social theory*, University of Minnesota Press, Minneapolis.
Willett, G 2013, 'Australia: Nine jurisdictions, one long struggle', in C Lennox & M Waites (eds), *Human rights, sexual orientation and gender identity in the Commonwealth: Struggles for decriminalisation and change*, School of Advanced Study, University of London, London, pp. 207–229.
Willett, G, Murdoch, W, & Marshall, D 2011, *Secret histories of queer Melbourne*, Australian Lesbian and Gay Archives, Parkville.
Wotherspoon, G 1989, '"The greatest menace facing Australia": Homosexuality and the state in NSW during the Cold War', *Labour History*, vol. 56, pp. 15–28.
Yue, A 2012, 'Queer Asian mobility and homonational modernity: Marriage equality, Indian students in Australia and Malaysian transgender refugees in the media', *Global Media and Communication*, vol. 8, no. 3, pp. 269–287.

Chapter 2

Policing the colony

The uneven histories of queer criminalisation

Introduction

The state has been, and continues to be, a network of institutions through which violence against queer people has been enacted in order to sustain the national space as heterosexual space (Warner 1993). Policing, as a particularly pronounced site of 'hegemonic masculinity' (Aiello 2014; Connell 1995), has played an important role in this historical process. Through the use of various mechanisms of surveillance, violent intervention, and coercive containment to govern 'appropriate' expressions of gender and sexuality, police have contributed not only to the erasure and exclusion of LGBT people, but also to the reproduction of ideas of queer deviancy, criminality, and threat. Policing has thus played a significant role in not only producing 'homosexuality', but also establishing it as inferior to heterosexuality. While the latter is pervasive in all aspects of social, cultural, and political life, it is simultaneously invisible by virtue of its normalisation, institutionalisation, and idealisation. In contrast, queerness is frequently marked as excessive, hyper-visible, and perpetually 'out of place'—a construction that is affirmed and reproduced by police practices (Boon-Kuo et al. 2018). Policing is thus not merely a repressive apparatus of power, but a productive one. It is actively involved in reconstituting the heteronormative social order.

To present a historicised critique of policing solely based on its gendered and sexual disciplinary techniques and effects would result in a myopic view of the institution's relationship to dominant structures of power. In settler colonies such as Australia, policing has facilitated processes of dispossession (Cunneen & Tauri 2015) and the development of capitalism (Connell & Irving 1980; McCulloch 2001). Rather than being analogous or separate processes, queer experiences of policing and punishment are also shaped by and through these systems of subjugation. This chapter provides the necessary historical context for understanding the broader social and political functions of policing, in order to advance a critical analysis of police power.

A 'civilising process': policing the colony

From its beginning, policing in the Port Phillip District, which became the state of Victoria in 1851, was deeply shaped by the settler colonial need to overcome Aboriginal resistance to dispossession (Attwood 1989; Finnane 1994; Reynolds 1989). In a historical context of convict transportation and frontier warfare, policing was conceived by the British and developed in the south-eastern part of the continent to most closely resemble a paramilitary force. Unlike their counterparts in England at the time, the settlement's first police units were heavily armed and militaristic (Connell & Irving 1980; Haldane 1995; McCulloch 2001). Upon deployment in 1836, the first task of police in the Port Phillip District was to keep Aboriginal people off land deemed fit for pastoral use (Moore 1991). The governance and control of Aboriginal people was largely the task of the Native Police Corps, established in the 1830s to aid the process of European settlement and enhance 'the civilising process' (Finnane 1994). Although the official mandate of police included the 'protection' of Aboriginal people and the minimisation of conflict (Victoria Police 1980), the various early Native and Mounted Police units were involved in numerous massacres (McCulloch 2001; Nance 1981). Historian Lyndall Ryan (2010, p. 267) reports that at least 13 'military-style' massacres were carried out by the Native Police and the Mounted Police in Port Phillip during the period 1836–1851, in reprisal for the alleged killing of settlers or, more often, sheep and cattle. Reflecting the 'logic of elimination' that underpins settler colonialism (Wolfe 1994), the first police units in Victoria actively contributed to the genocidal violence of the frontier and played an integral role in projects of land theft and denial of Aboriginal sovereignty.

While Australian police history reveals its origins as a settler colonial project, it also establishes the centrality of reform to police legitimacy and power. An official account of Victorian police history emphasises that 'experimentation' and adaptation have been inherent in the historical development and expansion of the force (Victoria Police 1980, p. 111). Victoria Police, as we now know it, was conceived as a reform to the disparate police forces that were deployed in the early years of the colony, which included the Native, Border, Mounted, and Melbourne Police (Victoria Police 1980). By 1852, not only was there no longer a perceived need for the Native Police, but the dramatic reduction of the Aboriginal population in the 15 years following British settlement also meant that such a force was no longer possible (McCulloch 2001). As the lethal effects of settlement became apparent in the 1850s, Port Phillip District was facing other significant social and economic changes with increasing perceptions of 'urban disorder' and an emergent gold-rush era (Finnane 1994). The early assortment of largely autonomous police forces that reported to no central authority rapidly became seen as an inadequate system of security in this new social context (Haldane 1995; Victoria Police 1980).

The massive influx of diggers into Victoria in the 1850s prompted officials to recruit 50 trained police officers from the London Metropolitan Police and to establish a government inquiry to develop a program of police reform. The Snodgrass Committee tabled its report in September 1852, which criticised existing forces as 'utterly inadequate' and recommended the formation of a single force under the command of one man—the Inspector General of Police (Haldane 1995). The Police Regulation Bill was modelled on Sir Robert Peel's London Metropolitan Police Act, which avoided the militaristic language associated with the Irish Constabulary model in favour of civil terminology. Historian Mark Finnane (1994, p. 28) argues that the development of a centralised police force in Victoria in the 1850s made 'a substantial contribution to the capacity of colonial government to rule in unstable times'. The amalgamation of the various forces into a single unit in the 1853 Police Act to form Victoria Police was an Australian first, ushering in 'a new era of policing' (Victoria Police 1980), and other Australian and New Zealand jurisdictions adopted the Victorian police rules as a model (Finnane 1994). According to police historian Robert Haldane (1995, p. 29), Victoria comprised a 'vanguard' and 'progressive' force relative to its interstate neighbours, even as 'instances of corruption, brutality, inefficiency and maladministration' abounded during this period (see also McQuilton 1987).

Despite the ideals of a 'civil force' in the mid-nineteenth-century Victoria, policing in practice continued to be militaristic. Up until the 1880s, Chief Commissioners of Victoria Police were either former military or proponents of the Irish Constabulary model (McQuilton 1987). The discovery of gold in 1851 brought about rapid economic and political changes in the colony and 'provided the authorities with new enemies to overcome', namely those working as independent miners or 'diggers' (McCulloch 2001, p. 35). Routine police harassment of diggers for unpopular mining licencing fees precipitated the infamous 1854 Eureka Stockade in Ballarat, which was constructed to protect diggers from the predations of police (Connell & Irving 1980; McCulloch 2001). More than 250 police officers and soldiers mounted an attack on the Stockade, and about 30 miners and 4 soldiers were killed in the ensuing battle. Afterwards, the Mounted Police were accused of gratuitous violence and were not again used for law enforcement in Victoria (McCulloch 2001). The Eureka Stockade cemented police as a crucial agent of the maintenance of class divisions, clearly revealing the force as a defender of ruling-class interests.

In the 1880s, policing in rural areas of the state became less militaristic (McCulloch 2001).[1] This is often credited to the pressure for reform caused by the 1881 Royal Commission into policing and the forethought of individual police (Haldane 1995; Victoria Police 1980). However, as Jude McCulloch (2001) points out, police reform also occurred at a time of significant economic restructuring along the lines of industrial capital, such that major class divisions came to revolve not around land so much as capital (see also

Connell & Irving 1980). Accordingly, police redirected their focus to the urban context where workers' movements were on the rise. In 1917, Victoria Police was partially unionised, which established the Police Association. As Finnane (1994) describes, the 'muted' and 'limited' goals of the Police Association were 'to conserve and further the interests of the Victoria Police Force', promote 'good fellowship' among its members, and provide 'efficiency and assistance to the administration'. From its outset, the Police Association was a conservative union and it failed to support the one and only police strike action in Australia's history. In 1923, 600 Victoria Police officers refused to work over poor conditions and their participation in the strike ultimately ended their policing careers (Finnane 1994; Haldane 1995). The Police Association's criticism of the strike ensured that the organisation was distinguished from radical labour movements of the time. In the 1980s, it waged a campaign that succeeded in abolishing the Victorian Police Complaints Authority, illustrating the power of the Police Association to influence criminal justice policy and shield police from accountability processes (Finnane 1994). Its conservative reputation continues to this day.

'A crime not fit to be named': legal erasure and the policing of perversion

Modern policing has developed to advance colonial and capitalist interests. It has also shaped, and been shaped by, a 'heteropatriarchal' society (Harris 2011). Traditionally, women and other sexual and gender 'deviants' have been excluded from employment within police organisations; they have been denied protection, or received little of it, from their most frequently experienced harms; and otherwise they have been reprimanded and punished for such deviancy (Allen 1987). In Australia, as in many other Western contexts, criminality and sexual perversion have long been understood to exist in a tautological relationship. In 1851, English statutes and case law outlawing a range of homosexual offences were applied to the new colony of Victoria. Initially, the 'abominable crime of buggery' was punishable by death and following that, men or boys could be sentenced to up to 15 years in prison for having consensual sex (Human Rights Law Centre 2014, p. 12).[2] Over the next century, other 'crimes' were invented to police 'vice', or behaviours deemed 'perverse', which later morphed into signifiers of a particular subject position: 'the homosexual' (Foucault 1978; Willett 2008; Wotherspoon 1991). The offence of gross indecency was adopted in Victoria in 1919 and 'loitering' or soliciting for 'immoral purposes' was outlawed in 1961; both of these offences targeted 'deviant' sexual practices and gender presentations. The 1950s saw the beginning of vice squads and the intensification of policing methods 'to curb and control homosexuality', including entrapment via 'agent provocateurs' and blackmail (Featherstone & Kaladelfos 2016, p. 162). State surveillance and prosecution of homosexual men drew from and reinforced emergent discourses of homosexuality in Australia as 'a problem for domestic security and national morality' (Featherstone & Kaladelfos 2016, p. 162), or as 'crime, sin or bio-medical disorder' (Willett 2008, p. 120). For women, their queer desires were deemed 'filthy, obscene or mad' (Ford 2008).

Sexual and gender categories are not neutral or natural phenomena. As the above discussion of the political construction of queerness as threatening, deviant, and so forth highlights, institutional practices and discourses play a powerful role in shaping our understandings of these social categories. Prior to the legal recognition of the existence of the 'homosexual', same-sex sexual practices were considered simply to be individual and isolated behaviours, rather than emblematic of an actual 'type' of person (Aldrich 2003). Historians have tracked the emergence of 'modern' notions of sexuality in the nineteenth and twentieth centuries in the West, particularly the dominant assumption that sexual acts and desires constituted the essential identity of the modern subject (Halperin 1990; Katz 1983). As French philosopher Michel Foucault (1978) summarises, sex came to be regarded as 'the truth of the self'. Subsequently, others have emphasised how modern notions of sexuality developed within and through—rather than alongside—powerful classificatory systems of race and gender (Kunzel 2008; Riggs 2006; Somerville 2000; Stoler 1995). From this perspective, sexuality is always already racialised, gendered, and so on. While all these categories of differentiation are fundamentally unstable, rather than fixed or essential, this is not to say that they have no significance in the world. Socially constructed traits certainly maintain their power and permanence—the effects of such categories are unquestionably real. The central problem is not the existence of such categories; rather, it is the way they are located within value systems and used to create social hierarchies and determine the distribution of material resources (Stanley 2011).

Sodomy laws often serve as historical markers for queer criminalisation, largely because they generated more concrete historical records than other forms of surveillance, governance, and violence targeted at LGBT people. However, sodomy laws were not applied evenly among men having sex with men; nor were they applied to women. The perception of sodomy laws as the cornerstone of queer criminalisation is complicated by markers of race, class, gender, and relationship to the colonial nation state (Mogul et al. 2011). All these markers have long served to identify who is and who is not a presumptive 'criminal' in the Australian context.[3] Riggs (2006, p. 23) points out that while the term 'homosexual' came to be used in Australia to describe a group of people who were labelled as deviant or pathological, their deviance was not taken to be representative of the white race in general. In contrast, Aboriginal people were constructed as 'sexually available', 'sexually deviant', and otherwise 'perverted' (Behrendt 2000; Connors 2017; Gays and Lesbians Aboriginal Alliance 1993). Moreover, historian Ruth Ford's (2008) research into cases of women accused of same-sex desire and/or living as men in south-eastern Australia in the first half of the twentieth century highlights an inextricable relationship between homophobia and misogyny. It also reiterates the ways in which race, class, gendered appearance, and geographical location mediate individual experiences with the law (Ford 2008).

Historical investigations of queer criminalisation often fail to capture the different modes of state control and discipline applied to women and trans people. It is well noted that historical accounts of policing women's queer sexual practices are relatively few compared to those of men (Chesser 2008b; Ford 2000, 2008; Willett et al. 2011). There is, however, significant documentation of intimate and 'queer' relationships among convict women incarcerated in 'female factories' in Tasmania or among the 'criminal class' in Melbourne in the nineteenth century (Casella 2000; Nolan 2013; Piper 2015). In *Parting with My Sex*, historian Lucy Chesser (2008a) catalogues numerous examples of policing (and public scandal surrounding) 'cross-dressing and gender blurring' in Australian history. This literature reminds us of the historical specificities of queer practices and the social and cultural meanings ascribed to them. As noted above, sexual and gender identities are constructed through a confluence of discourses, and sometimes the perceived absence or invisibility of lesbian and trans histories is an issue of language and terminology. Particular practices and sexual or gender identities may be categorised differently at different times. As Stanley (2011, p. 5) argues, 'gender identification is always formed in relation to other forms of power and thus the words we use to identify others and ourselves are culturally, generationally, and geographically situated'. For example, perhaps some of those referred to as 'women living as men' or 'female impersonators' in 1950s Melbourne would today be captured by the term 'trans'. However, these projects of historical recuperation are fraught—they primarily serve to highlight that sexual and gender identities are socially constructed.

The relative invisibility of lesbian sexualities is also a product of the frequent use of legal records to construct histories of queer criminalisation. Historically, policing practices criminalised lesbian sexuality less vigorously than that of gay men (Mason 1995; Robson 1990; Valverde 2007). Throughout its legal history in Britain, sodomy was described as 'a crime not fit to be named' and women were explicitly excluded from the statute because of fear that verbalising such acts would make otherwise ignorant women aware of, and thereby more prone to engage in, such behaviour (Valverde 2007). In 1921, the British House of Lords rejected the criminalisation of lesbian acts because it was feared that the law would bring sexual practices to the attention of women who had never conceived of them before. This legacy extends to British settler colonies including Canada, the USA, and Australia, where sodomy laws technically applied to women, but were rarely enforced (Ford 2008; Valverde 2007). However, this does not signal that lesbian sexualities escaped state control. The exclusion of women from sodomy laws reflects an alternative form of regulation premised on silencing or erasure;

such legal silences may constitute a deliberate attempt to regulate lesbian sexuality through denial of its existence. As Lamble (2009, p. 112) argues:

> The capacity to 'not see' or 'not know' queer bodies and sexualities is not simply a matter of inadvertent omission, but involves wilful acts of ignorance. Particular facts must remain unspoken, details unquestioned, lines of thinking unpursued ... Legal invisibility ... [is not] simply the consequence of state indifference or repression, ... legal discourses and organisational rationalities [also] constitute queer bodies and sexualities as unthinkable and unknowable.

While gay men were policed and prosecuted for sodomy and other 'homosexual offences', alternative laws or mechanisms of regulation were more likely to be used to criminalise, regulate, and erase lesbian desires and gender non-conforming identities. For example, Ford (2008) documents how the lesbian working-class bar scene in 1950s Melbourne was routinely subject to police harassment, threats, and inaction when staff and patrons were abused by members of the public. Women were policed to ensure compliance with cross-dressing laws that stipulated women must have at least three items of feminine clothing at all times. Outside of criminal legal mechanisms, sexual and gender 'deviance' was also subjected to medical/psychiatric intervention in mid-twentieth-century Australia, sometimes resulting in incarceration (Ford 2003; Reynolds 2002). This suggests that historically, lesbians and trans people did not escape surveillance or punishment. Rather, it reveals that policing (in its various forms) has played a central role in shoring up—often violently—a dominant sexual and gendered social order.

'We knew police were simply ignoring the law reform': from criminalisation to protection?

The incremental law reforms that removed explicit homosexual offences from the various state and territory criminal statutes are frequently held up as significant markers of progress in LGBT rights history in Australia. The first Australian state to decriminalise homosexual sex between men was South Australia. This decision was spurred by a suspicious death that is widely believed to have involved members of the Vice Squad (Hodge 2012). Dr George Duncan, a legal academic at the University of Adelaide, drowned on 10 May 1972 'in the close vicinity' of Adelaide's most popular beat (Reeves 2016). Duncan's death sparked lesbian and gay outrage and broader public concern about police abuse of powers and within just 11 weeks of Duncan's death, a bill was introduced into South Australia's Legislative Council that began the process of homosexual law reform (Reeves 2016). A watered-down version of the bill was passed in 1975. Following South Australia and the Australian Capital Territory, Victoria was the next jurisdiction to enact homosexual law reform in 1981. The campaign for decriminalisation in Victoria was the first in Australia that was authored and propelled by homosexual organisations, principally the Homosexual Law Reform Coalition (HRLC) (Boucher & Reynolds 2018). As others gradually followed suit over the next decade, Tasmania became the last Australian jurisdiction to remove sodomy from its criminal statute. In 1994, Tasmania had legislative reform forced upon it by the United Nations Human Rights Committee, following a case brought against it by gay activist Nicholas Toonen (Morgan 1993–1994).

The 'decriminalisation of homosexuality' is somewhat of a misleading phrase, however, as these legal reforms did not signal an end to the policing and punishment of sexual and gender deviance. Historians Boucher and Reynolds (2018, p. 458) argue that the conventional story of legal equality and sexual citizenship in Australia posits decriminalisation as:

> The first stage of a putatively obvious teleology of legal and social reform even though the reforms concerning male homosex in each state de- and re-criminalised sex in different ways; ages of consent varied, the statutes regarding public intimacy between men remained inconsistent across different jurisdictions, and practices of policing sex in public remained unpredictable.

Across Australia, both the campaigns for decriminalisation and the legislative reforms themselves varied significantly in style and approach (Holmes & Pinto 2013). Legal and social change for men having sex with men was thus stilted, uneven, and sometimes contradictory—troubling any assumption of linear progress and highlighting the limitations of a liberal reformist approach.

Since the early 1970s in Victoria, when activists began lobbying for homosexual law reform, political fault lines have existed within the movement. For instance, Victoria's first known sexual identity-based activist group, Society Five, mounted arguments for reform on the basis of liberal ideals of 'fairness' and 'right to privacy', and the group explicitly asserted that it was 'reformist rather than revolutionary' (Carbery 2014). While some sought 'modest legislative protection' for sexual acts conducted in the private sphere, others such as Gay Liberationists sought 'a more radical reconfiguration of the social and sexual order' (Boucher & Reynolds 2018, p. 460). These debates played out within the HRLC, which formed after the highly publicised arrests at Black Rock Beach in the summer of 1976–1977 and later became the Gay Legal Rights Coalition (GLRC) after law reform was achieved in 1981. When I interviewed Alison Thorne, former Vice President of GLRC, she reflected that its members predominantly worked within a liberal framework, focusing on lobbying politicians in order to achieve legislative and policy change.

Although she was invested and involved in the struggle against criminalisation, including legal strategies, her analysis differed:

> I came at it from more of a liberationist perspective. I wasn't quite so interested in the lobbying of politicians, but more the idea that by fighting to win reforms we can understand some of the limits of our existing system. Any reforms that we do win are only as good as long as we can hang onto them. We're in a period now where I think some people are starting to see that some of the reforms that maybe were won in the '70s and '80s were not quite as entrenched as people may have thought.

Thorne's comments remind us that LGBT rights gains are less a product of inevitable progress in a liberal democracy than an ongoing struggle for social and political change. Sexual citizenship in Australia remains tenuous and the protections afforded to a privatised and 'respectable' version of homosexuality do not necessarily extend to other facets of queer and trans lives.

While historian Graham Willett (2000, p. 156) has hailed the Victorian legislation as the 'best ... reform package ... in the English-speaking world', others challenge the notion that it signalled wholesale decriminalisation. Homosexuality may have no longer been explicitly criminalised, but the new offence of 'soliciting for immoral sexual purpose' that was created in this reformist moment was targeted at the same 'deviant' groups (Boucher & Reynolds 2018). Furthermore, legal change did not easily translate into police practice. Former President of H/GRLC, Jamie Gardiner (2015), outlined how reports of police harassment and charges for 'loitering for homosexual purposes' continued in the weeks and months after the law reform came into effect in Victoria on 1 March 1981. As he summed it up: 'We knew police were simply ignoring the law reform' (Gardiner 2015).

Numerous scholars have documented how queer public sex practices, such as beat activity, continued to be aggressively policed long after the decline of sodomy laws (Dalton 2007, 2008; Johnson 2008, 2010; Swivel 2001). Victoria Police continued to conduct entrapment operations with plain-clothes officers at beats well into the 1990s (Iveson 2007). Even in 2002, 'Operation Dalliance' led to the arrest of over 100 men at Flinders Street Station in Melbourne in acts of entrapment and surveillance (Dalton 2008, p. 99). The persistent police focus on public sex between (predominantly) men suggests that sexual citizenship gains are not without limits. Instead, they tend to reinforce rather than challenge dominant norms of intimacy (such as monogamous coupling through marriage), allowing for increased regulation and new forms of exclusion for sexual dissidents (Bell & Binnie 2000; Dreher 2016; Pendleton & Serisier 2012). It also highlights that the criminalisation of homosexuality was not ended, but reworked—in part along the lines of privacy and sexual respectability (Boucher & Reynolds 2018). The last decade of the twentieth century in Australia also heralded the advent of prosecutions for 'reckless' HIV transmission in different Australian states, presenting new avenues through which homosexual conduct could be criminalised and the queer body could be reproduced as deviant and threatening (Houlihan 2007, 2011).

Although sustained LGBT advocacy has successfully created pressure for police organisations in the majority of Australian jurisdictions to adopt the language of LGBT rights in their policies and public relations (Russell 2018), to imply that the days of 'policing perversion' are over would be, in Dwyer's (2014, p. 150) words, 'erroneous and simplistic'. In the UK, Moran (2012) argues that there has been a reduction in the targeting of some LGBT people by police, but only those deemed respectable sexual citizens. The development of LGBT–police partnerships in contexts such as Australia and the UK has largely focused on ending the formal targeting of gay men and improving police responses to homophobic hate crime, as I discuss in Chapter 6. Meanwhile, other forms of anti-queer violence linked to racism or socioeconomic and mental health status have often been neglected, such as the criminalisation frequently associated with homelessness, unemployment, sex work, the drug trade, and addiction (Lamble 2014). For instance, LGBTI advocate and senior lawyer at the Human Rights Law Centre Lee Carnie recounted in interview that although there was a lack of empirical data,

> anecdotally we hear that trans women who are sex workers are over-policed, but also that trans women—particularly trans women of colour—are disproportionally represented as victims of crime ... and because they are over-policed, they are less likely to report.

This was reinforced in my interview with Jane Green, a queer sex worker activist and representative of Vixen Collective (Victoria's peer only sex worker organisation). They explained that in their efforts to improve police responses to sex workers, they continue to confront:

> A police culture that is incredibly entrenched and rigid and has negative views about our community and views us all as criminals, despite the fact that our work is legal in Victoria now. And when I say that, I mean I had the police unit that we deal with primarily call me a criminal to my face.

I raised with Green the idea that there seemed to have been a significant shift in the past two decades, as 'quite a sanitised version of lesbian and gay identity has been somewhat able to escape this stigma of criminality'. Green responded by stating that 'it's a very slow process, and ... a process that's taking a lot longer for sex workers'. However, given the emphasis of the politics of respectability in much LGBT rights campaigning (Richardson 2005), it is unclear if these gains will extend to other stigmatised groups, including sex workers. As Lamble (2014) points out, the reduction in the policing of more privileged sections of the LGBT community has occurred alongside a massive increase in the targeted policing of others, particularly those from poor, racialised, and migrant communities.

In Australia, Aboriginal and Torres Strait Islander people continue to bear the brunt of the violence of policing (Blagg 2008; Cunneen 2001; Klippmark & Crawley 2018). This reinforces the importance of advancing intersectional queer politics and analysis (Cohen 1997). For instance, in the midst of grassroots protests following the highly publicised police assault of a white queer youth, Jamie Jackson Reed, at the 2013 Sydney Mardi Gras (Australia's major LGBT pride event, discussed in Chapters 4 and 5), Wiradjuri man Ray Jackson, a prominent activist against Black deaths in custody, argued for building stronger links between Aboriginal and LGBT activists:

> For 225 years both our mobs have been discriminated against, ostracised and abused by the police. As I said at that rally, it is high time that both our groups worked together … to curb the violence of the police … In the Aboriginal mobs there's gay people, so we cross over. And there's no use that you fight your battles with the police from the gay point of view, and we fight our battles with the police, which is the same battle from the Aboriginal point of view.
>
> (Copland 2013)

While many queer activists have consistently named the coercive and regulatory functions of policing, Ray Jackson issues a challenge to the 'single-issue' politics that have often dominated lesbian and gay campaigns that focus solely on sexual oppression. Any discussion of the policing of sexuality and gender cannot be divorced from an understanding of policing as a settler colonial project. The coalitional politics that Jackson espouses requires LGBT critiques of policing to extend beyond individual and high-profile incidents of anti-queer violence to encompass broader recognition of the violence of policing that is continually visited upon the bodies of Aboriginal people and others marginalised by their race, class, disability, gender, sexuality, or any combination of these. As I discuss in Chapter 6, LGBT experiences of violence—including at the hands of police—are most frequently unreported, largely because they are normalised and institutionalised. However, violence is not evenly spread among LGBT people. Sexual and gender identities are always racialised, classed, and gendered, which effects how they are policed, and how the public responds when the violence of policing is exposed.

The next chapter examines in close detail the highest-profile instance of LGBT criminalisation in Melbourne in the post-law reform era: the 1994 Tasty nightclub raid. This case illustrates the continuities in paramilitary policing in Victoria and in LGBT efforts to name and push back on police violence and targeting. The fallout from the Tasty raid laid bare the institutionalised homophobia of policing in a way that has not been repeated since. The chapter also begins to critically explore the identity politics and sexual citizenship claims that were gaining visibility during the 1990s, particularly the notion of lesbian and gay respectability as a basis for claims to equal treatment.

Notes

1 This shift followed the notorious saga centring Irish bushranger Ned Kelly in north-eastern Victoria, which was grounded in class conflicts over policing and land.

2 In 1864, the death penalty was restricted to cases that involved force or a person under the age of 14. In 1949, the death penalty was abolished for sodomy in Victoria.

3 While there are very little publicly available data on the number of arrests and prosecutions for consensual homosexual behaviour historically, biographical accounts offer unique insights into the uneven application of sodomy laws. For example, in his autobiography, gay dancer and performer Noel Tovey (2004) writes of his wrongful conviction for buggery in 1951 as an Aboriginal teenager in Melbourne coerced into confessing by police. He details the disadvantaged young men he met in prison who engaged in same-sex activity sometimes as a means of survival, and the high-profile prosecutions of his friends in Melbourne who were 'female impersonators' to serve as an example or warning to others.

References

Aiello, MF 2014, 'Policing the masculine frontier: Cultural criminological analysis of the gendered performance of policing', *Crime Media Culture*, vol. 10, no. 1, pp. 59–79.

Aldrich, R 2003, *Colonialism and homosexuality*, Routledge, London.

Allen, J 1987, 'Policing since 1880: Some questions of sex', in M Finnane (ed.), *Policing in Australia: Historical perspectives*, New South Wales University Press, Kensington, pp. 188–222.

Attwood, B 1989, *The making of the Aborigines*, Allen & Unwin, Sydney.

Behrendt, L 2000, 'Consent in a (neo)colonial society: Aboriginal women as sexual and legal "other"', *Australian Feminist Studies*, vol. 15, no. 33, pp. 353–367.

Bell, D & Binnie, J 2000, *The sexual citizen: Queer politics and beyond*, Polity Press, Cambridge.

Blagg, H 2008, *Crime, Aboriginality and the decolonisation of justice*, Hawkins Press, Annandale.

Boon-Kuo, L, Meiners, ER, & Simpson, P 2018, 'Queer interruptions: Policing belonging in the carceral state', in P Aggleton, R Cover, D Leahy, D Marshall, & ML Rasmussen (eds), *Youth, sexuality and sexual citizenship*, Routledge, Oxon, pp. 34–49.

Boucher, L & Reynolds, R 2018, 'Decriminalisation, apology and expungement: Sexual citizenship and the problem of public sex in Victoria', *Australian Historical Studies*, vol. 49, no. 4, pp. 457–474.

Carbery, G 2014, *Towards homosexual equality in Australian criminal law—a brief history*, Australian Lesbian and Gay Archives Inc, viewed 7 December 2018, www.alga.org.au/files/towardsequality2ed.pdf.

Casella, EC 2000, '"Doing trade": A sexual economy of nineteenth-century Australian female convict prisons', *World Archaeology*, vol. 32, no. 2, pp. 209–221.
Chesser, L 2008a, *Parting with my sex: Cross-dressing, inversion and sexuality in Australian cultural life*, Sydney University Press, Sydney.
Chesser, L 2008b, '"What they were doing with their clothes off I don't know": Homophobia, lesbian history and responses to "lesbian-like" relationships, 1860s–1890s', in S Robinson (ed.), *Homophobia: An Australian history*, The Federation Press, Sydney, pp. 39–62.
Cohen, CJ 1997, 'Punks, bulldaggers, and welfare queens: The radical potential of queer politics?', *Gay and Lesbian Quarterly*, vol. 3, no. 4, pp. 437–465.
Connell, RW 1995, *Masculinities*, Allen and Unwin, Sydney.
Connell, RW & Irving, TH 1980, *Class structure in Australian history: Documents, narrative and argument*, Longman Cheshire, Melbourne.
Connors, L 2017, 'Uncovering the shameful: Sexual violence on an Australian colonial frontier', in R Mason (ed.), *Legacies of violence: Rendering the unspeakable past in modern Australia*, Bergahn Books, New York, pp. 33–52.
Copland, S 2013, 'Interview with Ray Jackson', *Simon Copland*, web log post, 27 March, viewed 8 December 2018, http://simoncopland.com/2013/03/27/interview-with-ray-jackson.
Cunneen, C 2001, *Conflict, politics and crime: Aboriginal communities and the police*, Allen & Unwin, Sydney.
Cunneen, C & Tauri, J 2015, *Indigenous criminology*, University of Chicago Press, Chicago.
Dalton, D 2007, 'Policing outlawed desire: "Homocriminality" in beat spaces in Australia', *Law Critique*, vol. 18, pp. 375–405.
Dalton, D 2008, 'Gay male resistance in "beat" spaces in Australia: A study of outlaw desire', *The Australian Feminist Law Journal*, vol. 28, pp. 97–119.
Dreher, T 2016, 'The "uncanny doubles" of queer politics: Sexual citizenship in the era of same-sex marriage victories', *Sexualities*, vol. 20, no. 1–2, pp. 176–195.
Dwyer, A 2014, 'Pleasures, perversities, and partnerships: The historical emergence of LGBT–police relationships', in D Peterson & VR Panfil (eds), *Handbook of LGBT communities, crime, and justice*, Springer, New York, pp. 149–164.
Featherstone, L & Kaladelfos, A 2016, *Sex crimes in the fifties*, Melbourne University Press, Carlton.
Finnane, M 1994, *Police and government: Histories of policing in Australia*, Oxford University Press, South Melbourne.
Ford, R 2000, Contested desires: Narratives of passionate friends, married masqueraders and lesbian love in Australia, 1918–1945, doctoral thesis, La Trobe University, Melbourne.
Ford, R 2003, 'Sexuality and "madness": Regulating women's gender "deviance" through the Orange asylum in the 1930s', in C Coleborne & D MacKinnon (eds), *Madness in Australia: Histories, heritage and asylum*, University of Queensland Press, Brisbane, pp. 109–119.
Ford, R 2008, '"Filthy, obscene and mad": Engendering homophobia in Australia, 1940s–1960s', in S Robinson (ed.), *Homophobia: An Australian history*, The Federation Press, Sydney, pp. 86–112.
Foucault, M 1978, *The history of sexuality, vol. 1: An introduction*, trans. R Hurley, Random House, New York.

Gardiner, J 2015, 'Repealed? So what!', unpublished paper presented at *Australian Homosexual Histories Conference*, 13–14 November, Adelaide.

Gays and Lesbians Aboriginal Alliance 1993, 'Peopling the empty mirror: The prospects for lesbian and gay Aboriginal history', in R Aldrich (ed.), *Gay perspectives II: More essays in Australian gay culture*, University of Sydney, Sydney, pp. 1–62.

Haldane, R 1995, *The people's force: A history of the Victoria Police*, Melbourne University Press, Carlton South.

Halperin, DM 1990, *One hundred years of homosexuality and other essays on Greek love*, Routledge, New York.

Harris, AP 2011, 'Heteropatriarchy kills: Challenging gender violence in a prison nation', *Washington University Journal of Law & Policy*, vol. 37, no. 1, pp. 13–65.

Hodge, D 2012, 'Police persecution of Adelaide's homosexual culture: 1945–1972', *Flinders Journal of History and Politics*, vol. 28, pp. 45–76.

Holmes, K & Pinto, S 2013, 'Gender and sexuality', in A Bashford & S Macintyre (eds), *The Cambridge history of Australia, volume 2: The Commonwealth of Australia*, Cambridge University Press, Melbourne, pp. 308–331.

Houlihan, A 2007, (Ill-legal) lust is a battle field: HIV risk, socio-sexuality and criminality, doctoral thesis, Griffith University, Queensland.

Houlihan, A 2011, 'Risky (legal) business: HIV and criminal culpability in Victoria', *International Journal of Liability and Scientific Enquiry*, vol. 4, no. 4, pp. 305–327.

Human Rights Law Centre (HRLC) 2014, *Righting historical wrongs: Background paper for a legislative scheme to expunge convictions for historical consensual gay sex offences in Victoria*, HRLC, Melbourne, viewed 14 January 2019, www.hrlc.org.au/reports/righting-historical-wrongs-background-paper-for-a-legislative-scheme-to-expunge-convictions-for-historical-consensual-gay-sex-offences-in-victoria.

Iveson, K 2007, *Publics and the city*, Blackwell Publishing, Malden.

Johnson, P 2008, '"Crimes against morality": Law and public sex in Australia', *Alternative Law Journal*, vol. 33, no. 3, pp. 150–159.

Johnson, P 2010, 'The enforcement of morality: Law, policing and sexuality in New South Wales', *The Australian and New Zealand Journal of Criminology*, vol. 43, no. 3, pp. 399–422.

Katz, J 1983, *Gay/lesbian almanac: A new documentary*, Harper & Row, New York.

Klippmark, P & Crawley, K 2018, 'Justice for Ms Dhu: Accounting for Indigenous deaths in custody in Australia', *Social & Legal Studies*, vol. 27, no. 6, pp. 695–715.

Kunzel, R 2008, *Criminal intimacy: Prison and the uneven history of modern American sexuality*, University of Chicago Press, Chicago.

Lamble, S 2009, 'Unknowable bodies, unthinkable sexualities: Lesbian and transgender legal invisibility in the Toronto women's bathhouse raid', *Social and Legal Studies*, vol. 18, pp. 111–130.

Lamble, S 2014, 'Queer investments in punitiveness: Sexual citizenship, social movements and the expanding carceral state', in J Haritaworn, A Kuntsman, & S Posocco (eds), *Queer necropolitics*, Routledge, Oxfordshire, pp. 151–171.

Mason, G 1995, '(Out)laws: Acts of proscription in the sexual order', in M Thornton (ed.), *Public and private: Feminist legal debates*, Oxford University Press, Oxford, pp. 66–88.

McCulloch, J 2001, *Blue army: Paramilitary policing in Australia*, Melbourne University Press, Carlton.

McQuilton, J 1987, 'Police in rural Victoria: A regional example', in M Finnane (ed.), *Policing in Australia: Historical perspectives*, New South Wales University Press, Kensington, pp. 35–58.

Mogul, J, Ritchie, AJ, & Whitlock, K 2011, *Queer (in)justice: The criminalisation of LGBT people in the United States*, Beacon Press, Boston.

Moore, D 1991, 'The origins of the police mandate: The Australian case reconsidered', *Police Studies*, vol. 14, pp. 107–120.

Moran, LJ 2012, 'The changing landscape of policing male sexualities: A minor revolution', in P Johnson & D Dalton (eds), *Policing sex*, Routledge, London, pp. 11–22.

Morgan, W 1993–1994, 'Identifying evil for what it is: Tasmania, sexual perversity and the United Nations', *Melbourne University Law Review*, vol. 19, no. 3, pp. 740–757.

Nance, B 1981, 'The level of violence: Europeans and Aborigines in Port Phillip, 1835–1850', *Historical Studies*, vol. 9, no. 77, pp. 532–552.

Nolan, B 2013, 'Up close and personal: Lesbian sub-culture in the female factories of Van Diemen's Land', *Journal of Lesbian Studies*, vol. 17, no. 3–4, pp. 291–304.

Pendleton, M & Serisier, T 2012, 'Some gays and the queers', *M/C Journal*, vol. 15, no. 6, viewed 12 September 2018, www.journal.media-culture.org.au/index.php/mcjournal/article/view/569.

Piper, AJ 2015, '"I'll have no man": Female families in Melbourne's criminal subcultures, 1860–1920', *Journal of Australian Studies*, vol. 39, no. 4, pp. 444–460.

Reeves, T 2016, 'Dr Duncan revisited', *Journal of Historical Society of South Australia*, vol. 44, pp. 117–126.

Reynolds, H 1989, *Dispossession: Black Australians and white invaders*, Allen & Unwin, Sydney.

Reynolds, R 2002, *From camp to queer: Remaking the Australian homosexual*, Melbourne University Press, Carlton.

Richardson, D 2005, 'Desiring sameness? The rise of a neoliberal politics of normalisation', *Antipode*, vol. 37, no. 3, pp. 515–535.

Riggs, DW 2006, *Priscilla, (white) queen of the desert: Queer rights/race privilege*, Peter Lang Publishing, New York.

Robson, R 1990, 'Lesbianism in Anglo-European legal history', *Wisconsin Women's Law Journal*, vol. 5, pp. 1–42.

Russell, EK 2018, 'Carceral pride: The fusion of police imagery with LGBTI rights', *Feminist Legal Studies*, vol. 26, no. 3, pp. 331–350.

Ryan, L 2010, 'Settler massacres on the Port Phillip frontier, 1836–1851', *Journal of Australian Studies*, vol. 34, no. 3, pp. 257–273.

Somerville, SB 2000, *Queering the color line*, Duke University Press, Durham.

Stanley, EA 2011, 'Fugitive flesh: Gender self-determination, queer abolition and trans resistance', in EA Stanley & N Smith (eds), *Captive genders: Trans embodiment and the prison industrial complex*, AK Press, Oakland, pp. 1–11.

Stoler, A 1995, *Race and the education of desire: Foucault's History of Sexuality and the colonial order of things*, Duke University Press, Durham.

Swivel, M 2001, 'Public convenience, public nuisance: Criminological perspectives on the beat', *Current Issues in Criminal Justice*, vol. 5, pp. 237–249.

Tovey, N 2004, *Little black bastard: A story of survival*, Hodder, Sydney.

Valverde, M 2007, 'Bodies, words, identities: The moving targets of the criminal law', in M Dubber & L Farmer (eds), *Modern histories of crime and punishment*, Stanford University Press, Stanford, pp. 224–251.

Victoria Police 1980, *Police in victoria, 1836–1980*, Victoria Police, Melbourne.

Warner, M 1993, *Fear of a queer planet: Queer politics and social theory*, University of Minnesota Press, Minneapolis.

Willett, G 2000, *Living out loud: A history of gay and lesbian activism in Australia*, Allen & Unwin, Sydney.

Willett, G 2008, 'From "vice" to "homosexuality": Policing perversion in the 1950s', in S Robinson (ed.), *Homophobia: An Australian history*, The Federation Press, Sydney, pp. 113–127.

Willett, G, Murdoch, W, & Marshall, D 2011, *Secret histories of queer Melbourne*, Australian Lesbian and Gay Archives, Parkville.

Wolfe, P 1994, 'Nation and miscegenation: Discursive continuity in the post-Mabo era', *Social Analysis*, vol. 36, pp. 93–152.

Wotherspoon, G 1991, *'City of the plain': History of a gay sub-culture*, Hale and Iremonger, Sydney.

Chapter 3

Over-policing and the production of good queer victims

The Tasty nightclub raid

Introduction

On 7 August 1994, 40 Victoria Police officers detained and strip-searched 463 patrons and staff under a single warrant at 'Tasty', a gay event regularly held at the Commerce Club in Flinders Lane, Melbourne. The club was reportedly frequented not only by predominantly white, professional gay men, but also by lesbians, trans women, and 'straights' (Willett 2011). Six charges were laid as a result of the raid (including five charges for drug possession), yet only one charge stuck—for hindering police. During the raid, individual officers failed to wear visible identification and ignored existing guidelines for searches. In the fallout from the raid, relations between police and the 'gay community' were described as being 'at an all-time low' (Freeman-Greene 1997, p. 18). Victoria Police received widespread criticism and condemnation in both mainstream and lesbian and gay press for the raid—named 'Operation Maze' after the 'grope maze' section of the venue—at a time when their general reputation and image in the media was overwhelmingly negative. In contrast, lesbian and gay Tasty patrons were often represented as respectable, 'ordinary law-abiding citizens' (Smith 1994) with a legitimate claim to victimhood. This claim was vindicated when those temporarily detained and strip-searched at the Tasty nightclub brought a successful civil suit against Victoria Police in 1996.

Focusing on the Tasty raid, this chapter investigates some of the key questions that concern this book: how do LGBT people come to embody legitimate victimhood, and on what basis? And what are the social and political effects of such a process? Simultaneously, how do police seek to control their image and garner legitimacy following high-profile incidents of police violence? And what factors enable or constrain their success? The Tasty raid is a useful case through which to explore these questions because of the large scale of the raid, the extensive media coverage it generated, and its constructed significance for local queer history. I have seen it referred to many times as 'Melbourne's Stonewall' (e.g. Freeman-Greene 1997)—a stretched reference to the infamous 1969 rebellion that followed a police raid on the Stonewall Inn in New York City, a gay bar that catered to a diverse crowd, including 'street queens' and homeless queer youth (Hanhardt 2013). In reality, the Tasty raid played out very differently to Stonewall, as relatively privileged lesbian and gay people utilised liberal rights frameworks and formal legal channels to challenge police harassment, rather than direct and violent confrontations with police in the streets. Nonetheless, the local importance of the Tasty raid for queer *and* police history was augmented by the official apology issued by Victoria Police on the 20th anniversary of the raid—an event I analyse in more depth in Chapter 7. In this chapter, I examine both mainstream and lesbian and gay media coverage of the Tasty raid in the mid-1990s in order to analyse conventional representations and understandings of the raid and its key actors: namely lesbian and gay Tasty patrons and Victoria Police. I use criminologist Nils Christie's (1986) framework of the 'ideal' victim to explore how lesbian and gay people came to be understood as legitimate victims in the aftermath of the raid—deserving recognition, sympathy, and redress—and the social and political implications of this process. The category of the ideal victim, as I will discuss, is constructed through the use of a variety of idealised moral qualities, such as innocence and respectability.

By analysing the production of victim identities in this case, I want to extend existing understandings of the significance of the Tasty raid for the politics of queer history beyond the continuation of homophobic policing (cf. Groves 1995). Instead, I want to explore the ways in which sexual politics interact with constructions of 'respectability' (Skeggs 1997) in the contexts of criminalisation, policing, and state protection. Bringing the concept of homonormativity into conversation with the notion of ideal victimhood, I argue that the successful construction of legitimate victimhood by lesbian and gay Tasty patrons was achieved largely through classed signifiers of respectability and the paradigm of sameness: that is, the idea that homosexuals are the same as our heterosexual counterparts, which becomes the basis of claims for rights and protection. Among the benefits of this homonormative construction was that it helped to impede police efforts to control media narratives and secure legitimacy in the aftermath of the Tasty raid. However, by casting hyper-visible queerness as outdated, irrelevant, and a threat to lesbian and gay efforts to achieve sympathy and recognition, this construction of 'respectability' failed to deeply challenge homophobia. The case thereby offers unique insights into some of the ways in which LGBT people may achieve legitimacy as victims in a heteronormative context and how this might come at the cost of a structural analysis of sexuality, power, and violence. It also highlights how state institutions navigate and avoid accountability for violence enacted upon a specific and historically targeted group.

'Treated like scum': the Tasty raid

Those detained and strip-searched by police at the Tasty nightclub described the raid as frightening, homophobic, threatening, abusive, and humiliating. By all reports, they were 'treated like scum' (Tozer 1994, p. 6). During the raid police told patrons to put their hands against the wall, to be silent and still—if they moved, police reportedly yelled, pushed and shoved them, or shone torches in their faces (Conroy 1994a). People were called 'faggots' by a number of officers (Dean 1996; Deputy Ombudsman of Victoria 1994). When I interviewed Sally Gordon, a Tasty patron who became the lead plaintiff in the subsequent civil suit against Victoria Police, she described police coming into the club 'like a pack of storm troopers' and acting 'really, really aggressive'. She recounted asking police three times to see their search warrant and being told in response to 'shut the fuck up', and witnessing one man who refused to be strip-searched pushed down the stairs by an officer.

In an unusual fashion, this abuse of state power was witnessed by hundreds of people at the nightclub, some of whom were well connected and highly articulate lesbians and gay men with various resources at their disposal. As lawyer and Tasty patron Gary Singer mentioned when I interviewed him, the Tasty raid 'was a pretty unique situation, because [there were] more witnesses than police, which is a really unusual dynamic, because normally [there is] one victim and a group of police tell another story'. In the days following the raid, it came to be portrayed in both mainstream and lesbian and gay press as 'over the top', degrading, dangerous, intimidating, discriminatory, and unacceptable (e.g. Forell 1994; Ryle et al. 1994; Spindler & Connellan 1994). Feelings of shock, anger, fury, outrage, and disgust directed towards police from Tasty patrons, family members, the wider LGBT community, and other supporters circulated in letters to newspaper editors and reporting on the raid, along with demands for an end to police harassment (e.g. Alexander 1994; Cummins 1994; Wilson 1994).

The Tasty raid quickly generated an independent investigation by the Deputy Ombudsman of Victoria and an internal police investigation. The Deputy Ombudsman's (1994) investigation found that police rejection of alternative strategies partly reflected a stereotyping of homosexual behaviour; he also noted that police failed to consult the Police Lesbian and Gay Liaison Committee before the raid.[1] In his examination of allegations that the decision to instigate the raid, and the manner in which it was carried out, had been influenced by homophobia, the Deputy Ombudsman (1994, p. 1) concluded that 'the raid was discriminatory but was not, insofar as can be ascertained, based on prejudice against homosexuals'. Without finding a clear motivation of homophobia, the report nevertheless stated that 'the Club was treated differently because it's a gay club' (Deputy Ombudsman of Victoria 1994, p. 65). Groves (1995) argues that the Deputy Ombudsman's findings were disappointing and inconsequential for LGBT people because of the disavowal of homophobic intentions and the failure to rule out the possibility of a similar raid occurring again. He further points out that, regardless of internal police efforts to reform their strip-searching policy, previous guidelines were not followed during the Tasty raid (1995, p. 27); this highlights the gap between police policy and practice, and the lack of consequences for the abuse of power.

As mentioned above, the Tasty raid catalysed a civil suit against police, led by lawyer Gary Singer. When I interviewed Singer, he described:

> While the [raid] had been happening, I was thinking: 'This is what all my criminal [law] clients tell me happens with the police; you have this police brutality, this complete show of force'. And I thought: 'I'm not going to cause strife there [during the raid], because you're just asking for trouble with the police'. So, I thought my way of revenge would be to investigate my rights and to sue them for false imprisonment tomorrow.

Singer had the advantage of significant legal knowledge and experience and was able to immediately connect his atypical experience on the 'other side' of the law with broader patterns of police violence most often targeted at his socio-economically disadvantaged clients. Sally Gordon reiterated that during the raid, 'the lawyers [who were present] like Gary Singer—they absorbed every goddamn detail of what was going on'. With the help of a barrister, Jack Keenan QC, Singer aided Gordon in successfully filing a civil suit against the police, which was heard in the Victorian County Court over roughly two months in early 1996.[2] The court awarded Gordon AUD$10,000 compensation, and Judge Ostrowski ruled that the execution of the raid was 'unreasonable' (Conroy & Adams 1996). A class action followed involving more than 250 plaintiffs claiming false imprisonment and assault, which ultimately cost the metropolitan Victoria Police Department AUD$6 million in compensatory damages (Waghorne & Macintyre 2011, p. 161). However, the significance of the successful legal challenge surpasses financial terms. When I asked Gordon what the Tasty raid case means to her today, she responded:

> Whether you want to call it a part of human rights history in Victoria and Australia, whether you want to call it history in the gay community … I think that all institutions like the police force, if we live in a democratic country, they need to be called to account when their behaviour is way out of whack … I hope that the 463 people [at the raid]—because it wasn't just me—and the wider community get a sense of pride from the pressure we applied for something that was absolutely, totally wrong; and that was the police behaviour on that night.

While Gordon is clear in her condemnation of police conduct during the Tasty raid and steadfastly characterised Victoria at the time as a 'police state', she is also adamant that policing has 'definitely changed in Victoria' since then. Indeed, the Tasty raid occurred at a time of significant expansion of police powers and 'tough on crime' governance, as well as increased scrutiny of police violence and impunity.

'They see fags as an easy target': paramilitary policing and institutionalised homophobia

In the immediate aftermath of the civil suit, legal scholar and barrister Ian Freckelton contested the notion that the case was straightforwardly 'an emphatic victory' or an 'example of justice at work', as it was depicted in the media (Freeman-Greene 1997, p. 19). Freckelton (1996) argues that the damages awarded were low and that the case failed to make police accountable or break down an entrenched police culture of disrespecting the rights of minority groups, excessive use of force, and 'inappropriate loyalty'. Scholarship on police culture suggests that police organisations are frequently characterised by intolerance and prejudice, conservatism, and mutual solidarity—or a culture of 'cover up' (Chan 1997; Waddington 1999). While police culture is not static and homogenous, nor is it entirely disconnected or insulated from the wider society that surrounds it (Loftus 2007); the traditional 'cult' of white, heterosexual masculinity within police organisations is particularly difficult to shift (Smith & Gray 1985). Victoria Police continues to come under scrutiny for a toxic organisational culture of sexual harassment and bullying (e.g. Victorian Equal Opportunity & Human Rights Commission 2015). Of course, when viewed through a historical lens, policing in Victoria has always used violent and repressive techniques to contain resistance to or deviance from the dominant social order, both within and outside of the force. Lesbian and gay liberation movements in Australia were conceived and developed in a context of severe state hostility towards sexual and gender transgressions: queer spaces in Melbourne have a long history of police surveillance, intrusion, and violence (Human Rights Law Centre 2014; Tovey 2004). As gay activist and Tasty patron Stephen Jones argued, police 'see fags as an easy target, they know we're used to being harassed by them' (Bonwick 1994).

Police reportedly harassed people at Tasty events both before and after the raid in August 1994. The *Age* reported that there had been numerous incidents involving individual police 'swaggering into the club' and subjecting staff and patrons to 'homophobic taunts' prior to the raid, and further claims of police harassment by Tasty patrons emerged six months after the raid in February 1995 (Hill 1995). This suggests that the Tasty raid was not strictly an isolated event, but rather part of a broader pattern of police harassment of LGBT people. For those impacted by police harassment, the wide media coverage of the raid provided an opportunity to voice long-standing concerns about systemic oppression. Letters appeared in the *Age* in the days after the event arguing that 'it's hard to interpret police behaviour as anything more than homophobia', and that the raid 'reveals almost an institutionalised police homophobia' (Clifton 1994, p. 20; Daye 1994, p. 20). These accounts and analyses reflect how police harassment and violence were not new experiences for many LGBT people who attended Tasty nightclub.

The Tasty raid was linked to a pattern of paramilitary policing, which fuelled perceptions of escalating state repression in Victoria at the time (O'Leary 1994; Waghorne & Macintyre 2011). In brief, paramilitary policing involves the use of high levels of force, often against groups of people conceived as 'enemies' (McCulloch 2002). Between 1984 and 1995, roughly the decade preceding the Tasty raid, there were 35 police shooting fatalities in Victoria and in the first nine months of 1994 alone, Victoria Police shot and killed eight people; in comparison, New South Wales police shot and killed four people in the six years leading up to 1994 (McCulloch 2001, p. 100). The disproportionate rate of police shootings in Victoria and the apparent lack of police accountability led to, as criminologist Jude McCulloch (1990, p. 160) describes it, 'a new level of fear and distrust between the police and the community'. State Premier Jeff Kennett came to power in 1992 and continued to 'ratchet up police powers' and trial new police weapons; a number of well-publicised incidents of police violence followed (Waghorne & Macintyre 2011, p. 160). Just one day before the findings of the Deputy Ombudsman's investigation into the Tasty raid were released, Victoria Police was found to have used excessive force on protesters at Richmond Secondary College in December 1993 and anti-logging demonstrators in East Melbourne in February 1994 (McCulloch 2001, pp. 116–149, pp. 195–213). One Tasty patron linked the raid to the series of police shootings and increasing 'police brutality in general', arguing in a letter to the lesbian and gay newspaper *Melbourne Star Observer* that 'Victorian law enforcement under Kennett has piece by piece been becoming more and more absolute' (Ravel 1994).

In this context, the tension between maintaining institutional legitimacy and patterns of illegitimate behaviour proved ultimately unmanageable for Victoria Police. The Tasty raid heightened media and institutional scrutiny of policing practices, reinforcing widely held perceptions that Victoria Police had 'lost the plot' (Clifton 1994), were 'increasingly regarding themselves as being beyond the law' (Spindler & Connellan 1994), and were 'out of control and must be reined in' (*Gayzette* 22 August 1994, p. 1). Concerns regarding police powers were also linked to underlying homophobia; as one letter in the *Age* argued, 'the police picked a minority group to try out their new powers to see if they could get away with it' (Webster 1994, p. 20). The negative image of police circulating in the media around the time of the Tasty raid, and the lack of public support that it both indicated and encouraged, represented a significant problem for Victoria Police in carrying out its core tasks. To be effective in its aims, policing requires the ongoing support, consent, and cooperation of the public, which rests upon the perception that the police organisation and the power it exercises are legitimate (Bottoms & Tankebe 2012; Tyler 2006). Media and communications are central to the legitimation of policing; legitimation involves the careful construction and reconstruction of image (Lee & McGovern 2014, p. 38; Reiner 2003). The negative image of Victoria Police in the media and their lack of public support may have contributed to creating the conditions necessary for LGBT people to gain media and public sympathy for their plight as victims of police violence, in a way that was largely unprecedented.

Ideal subjects? The new politics of lesbian and gay victimhood

Popular depictions of Victoria Police as 'out of control' combined with representations of lesbian and gay Tasty patrons as respectable and 'innocent' victims to shape wider public reactions to the raid: reactions of shock, disgust, and condemnation. In so doing, the emotionality of moral panics about sexuality—usually directed at queers (Irvine 2007)—was diverted towards the police, reinforcing a perceived lack of public trust in the force. Meanwhile, lesbians and gay men garnered sympathy and support from mainstream media and others who came to view them as worthy of state protection, rather than as a criminalised class. In other words, queer subjects were able to emulate and rework constructions of worthy or 'ideal' victimhood.

Within criminology, the concept of the 'ideal' victim refers to an idealisation of what it means to be a victim (Christie 1986). Ideal victims are not necessarily those most likely to experience harm and violence, but those who, when harmed or negatively impacted, are '*most readily given the complete and legitimate status of being a victim*' (Christie 1986, p. 18, emphasis in original). Christie (1986) suggests that the successful construction of ideal victimhood relies on the projection of imagined qualities of respectability and blamelessness, among others. The status of ideal victimhood is profoundly shaped and given meaning by shifting social and economic conditions (Green 2011). Whether an individual or group is regarded as respectable or innocent is therefore likely to be connected to privileged (and unfixed) markers of identity in a specific context, such as those based on class, race, gender, ability, and sexuality.

Historically, LGBT people are not ideal victims. Those seen to be outside the bounds of heteronormativity are more likely to be blamed for their own victimisation and held to 'moral account', irrespective of the specific ways in which they are violated (Mason 2007). This phenomenon has been well documented in the context of homophobic violence and sexual assault, where victims who are seen as morally deficient in some way are too often assumed to deserve their own violation: sex workers, trans women, women or effeminate men perceived to be 'asking for it', queers who are HIV positive, and/or men who visit 'beats' (Mason et al. 2004; Tomsen 2006). The traditional categories of worthy and unworthy victims are complicated by the Tasty raid because a group traditionally ineligible for legitimate victimhood (LGBT people and others frequenting a sex-on-premises nightclub) were able to convincingly claim the status of worthy victims. A possible reason for this may be the context of heightened criticism of Victoria Police and its use of paramilitary tactics, as discussed above. In the case of the Tasty raid, Victoria Police was seen to have 'lost the plot' (Clifton 1994) and the Deputy Ombudsman's inquiry targeted the police organisation as a whole, rather than simply individual 'bad apples' among the ranks, which is usually the default framework for understanding police misconduct. The perceived deviancy of Victoria Police was reflected at levels as high up as the State Premier, who publicly described the Tasty raid as 'extreme' and 'disturbing' (Conroy 1994c, p. 3). In this instance, the perceived deviancy of the police may have outweighed the sexual deviancy of Tasty patrons, who should have been excluded from the category of 'ideal victims', enabling them instead to occupy that category.

Despite needing a relative degree of 'weakness' to establish themselves within public sympathies, ideal victims must still, as Christie (1986, p. 21, emphasis in original) points out, be 'strong enough to be listened to, or dare to talk', but '*weak enough not to become a threat to other important interests*'. Ideal victims then cannot make a demand for fundamentally transformative changes. Their claim must be about restoring and reaffirming pre-existing social and cultural norms (such as privacy, tolerance, and individual rights) that were violated during the event of their victimisation. This suggests that one way in which LGBT people may be able to approach ideal victimhood is through appealing to established norms, including heterosexual ideals.

'Good queer subjects' can be promoted through downplaying or disallowing the aspects of queer practices and identities that may be seen as threatening to the heteronormative order. As outlined in the introductory chapter of this book, this trend in sexual politics has been referred to as 'homonormativity' (Duggan 2004), whereby good queer subjects are constructed through cultural markers of upward (class) mobility, whiteness, and heteronormativity, such as marriage and nuclear family structures (Agathangelou et al. 2008). In the Australian context, criminologist Stephen Tomsen (2001, p. 238) takes account of a pattern of increasing affluence for a (limited) number of lesbian and gay people, which has contributed to the emergence of 'gentrified' middle-class gay and lesbian cultural identities. The construction of these identities based on established norms, Tomsen (2001) suggests, has led to moral judgements about 'good' and 'bad' victims of homophobic violence, redrawing and evoking simplistic dichotomies between deserving and undeserving, responsible and irresponsible, respectable and unrespectable citizens (Phelan 2001). 'Bad victims' are the antithesis of 'ideal' victims, failing the tests of 'proper self-management' and therefore seen as being 'unfashionably oblivious to risk' (Moran & Skeggs 2004; Race 2012; Tomsen 2001). The emergence of these moral categories suggests that there has not necessarily been a move away from blaming LGBT people for their victimhood (or denying them victim status), but that a new division has been produced between 'good' and 'bad' victims of homophobic violence through neoliberal logics of risk and self-responsibility. In other words, moralising representations of victims that rely on classed, gendered, and racialised markers of respectability and blamelessness may contribute to the reproduction of hierarchies of victimisation, whereby some victims are perceived as more legitimate or blameless than others. This process may leave out others who experience violence but do not fit the narrow criteria for sympathy, pity, or compassion (Jenness 2004; Mason 2014; Morgan 2002).

The projection of a new public image of 'respectable' lesbians and gay men ruptures the traditional view of these marginal groups as deviants deserving the harsh repression by the police that they experience. Instead, in the public discourse that followed the Tasty raid, good queer subjects transitioned out of the realm of criminalisation and into that of state and legal protection.

'It's not a drug den': the production of respectable queerness

Discussions of the Tasty raid in both mainstream and lesbian and gay press were marked at various points by important challenges to institutionalised homophobia and state and police power (Bonwick 1994; Clifton 1994; Daye 1994; Webster 1994). However, the media also projected images of lesbians and gay men that relied upon and reinforced norms of respectability, including normative notions of gender, middle-class values, and privatised sexuality. I use the notion of privatised sexuality in relation to the consumerist sexual identity associated with homonormativity, and in the sense of affirming the private or personal realm as the proper and appropriate place for sexual expression, which reproduces the notion that queer public sex cultures are inherently dangerous and deviant (Berlant & Warner 1998; Morgan 1993–1994). For example, it is often noted that many—though certainly not all—Tasty patrons were professional-class lesbians and gay men, such as lawyers and doctors (Freeman-Greene 1997; Willett 2011). In contrast, the fact that Tasty was a sex-on-premises venue that could be described, in the words of Willett (2011, p. 158), as 'sleazy, or avant-garde, or just "out there"' scarcely received a mention in the press. To be sure, the selective framing of the Tasty raid in the media is likely to reflect strategic attempts by some LGBT people and their advocates to foreground specific traits and factors—while minimising others—in order to garner sympathy and support for raid victims. This is what Mariana Valverde (2010, p. 220) refers to as 'tactical speech': simplistic framing and language designed to communicate directly and persuasively to a broader audience. While it may be effective in reaching a larger number of people, tactical speech also carries the risk of erasing complexity and reinforcing existing assumptions and dominant ideas (about class and respectability, for example). It therefore requires closer interrogation.

Particular representations in the mainstream media of lesbians and gay men who experienced the Tasty raid relied on establishing their conformity with norms of middle-class respectability. In what appears to be the lengthiest article published in the mainstream press on the Tasty nightclub raid,[3] and thus the most detailed (though not unusual) in constructing a normalising narrative of lesbian and gay respectability and victimhood, reporter Suzy Freeman-Greene (1997) profiles two white gay and lesbian Tasty patrons, Robert Gould and Sally Gordon (the lead plaintiff in the civil suit), and makes mention of another, lawyer Gary Singer. Included in the *Sydney Morning Herald's* lift-out magazine *Good Weekend*, the article describes how

> Robert Gould, a respected gallery owner and art dealer, spends his life surrounded by beauty. In his long, white gallery on Toorak Road hang works by Nolan, Blackman, Tucker and Rees (…) Gould is a well-dressed man with a big smile. He talks quietly, but the outrage is still present in his voice when he recalls the night he and his friends went dancing at Tasty (…) He views the incident as primarily a civil rights issue, an attitude shared by his lawyer and fellow raid-victim, Gary Singer (…) who is a partner in the law firm Simon Parsons and Co.
>
> …
>
> Sydney woman Sally Gordon, the tall, no-nonsense business development manager of brewing company Lion Nathan Australia (…) was raised with a healthy respect for the police. [Now she is a] career woman who has been active in the Sydney gay community for many years.
>
> (Freeman-Greene 1997, pp. 20–22)

The Tasty patrons featured in this article are represented as responsible, hard-working, career-driven professionals: a respected gallery owner and art dealer; a partner in a law firm; a no-nonsense business development manager. This mirrors other representations of Gordon in the *Age* as an 'executive from Sydney who visited Melbourne regularly on business' at the time of the raid (Conroy 1996). Other descriptors such as 'well-dressed' and 'surrounded by beauty' in a 'long, white gallery on Toorak Road' add sophistication, cleanliness, and middle-class aesthetics to the story. The note that Gordon was raised with a 'healthy respect for the police', also mentioned in an earlier article in the *Age* and something she reiterated in her interview with me, evokes law-abiding citizenship and a respectable background and upbringing.[4] Freeman-Greene also conveys how the raid continues to impact Gould and Gordon through affective metaphors. Gould's 'outrage' is ascribed, presumably, to the tone of his voice, and Gordon is reported as saying, 'I know this sounds silly … but if I just see a policeman or woman on the streets there [in Melbourne], the hairs on the back of my neck stand up' (Freeman-Greene 1997). Markers of particular material conditions and class status are combined with emotional rhetoric to present lesbian and gay Tasty patrons as legitimate victims and good queer subjects. As respectable sexual citizens, they are reconstituted as blameless and worthy of compassion.

Foregrounding classed signifiers of respectability in claims for recognition, belonging, and protection can recode 'good' forms of sexual citizenship (Agathangelou et al. 2008, p. 122). However, this sexual governance can simultaneously marginalise those who fall outside of this social construction. LGBT people and others who fail to perform the imaginary of responsible citizenship—such as those who are unemployed, or engaged in work or behaviour that is stigmatised or criminalised, such as sex work—may not be regarded as respectable and therefore blameless victims in the same way. Instead, they may be morally judged as 'bad victims' who fall short of 'proper self-management' (Tomsen 2001). The effects of constructions of respectability and 'ideal' victimhood may also conceal the more regular and mundane applications of state violence and coercion, or even surreptitiously condone the same practices when used on those who exist outside the boundaries of respectability or responsible citizenship, such as those who are criminalised or otherwise routinely regarded as deviant. For example, an editorial that appeared in the *Age* (21 May 1996, p. 12) during the civil suit argued that the 'heavy methods' used by police at the Tasty raid 'almost certainly have a place against heavy criminal elements', but that 'nothing in the evidence suggests that police were likely to encounter such elements at the Tasty nightclub'. In other words, it is not the methods that are the problem, but on whom they are applied. This raises questions as to how the distinctions are to be made between those who deserve such abusive treatment by police and those who do not. When I interviewed Sally Gordon, she emphasised with incredulity the distinction between Tasty and other sites of criminality through a subtle and implicit differentiation between illicit drug dealing and drug taking, in order to make the overarching point that police behaviour at Tasty was highly inappropriate and excessive. As she exclaimed: 'It's not a drug den, it's not a place where … there's [drug] dealing going on, which I believe was their excuse for going in there. I mean, what a lot of rot!' Gordon reinforces the notion that Tasty patrons were undeserving targets of such 'heavy' police methods through disassociating them from 'heavy criminal elements'—here associated with drug dealing. This distinction helps to cement Tasty patrons' status as legitimate victims of wrongful state intrusion, but it also implies that others tainted by the spectre of criminality (as many sexually and gender nonconforming people continue to be) might not be so successful in winning popular support in similar circumstances.

'The clichéd image of mincing and effeminate poseurs': policing gender, policing sex

The prospect of inclusion in categories of respectability remains precarious for non-heterosexual citizens. The emphasis on asserting legitimate victimhood through association with shifting boundaries of respectability can create pressure to disown what Tomsen (2006) terms 'morally embarrassing victims'. It may entail distancing sexual identities from stigmatised behaviours or practices associated with queerness in a given context, in order to enable queers to approach, if not meet, the terms and criteria for social belonging and state protection. This reproduces the divide between victims who are perceived as 'deserving' of public sympathy and legal redress, and those who are not. Two examples in the context of media coverage of the Tasty raid reflect this disassociation: the issue of 'beats'—public sex environments frequented predominantly by gay men—and expressions of male femininity. Significant issues arising from the policing of beats, including harassment, violence, and entrapment, were being reported in the lesbian and gay media around the time the Tasty raid occurred (*Melbourne Star Observer* 2 September 1994, p. 3; Joyce 1997), but in the mainstream media, these connections were not made.

In *Publics and the City*, Kurt Iveson (2007) shows how the regulation of beats became an object of sustained and sometimes heated public debates during the 1980s and 1990s in Melbourne, involving contests between beat users, police, health workers, council officials, politicians, and the mainstream media. This dynamic discourse, Iveson (2007, p. 84) argues, positioned beats 'as a response to the dominant, and often violently enforced, heterosexuality of public space in Melbourne'—arguably much like gay nightclubs. However, coverage of the Tasty raid in the mainstream press largely ignored the issue, failing to link police harassment, entrapment, and violence at beats to a police raid on a gay nightclub that, at times, reportedly included a sex-on-premises space. As an exception to the generalised elision of the issue, when the policing of beats is mentioned in Freeman-Greene's (1997) feature article, it is quickly dismissed: 'lesbians and many gay men don't even visit beats, it's hard not to see this focus on toilet sex as somewhat limited. Joseph O'Reilly, who is also president of the Victorian AIDS Council, says beats are a trivial issue'. O'Reilly's trivialisation of the issue of beats, through its categorisation as 'toilet sex', is particularly troubling given the significant efforts of public health workers in the 1990s to establish destigmatising and harm-minimisation approaches to beat use, including HIV prevention (Iveson 2007). In opposition to these efforts, O'Reilly's comment contributes to the diminishment and demonisation of queer public sex cultures, aligning with conservative and homophobic views on beats such as those promoted by some mainstream media outlets, local councils, and police (Berlant & Warner 1998; Iveson 2007). O'Reilly's comment indicates that the rise of sexual citizenship, with its attendant claims for respectability, is compromised by the existence of public sex practices (Dalton 2008).

In another instance, male femininity is explicitly disavowed and degraded in media coverage of the Tasty raid. A reporter with the *Age*, Andrew Masterson (1994), visited the Tasty nightclub one week after the raid and describes the scene. He writes that 'in stark contrast to the clichéd image of gay clubs full of mincing and effeminate poseurs, by far the majority of the male dancers were muscular, clean-cut and dressed in jeans and t-shirts'. This description constructs the ostensible gender conformity of men at Tasty, drawing upon classed, racialised, and sexualised norms of hegemonic masculinity. He also provides an association with cleanliness that queers have traditionally been steadfastly denied. Notably in this instance, the reporter directly intervenes in representations of Tasty patrons and provides an authoritative 'outsider' account through witnessing the nightclub himself. Masterson goes to the Tasty nightclub in order to prevent gay victims of police violence from stigmatising assumptions or depictions of their gender deviance, thus bringing Tasty patrons closer to the status of ideal victim. Yet, by linking Tasty patrons to privileged notions of masculinity, the story reproduces and entrenches homophobia as 'mincing and effeminate poseurs' are reduced to a 'clichéd image'.

Both the disavowal of public sex and the affirmation of normative masculinity for gay male Tasty patrons contribute to the production of good queer subject positions that reinscribe heteronormative logics. By stripping away markers of femininity on gay male bodies, and some of the erotic and 'risky' dimensions of queer sexual practices, these representations trivialise and degrade non-heteronormative spaces and forms of sexual and gender expression. 'Perverse' sexual practices are momentarily addressed, but only so that they may be dismissed and degraded. Through these discursive manoeuvres, Tasty patrons can be constructed in ways that more closely align with prevailing ideals of respectable and responsible sexual citizenship—or as 'good victims' of homophobic violence.

'Ordinary law-abiding citizens': tactical speech and the trouble with sameness

Another important dimension of the discourse of respectability following the Tasty raid was the paradigm of 'sameness'. Both the mainstream and lesbian and gay press referred to Tasty patrons as 'ordinary people' and 'ordinary law-abiding citizens' (Smith 1994; Spindler & Connellan 1994), indicating an important conceptual shift towards an 'unmarked' liberal citizen, who does not bear any signifiers of sexuality, gender, race, or class (Davies 1998). Norms based on 'sameness' rather than difference—the idea that queers are 'just like' their straight counterparts—can advance claims to respectability in the fight for LGBT rights and social inclusion. However, a key limitation of the emphasis on sameness is that those whose queerness is viewed as 'excessive' or overly different (Harris 2006) become unlikely candidates for ideal victimhood and may not be seen as blameless in the same way that 'unmarked' others might. The paradigm of sameness accompanied the popular view that the Tasty raid could not be regarded as simply a 'gay rights' issue (Davies 1998). Instead, more universalising notions of civil and 'basic human rights' became key frames for interpreting and responding to the raid as a social and political event (Keogh 1994; Veitch 1994). While it may be possible to strategically mobilise both discourses of LGBT *and* human rights, which is precisely what my Tasty raid informants argued, the paradigm of sameness can reproduce heteronormativity. This is because it risks obscuring and diluting analyses of institutionalised homophobia through distancing the issue from sexual difference and how it comes to *matter* in specific contexts.

An opinion piece authored by Greg Connellan (1994) from Fitzroy Legal Service and published in the *Herald Sun* provides an example of some of the unintended consequences that may arise through the use of a human rights framework in attempts to reframe the issue away from the 'drug problem' (Delianis 1994), and generate compassion for Tasty raid victims. In so doing, Connellan (1994) argues:

> The images of herding small groups of people into rooms to be stripped of their clothes, dignity and most basic human right, must burn terror into the minds of all decent Victorians. The treatment of our fellow Victorians by our police in this manner ought to send the sound of crashing bells through the eardrums of the responsible ministers ... In the interests of all Victorians we must demand that our dignity and most basic human right be immediately afforded proper protection by our Victorian government.

The capacity of oppressed groups to generate compassion increases their chance of being coded as 'ideal' victims and assists them in their wider moral claim for respect and recognition (Mason 2007). However, as Connellan weaves together human rights, state protection, and the assumed decency of citizens, he fails to reckon with the significance of sexuality and gender in the context of the raid. Yet at the same time, the particular terms Connellan uses to engender compassion for 'our fellow Victorians' ('decent', 'responsible', and 'proper protection') recall popular conceptions of homosexuality as 'indecent', 'perverse', 'irresponsible', 'disordered', and 'dangerous'. These powerful and enduring constructions have enabled the subjection of queers to suspicion, surveillance, and punishment, as the previous chapter outlined. The Tasty raid itself can be understood as a manifestation of this disciplinary regime as it highlights how bodies that defy heterosexual norms are policed and punished (Davies 1998).

The construction of Tasty patrons as 'ordinary law-abiding citizens' (Smith 1994) also implies that the law is a neutral process, eliding a critical view to uneven processes of criminalisation. After all, law-abiding/law-breaking identities are socially and politically constructed categories deeply imbricated in power relations. Historically, lesbians and gay men are not 'ordinary people' or included in patriotic calls to support 'our fellow Victorians' (Connellan 1994); rather, they are stereotyped and marked as different or 'other'. In the context of social patterns of criminalisation, non-normative sexualities and gender expressions—alone or in combination with markers of race, class, and dis/ability—inform the manner in which different instances of similar conduct are interpreted (Boon-Kuo et al. 2018; Mogul et al. 2011).

While the focus of my analysis is upon conventional and popular representations of the Tasty raid via the media, it is important to note that these examples of public framing and 'tactical speech' also reflected the legal strategy used against Victoria Police. For instance, when I asked Gary Singer the reasons why Sally Gordon was selected as the lead plaintiff, or 'test case', he explained:

> Well, we wanted to have representation of women as well as men—and it was predominantly men who were in the club—but we wanted to have another angle. [The process involved] strategically looking at the pictures, the profile of the people, and [asking] how good are they as witnesses? You've got to take all that into account when assessing the process of litigation...
>
> ER: Do you look at things like, for example, if they had a past criminal record, then they wouldn't be a good lead?
>
> GS: Correct, yes. You look at their profile and you look at their strength as a witness, and also their ability to handle media scrutiny as well. So, those were factors that came into play [in preparing for the suit].

To be sure, Singer, and others who were prepared to take legal action following the raid, wanted to win. Taking on Victoria Police in the courts was a daunting task, which put people at considerable risk, including the possibility of unwanted 'outing' or further harassment from officers. As Sally Gordon pointed out, 'You don't go and sue the Victorian Police Force on a whim!' This helps to contextualise why more than a third of the 463 people detained and strip-searched during the raid did not come forward to claim compensation following the success of the civil suit. Gordon explained the social context within which many Tasty patrons existed:

> I was in my 30s and there were people in their late teens... young people going out for the first time who might be gay and lesbian, who were totally petrified [by the police] ... Back then there were [also] a lot of

> people who weren't out at work or weren't out to their families. I was, and I was lucky, but I'd only recently come out in the few years before that and I certainly kept it hidden at work for quite some time. So, a lot of people didn't want to do or say anything because it definitely wasn't cool to be gay at work—no way!

By drawing attention to some of the problems associated with representations of lesbian and gay respectability in the media, I do not want to deny or ignore the importance of LGBT people speaking out against the raid and challenging Victoria Police in the courts with the goal to hold police to account; nor do I intend to imply that the problems rest with individuals. While there are shifting patterns and cultures of affluence for a specific class of lesbians and gay men (Tomsen 2001), these are far from totalising. The benefits that accrue to the more homonormative expressions of sexual citizenship remain tenuous and subject to change (Chavez 2015). It is important to remember that a politics of victimhood emerged in part because the Tasty raid had traumatic impacts and activated genuine desires for state recompense and protection.

My aim is to raise questions about the political effects of such representations. What is gained and what is foregone when queer identities, practices, desires, and struggles are decentred for a focus on recognition for 'ordinary law-abiding citizens'? Rather than challenging enduring constructions of queer pathology and criminality, efforts to defend lesbian and gay raid victims in the media often proceeded through distancing them from 'excessive' queerness (Harris 2006) (and the stigma traditionally associated with it) and at times affirmed and extended homophobic ideas. The stress on respectability and sameness may therefore forego a structural analysis of sexuality, power, and violence. That is, the emphasis ignores the practices that produce, regulate, police, and punish sexual and gender difference in the reproduction of heteronormativity. While highlighting the 'ordinariness' of victims has the potential to garner compassion among certain groups, it may also, like respectability, have a regulative function by invisibilising sexual and gender difference and how they matter to law, citizenship, and the exercise of state violence. Through foregrounding the ordinariness of Tasty patrons, the specificity of queer experiences at the hands of the state may be downplayed.

'Relations have hit rock bottom': failing legitimation and police practices of denial

As already established, the Tasty raid occurred during a time of heightened media attention to police misconduct and use of excessive force. This pattern of police violence affected perceptions of public trust in police: one reporter suggested that 'relations between the Victoria Police and the community have, in some respects, hit rock bottom' (Ryle 1994). The raid was often framed within an ongoing pattern of police targeting sexual minorities. Many LGBT people speaking out saw police behaviour during and after the Tasty raid as anything but unusual. Neither its target nor its abusive approach was out of the ordinary. According to Tasty patron Stephen Jones, 'the raid is symptomatic of the way gay men and lesbians are treated in this State' (Bonwick 1994). Journalist and lesbian activist Philippa Bonwick (1994) pointed to the long-standing mistreatment of lesbian and gay people by the state government and located the raid as just one expression of that discrimination—albeit a highly visible one. The systemic analyses articulated by LGBT people were included in both the mainstream and lesbian and gay press.

In the fallout from the Tasty raid, Victoria Police reacted defensively. The force contested criticisms of its practices that were circulating in the press, and ultimately failed to maintain hold on media narratives. As the *Age* (21 May 1996, p. 12) editorialised about Victoria Police: they emerged with 'no credit from Tasty nightclub affair'. The demonstrable police lack of control over media representations of the Tasty raid is significant considering that police organisations occupy a privileged position as 'primary definers' of popular narratives of 'crime', 'justice', and 'social order'. Indeed, the concept of control is a 'cornerstone of much police public relations work'—control, or at least attempted control, over the dissemination of information and the reproduction of a positive police image (Lee & McGovern 2014, p. 34). In this instance, the mainstream press did not fully accept Victoria Police's version of events. While newspapers reported that the police were referring to the Tasty raid as 'a success', 'by the book', and 'a normal police operation' in the weeks following the raid, these were largely overshadowed by reports from Tasty patrons and their supporters that they had been humiliated, terrorised, and verbally abused; State Premier Jeff Kennett also made public comments criticising the raid (Alexander 1994; Conroy 1994c; Faulkner & Pegler 1994; Spindler & Connellan 1994). When told just days after the raid about allegations police had verbally abused patrons with anti-gay taunts, Kennett responded:

> if that was said, it is unacceptable. Unfortunately from time to time not only are expressions like that used, but I think some members of the police force in certain circumstances do use verbal abuse, or in fact physical abuse, beyond that which is necessary.
>
> (Johnston & Cummins 1994)

In the midst of the civil suit against Victoria Police, the Premier again criticised Victoria Police and the Tasty raid on radio 3AW: 'I don't know how that [raid] ever got off the ground. I don't know who gave the instruction for that … it seemed to be absolutely over the top' (Farouque et al. 1996). Despite Kennett's dramatic amplification of police powers as part of a broader law-and-order agenda in politics, his criticisms illustrate the significant public scepticism directed towards police—even among their biggest backers—in their attempts to frame the Tasty raid in their favour. It reflects how in this instance police failed to maintain control over the dissemination of information and the reproduction of a positive police image.

The management of police image through media is a public relations exercise that is fundamental to the exercise of police power. It includes attempts to filter and manage stories involving the police and the desire to present positive policing stories (Lee & McGovern 2014). For example, Victoria Police's liaison officer for the lesbian and gay community at the time, Chief Inspector Winther, argued that the Tasty raid was 'an isolated incident that would not damage the reputation of the police among Melbourne's gay and lesbian community' (Conroy 1994b). Despite serving as a 'liaison' between the lesbian and gay community and Victoria Police, Winther's response to the raid reflects his loyalty to the police force; the mandate to present a positive image of police supersedes any kind of 'commitment' to the LGBT community. His description of the Tasty raid as merely 'an isolated event' denies and downplays queer accounts of routine harassment, discrimination, and violence at the hands of Victoria Police, which were, by that time, well documented by the group Gays and Lesbians Against Discrimination (GLAD) (1994, pp. 15–16) in a report released only six months prior to the raid.[5] Winther's attempt to direct the discussion away from institutional and systemic issues was thus largely ineffective, reflecting the inability of police to gain strategic control over key messages and media narratives about the Tasty raid.

Following the Tasty raid, accusations of homophobia positioned police as not acting according to a 'shared moral purpose' with citizens, which is a vital component of police legitimacy (Smith 2007; Tyler 2006). As Bonwick (1994) pointed out, Victoria at the time regarded itself as 'enlightened' and 'progressive' in relation to its treatment of sexual minorities—a construction enabled in large part by comparison with the southern island state of Tasmania, which was yet to decriminalise sodomy. In order to appear morally aligned with the broader Victorian identification with discourses of tolerance, senior police officers repeatedly sidestepped accusations of prejudice using a combination of techniques to minimise or dismiss the existence of institutional or individual homophobia. For example, Chief Superintendent Graham denied claims that the Tasty raid was 'anti-gay behaviour', arguing that 'there is no suggestion whatsoever that it had to do with the gay and lesbian community' (*Brother/Sister* 26 August 1994, p. 1). Sergeant McNamara, the police officer who secured the warrant to carry out 'Operation Maze' at Tasty nightclub, had visited Tasty five months earlier after an anonymous tip-off regarding drug use, during which he and other officers encountered the 'grope maze' in the basement, described as 'a dimly lit corridor of booths where men went to have sex' (Conroy 1996). In his interview for the Deputy Ombudsman's investigation, McNamara said that while he found sexual activity in nightclubs to be 'personally offensive' and otherwise 'disgusting', he denied he was prejudiced against homosexuals, stating that 'he knew a number of gay people' (Deputy Ombudsman of Victoria 1994, p. 55).[6]

Triggered by the need to restore public confidence in police, the Deputy Ombudsman handed down his findings from the Tasty raid investigation later in 1994. Victoria Police publicly agreed with the Deputy Ombudsman's procedural findings that the raid on Tasty nightclub was poorly planned and breached regulations. Deputy Commissioner for Police Operations Brian Church stated in an article in the *Herald Sun*: 'I accept totally that we got it wrong, that the raid was ill-judged and that a lack of discretion was used' (Ryle et al. 1994). Church also relayed his particular 'pleasure' that the findings did not support the contention that the raid had been based on prejudice against homosexuals (Pinkney & Hall 1994). However, the Deputy Ombudsman did not rule out the possibility that the raid was homophobic in nature; as Matthew Groves (1995) reminds us, intention does not equal effect. Ultimately, the findings of the Deputy Ombudsman's investigation were not sufficient to restore police legitimacy in the aftermath of the Tasty raid. Moreover, police officers made a range of contradictory and inconsistent statements about the raid. For example, during the 1996 court case, Inspector O'Neill, the most senior officer present at the raid, still firmly believed his decision to strip-search all 463 staff and patrons at the Tasty raid was correct (Conroy 1996). The police failure to control media narratives of the raid and its persistence as a powerful memory of police violence in the collective memory of a queer movement undoubtedly contributed to the police decision to issue a formal apology on the 20th anniversary of the Tasty raid in 2014. The apology is analysed in depth in Chapter 7.

Conclusion

As many LGBT people pointed out at the time, the Tasty raid was historically consistent with the state's treatment of sexual and gender 'others'. While police actions during and after the raid certainly indicate a continuation of institutionalised homophobia, the ways in which lesbian and gay people were able to garner sympathetic press coverage and gain legitimacy as victims in this instance was relatively unprecedented. A closer examination of the construction of the Tasty raid in the media suggests that representations of Tasty patrons and Victoria Police were a culmination of many social, institutional, and political forces. These include both shifting patterns of affluence and cultural status for a number of lesbian and gay people who were affected, hyper-visible paramilitary policing trends, and the related circulation of a negative image of police. The damage to police reputation in the aftermath of the Tasty raid was reinforced by representations of Tasty patrons as upstanding sexual citizens and thereby legitimate victims. The construction of good gay subjects relied upon the dismissal and disregard of some of the most stigmatised signifiers of queer 'difference' in a heteronormative context.

My approach to the Tasty raid reveals new insights that complicate its assumed place in queer and policing history. Others have counterposed the Tasty raid with more recent community and partnership policing initiatives with the LGBT community, where the former becomes an example of the 'bad' policing of the past in opposition to the 'good' policing in more recent times (Dwyer & Ball 2009). However, as the chapter suggests, there are more complex dynamics in play between police, LGBT people, media, and perceptions and projections of legitimacy and respectability than can be captured in such a comparison. As I suggested in the introduction of this book, sexual citizenship and police legitimacy have become increasingly bound up together, necessitating close analysis of the specific conditions and discourses that allow some LGBT people to ascend to the realm of respectable citizenship (with its attendant rights to privacy and protection) and criminalised and stereotyped others to be cast further outside of it.

An exploration of symbols of respectability in both general and specific representations of lesbian and gay Tasty patrons in the media highlights the roles played by class, race, and gender signifiers in the establishment of an ideal (queer) victim status. This suggests that not all LGBT people experiencing victimisation at the hands of police would receive public compassion and sympathetic media coverage in the same way, particularly those who are routinely criminalised: dependent drug users, sex workers, or those who frequent beats. These are some of the key limitations and potential exclusions that flow from LGBT rights strategies that are premised on liberal constructs of citizenship and sameness in the face of state violence and denial. It also highlights the possibilities for reproducing the very conditions of heteronormativity that queer activists seek to undo.

The next chapter proceeds to the latter part of the 1990s and early 2000s to explore a central node in the consolidation of a 'mainstream' LGBT movement in Victoria. It investigates the history of 'Gay Pride' in Melbourne, tracing the continuities and breaks in radical activism as it increasingly wagers with the corporatisation and commodification of queer visibility. The emergence of an interstate queer anti-capitalist movement helps to map some of the defining debates within sexual and gender politics in a local context. Through broadening out the discussion beyond policing and legal developments to consider the changing social and economic conditions in which LGBT activism evolves, the following chapter provides important context and linkages between the strident LGBT challenges to the police violence of the Tasty raid and the celebration of official police participation in Pride March less than eight years later, which is closely analysed in Chapter 5. Perhaps most importantly, the next chapter establishes a diversity of political perspectives and modes of organising within a broader social movement based on sexuality and gender identity. This diversity both complicates and elucidates the shifting dynamics of sexual citizenship and the institutionalisation of an LGBT rights agenda.

Notes

1 For a history of the Police Lesbian and Gay Liaison Committee in Victoria, especially their advocacy around 'beats' during the 1990s, see Iveson 2007, pp. 97–106.
2 *Gordon v Graham & Ors.*, Victorian County Court, 20 May 1996.
3 At 2,941 words, this is the longest mainstream news article on the Tasty raid, to the best of my knowledge.
4 When I asked Sally Gordon in interview how her feelings or perceptions of police changed after the raid and the court case, she responded: 'I had a level of anxiety and I had a level of hatred towards police generally, be it in New South Wales or Victoria'.
5 Reflecting on the results of their survey, GLAD (1994, p. 17) concluded:

> The relationship between gay men and lesbians and the police force in Victoria is a major problem that must be fully addressed as a priority. Attempts to combat discrimination and violence in other areas of public life will founder so long as lesbians and gay men count police amongst the abusers.

6 The claim to be exempt from homophobia because of personal relationships with 'gay people' is a trope often used to disavow or dismiss individual accusations of oppressive behaviour and, accordingly, often discredited as a deflection of unexamined and unacknowledged complicity in the perpetuation of homophobia.

References

Agathangelou, AM, Bassichis, DM, & Spira, TL 2008, 'Intimate investments: Homonormativity, global lockdown, and the seductions of empire', *Radical History Review*, vol. 100, pp. 120–143.
Alexander, J 1994, 'The naked terror of a police raid', *Age*, 10 August, p. 14.
Berlant, L & Warner, M 1998, 'Sex in public', *Critical Inquiry*, vol. 24, no. 2, pp. 547–566.
Bonwick, P 1994, 'Victoria's rights and wrongs', *Age*, 13 August, p. 17.
Boon-Kuo, L, Meiners, ER, & Simpson, P 2018, 'Queer interruptions: Policing belonging in the carceral state', in P Aggleton, R Cover, D Leahy, D Marshall, & ML Rasmussen (eds), *Youth, sexuality and sexual citizenship*, Routledge, Oxon, pp. 34–49.
Bottoms, A & Tankebe, J 2012, 'Beyond procedural justice: A dialogic approach to legitimacy in criminology', *Journal of Criminal Law and Criminology*, vol. 102, pp. 119–170.
Chan, J 1997, *Changing police culture: Policing in a multicultural society*, Cambridge University Press, Cambridge.
Chavez, KR 2015, 'The precariousness of homonationalism: The queer agency of terrorism in post-9/11 rhetoric', *QED: A Journal in GLBTQ Worldmaking*, vol. 2, no. 3, pp. 32–58.
Christie, N 1986, 'The ideal victim', in EA Fattah (ed.), *From crime policy to victim policy: Reorienting the justice system*, Macmillan, Basingstoke, pp. 17–30.
Clifton, P 1994, 'Singled out', *Age*, 13 August, p. 20.
Connellan, G 1994, 'Stripping people's dignity: The case against', *Herald Sun*, 21 August, p. 15.
Conroy, P 1994a, 'Against the wall', *Age*, 11 August, p. 1.

Conroy, P 1994b, 'Deputy ombudsman may inquire into club raid by police', *Age*, 11 August, p. 6.
Conroy, P 1994c, 'Kennett in warning as Tasty raid row grows', *Age*, 12 August, p. 3.
Conroy, P 1996, 'The night they busted Tasty', *Age*, 21 May, p. 11.
Conroy, P & Adams, D 1996, 'Court set to hear gay nightclub raid claims', *Age*, 17 October, p. 4.
Cummins, A 1994, 'Gay fury at police raid strip-search', *Herald Sun*, 9 August, p. 11.
Dalton, D 2008, 'Gay male resistance in "beat" spaces in Australia: A study of outlaw desire', *The Australian Feminist Law Journal*, vol. 28, pp. 97–119.
Davies, S 1998, 'Just a passing attraction: The Tasty club raid and the vanishing homosexual', in A Howe (ed.), *Sexed crime in the news*, Federation Press, Annandale, pp. 104–123.
Daye, J 1994, 'Strip-search was selective', *Age*, 13 August, p. 20.
Dean, J 1996, 'Coff "backs up" Tasty', *Melbourne Star Observer*, 12 April, p. 1.
Delianis, P 1994, 'Stripping people's dignity: The case for', *Herald Sun*, 21 August, p. 15.
Deputy Ombudsman of Victoria 1994, 'Investigation of police raid on the Commerce Club (Tasty nightclub) on Sunday 7 August', Deputy Ombudsman of Victoria, Melbourne.
Duggan, L 2004, *The twilight of equality? Neoliberalism, cultural politics, and the attack on democracy*, Beacon Press, Boston.
Dwyer, A & Ball, M 2009, 'Policing sexualities', in RG Broadhurst & SE Davies (eds), *Policing in context: An introduction to police work in Australia*, Oxford University Press, South Melbourne, pp. 89–91.
Farouque, F, Conroy, P & Adams, D 1996, 'Tasty raid over the top', *Age*, 22 May, p. 5.
Faulkner, J & Pegler, J 1994, 'Gay club raid was by the book: Police', *Age*, 9 August, p. 4.
Forell, C 1994, 'Persecution can't be justified whatever your preference', *Age*, 22 August, p. 13.
Freckelton, I 1996, 'Suing the police', *Alternative Law Journal*, vol. 21, no. 4, pp. 173–190.
Freeman-Greene, S 1997, 'A night to remember', *Sydney Morning Herald*, 29 November, pp. 18–22.
Gays and Lesbians Against Discrimination (GLAD) 1994, *Not a day goes by: Report on the GLAD survey into discrimination and violence against lesbians and gay men in Victoria*, GLAD, Melbourne.
Green, S 2011, 'Crime, victimisation and vulnerability', in S Walklate (ed.), *Victims and victimology*, Routledge, New York, pp. 91–118.
Groves, M 1995, 'Not so Tasty', *Alternative Law Journal*, vol. 20, no. 3, pp. 123–127.
Hanhardt, CB 2013, *Safe space: Gay neighbourhood history and the politics of violence*, Duke University Press, Durham.
Harris, AP 2006, 'From Stonewall to the suburbs? Toward a political economy of sexuality', *William and Mary Bill of Rights Journal*, vol. 14, pp. 1539–1582.
Hill, K 1995, 'More police harassment claims by club patrons', *Age*, 7 February, p. 3.
Human Rights Law Centre (HRLC) 2014, 'Righting historical wrongs: Background paper for a legislative scheme to expunge convictions for historical consensual gay sex offences in Victoria', HRLC, Melbourne, viewed 27 December 2018,

www.hrlc.org.au/reports/righting-historical-wrongs-background-paper-for-a-legislative-scheme-to-expunge-convictions-for-historical-consensual-gay-sex-offences-in-victoria.

Irvine, J 2007, 'Transient feelings: Sex panics and the politics of emotions', *GLQ: A Journal of Lesbian and Gay Studies*, vol. 14, no. 1, pp. 1–40.

Iveson, K 2007, *Publics and the city*, Blackwell Publishing, Malden.

Jenness, V 2004, 'The dilemma of difference: Gender and hate crime policy', in A Ferber (ed.), *Home-grown hate: Gender and organized racism*, Routledge, New York, pp. 181–203.

Johnston, D & Cummins, A 1994, 'Strip search police face sack', *Herald Sun*, 12 August, p. 7.

Joyce, J 1997, 'Anti-gay police to be tackled', *Brother/Sister*, 9 January, p. 9.

Keogh, A 1994, 'Raid response 2', *Brother/Sister*, 26 August.

Lee, M & McGovern, A 2014, *Policing and media: Public relations, simulations and communications*, Routledge, Oxon.

Loftus, B 2007, 'Policing the "irrelevant": Class, diversity and contemporary police culture', in M O'Neill, M Marks, & A Singh (eds), *Police occupational culture: New debates and directions*, Elsevier Press, Amsterdam, pp. 181–204.

Mason, G 2007, 'Hate crime as a moral category: Lessons from the Snowtown case', *The Australian and New Zealand Journal of Criminology*, vol. 40, no. 3, pp. 249–271.

Mason, G 2014, 'The symbolic purpose of hate crime law: Ideal victims and emotion', *Theoretical Criminology*, vol. 18, no. 1, pp. 75–92.

Mason, G, Riger, S, & Foley, L 2004, 'The impact of past sexual experiences on attributions of responsibility for rape', *Journal of Interpersonal Violence*, vol. 19, no. 10, pp. 1157–1172.

Masterson, A 1994, 'Despite raid, the Tasty maintains the raging', *Age*, 15 August, p. 7.

McCulloch, J 1990, 'Police shootings and community relations', in J Vernon & S McKillop (eds), *The police and the community in the 1990s*, 23–25 October, Canberra, Australian Institute of Criminology, pp. 153–160.

McCulloch, J 2001, *Blue army: Paramilitary policing in Australia*, Melbourne University Press, Carlton.

McCulloch, J 2002, 'Civil litigation', in T Prenzler & J Ransley (eds), *Police reform: Building integrity*, Hawkins Press, Annandale, pp. 172–184.

Mogul, J, Ritchie, AJ, & Whitlock, K 2011, *Queer (in)justice: The criminalisation of LGBT people in the United States*, Beacon Press, Boston.

Moran, LJ & Skeggs, B 2004, *Sexuality and the politics of violence and safety*, Routledge, London.

Morgan, J 2002, 'US hate crime legislation: A legal model to avoid in Australia', *Journal of Sociology*, vol. 38, no. 1, pp. 25–48.

Morgan, W 1993–1994, 'Identifying evil for what it is: Tasmania, sexual perversity and the United Nations', *Melbourne University Law Review*, vol. 19, pp. 740–757.

O'Leary, K 1994, 'State repression', *Age*, 12 August, p. 14.

Phelan, S 2001, *Sexual strangers: Gays, lesbians, and dilemmas of citizenship*, Temple University Press, Philadelphia.

Pinkney, M & Hall, L 1994, 'Police hit over club strip raid', *Herald Sun*, 1 December, p. 3.

Race, K 2012, 'Framing responsibility', *Journal of Bioethical Inquiry*, vol. 9, no. 3, pp. 327–338.
Ravel, R 1994, 'Bad taste', *Melbourne Star Observer*, 19 August, p. 6.
Reiner, R 2003, 'Policing and the media', in T Newburn (ed.), *Handbook of policing*, Willan, Cullompton, pp. 259–281.
Ryle, G 1994, 'Policing must remain open to public scrutiny', *Age*, 1 December, p. 3.
Ryle, G, Conroy, P, & Farrant, D 1994, 'Police "got it wrong" in gay club raid', *Age*, 1 December, p. 3.
Skeggs, B 1997, *Formations of class and gender: Becoming respectable*, Sage, London.
Smith, DJ 2007, 'New challenges to police legitimacy', in A Henry & DJ Smith (eds), *Transformations of policing*, Ashgate, Aldershot, pp. 273–306.
Smith, DJ & Gray, J 1985, *Police and people in London*, Gower, London.
Smith, DM 1994, 'Raid response', *Brother/Sister*, 26 August, p. 8.
Spindler, S & Connellan, G 1994, 'An independent inquiry needed on police raid', *Age*, 11 August, p. 14.
Tomsen, S 2001, 'Queer and safe: Combating violence with gentrified sexual identities', in C Johnston & P Van Reyk (eds), *Queer city: Gay and lesbian politics in Sydney*, Pluto Press, Annandale, pp. 229–240.
Tomsen, S 2006, 'Homophobic violence, cultural essentialism and shifting sexual identities', *Social and Legal Studies*, vol. 15, pp. 389–407.
Tovey, N 2004, *Little black bastard: A story of survival*, Hodder, Sydney.
Tozer, M 1994, 'Bad hair raid', *Melbourne Star Observer*, 2 September, p. 6.
Tyler, TR 2006, *Why people obey the law*, Princeton University Press, Princeton.
Valverde, M 2010, 'Practices of citizenship and scales of governance', *New Criminal Law Review*, vol. 13, no. 2, pp. 216–240.
Veitch, P 1994, 'Legal action over raid', *Brother/Sister*, 26 August, p. 10.
Victorian Equal Opportunity & Human Rights Commission 2015, *Independent review into sex discrimination and sexual harassment, including predatory behaviour in Victoria Police: Phase One report*, State of Victoria, Carlton, viewed 27 December 2018, www.humanrightscommission.vic.gov.au/projects-initiatives/item/1056-independent-review-into-sex-discrimination-and-sexual-harassment-including-predatory-behaviour-in-victoria-police.
Waddington, PAJ 1999, *Policing citizens: Authority and rights*, UCL Press, London.
Waghorne, J & Macintyre, S 2011, *Liberty: A history of civil liberties in Australia*, NewSouth Publishing, Sydney.
Webster, J 1994, 'Club raid: The police got it wrong', *Age*, 14 August, p. 20.
Willett, G 2011, 'Tasty', in G Willett, W Murdoch, & D Marshall (eds), *Secret histories of queer Melbourne*, Australian Lesbian and Gay Archives, Parkville, pp. 157–158.
Wilson, C 1994, 'Legal claims on club raid grow', *Age*, 28 August, p. 3.

Chapter 4

'We don't just want a piece of the pie; we want a whole new pie'

Gay pride, pink dollars, and queer anti-capitalism

Introduction

At the Midsumma Pride March in Melbourne in 2012, I was part of a small group of young, predominantly white, queer activists handing out flyers and holding placards that read: 'No Pride in a Police State' and 'Police Racism Is a Queer Issue'. We wanted to challenge the renewed emphasis on LGBT–police partnerships and collaborations following the release of Victoria Police's (2011) 'Prejudice-Motivated Crime Strategy', which not only reproduced a narrow understanding of transphobia and homophobia based on 'individual behaviours and ignorance', but also, in our view, represented the 'progressive rhetoric' that had the potential to 'deflect our attention away from police brutality and a rapidly expanding criminal punishment system' (Queering the Air and the Abolition Collective 2012). I do not recall encountering any visible hostility from fellow marchers or spectators, but other local counter-protests—those made up of largely non-white and/or gender-diverse young people—have had different experiences. For instance, Maddee Clark (2015, p. 246) recounts an experience of being shouted at and told that they 'were not welcome and were too political' after arriving in a group at Pride March in 2011 with 'home-made banners, badges, and signs with pro-refugee slogans' to demonstrate solidarity with 'queer refugees and asylum seekers living under the mandatory detention laws in Australia'. Moreover in 2016, a small group of queer and trans activists disrupted the parade by sitting down in front of the National Australia Bank float to protest 'pink-washing', or the 'the use of support for mainstream "gay rights" as a veil to excuse other behaviours', such as financial complicity in the mandatory detention of asylum seekers (Clark 2016). This group attracted particularly hostile and antagonistic responses from the crowd, including insults, shoving, and aggressive attempts to remove them from the parade. Although disparate and only loosely connected, these brief examples demonstrate how Pride March remains an important site of queer protest, debate, and disruption in Melbourne, as it does elsewhere (Lamusse 2016; Russell 2018). They also suggest that some manifestations of LGBT activism are viewed as more legitimate than others.

While the previous chapter examined how LGBT people have used legal strategies and citizenship claims to contest a violent police incursion into queer space, these sporadic queer counter-protests are useful to remind us of the heterogeneity of sexual and gender politics in any given local context.

Since the establishment of the Victorian Annual Pride March in 1996, the event has often served as a space where queer critiques of LGBT alignments with 'conservative and nationalist discourses and projects' (Denike 2010, p. 85) are articulated and suppressed. These internal debates persist despite the efforts of organisers, participants, and spectators to distinguish and distance the event from 'politics'. This chapter briefly tracks the history of gay pride in Melbourne and the political fault lines that it reflects and produces within LGBT movements. It examines a particular queer countermovement during the period 1999–2002, which asserted a visible queer presence in a broader anti-capitalist movement in Australia, and an anti-capitalist presence within the LGBT movement. By eschewing the idea that institutional recognition is inherently positive and desirable, these queer anti-capitalist groups, comprised mostly of students, foregrounded coalitional politics and a materialist analysis of queer oppression to challenge the ascendance of liberalism and consumerism within sexual and gender politics. From a historical perspective, this chapter explores some of the shifts, ambivalences, and tensions within and around localised 'spaces of pride' (Ammaturo 2016), contextualised by national and transnational influences, connections, and breaks. It does this in order to further complicate one of the central arguments of the book—that LGBT movements are being brought into the fold of the state—since queers have always been one group that names and resists state and corporate exploitation and co-option (Bernstein Sycamore 2008; Conrad 2014; Warner 1999). The inclusions afforded to sexual citizens are thus differentiated, incomplete, and open to challenge.

'Not a tits, arse and crotch spectacular': protest and pride

Pride events happen in a number of international locations and form part of a diverse movement known as 'gay pride'. The goal of the gay pride movement may be summed up as 'the complete destigmatisation of homosexuality, which means the elimination of both the personal and the social shame attached to same-sex eroticism' (Halperin & Traub 2009, p. 3). The rather broad goal of gay pride allows room for multiple interpretations and permeations within and against this movement. A gay pride event may take the form of a parade, march, rally, festival, cultural activity, or any other event organised for LGBT people to promote queer visibility.

Many gay pride events internationally commemorate the 1969 rebellion that took place at the Stonewall Inn, a popular gay bar in Greenwich Village, in New York City. During the uprising, patrons resisted a routine bar raid and a series of riots ensued against violent police assault and repression (Hanhardt 2013). Within the USA (and beyond), 'Stonewall' is often seen to symbolise the birth of the 'gay rights' movement (Manalansan 1997; Stanley 2011). However, as Christina Hanhardt (2013) points out, the memory of Stonewall often omits the facts that it was a collective challenge to the police and that it was just the latest clash in an ongoing struggle. Dominant representations also frequently obfuscate the centrality of trans women of colour in leading this resistance.

The best-known Australian example of queer protest against policing and criminalisation is the 1978 demonstration in Sydney now known as 'the first Mardi Gras'. This protest was organised by the Gay Solidarity Group to coincide with the ninth anniversary of the Stonewall rebellion. On the night of 24 June 1978, more than 1,000 queer demonstrators marching down Oxford Street were met with police brutality and repression that resulted in 53 arrests and significant injuries. Back at Darlinghurst police station, arrestees were beaten in their cells and the following day the *Sydney Morning Herald* published their names, occupations, and addresses on the front page—effectively 'outing' those now known as 'the '78ers' in the homophobic climate of the late 1970s. The aggressive policing of the demonstration sparked a series of further protests and arrests, and the Mardi Gras was repeated the following year with double the numbers (Carbery 1995; Markwell 2002). The original 1978 protest occurred within a context of sustained over-policing of queer lives and spaces, and significant state indifference to anti-queer violence (Davis 2007; Featherstone & Kaladelfos 2016). Both these accounts of Stonewall and the first Mardi Gras highlight how historical events that are often singled out for commemoration in gay pride festivals today were not so much exceptional or isolated incidents, but reflected a broader pattern and context of routinised police violence and repression (Russell 2017).

The Victorian Annual Pride March has a different genealogy to the Sydney Mardi Gras. The first Pride March took place in Melbourne on 4 February 1996 as part of the lesbian and gay Midsumma festival that began in 1989. From its beginning, the Pride March represented multiple different and conflicting interests and aims. While it was conceived and developed in reference to local, national, and transnational movements rallying under the banner of 'gay pride', it was initially proposed by gay business owners to augment tourism (Joyce 1997; Markwell & Waitt 2009).

Pride March takes place in the bayside suburb of St Kilda, roughly a 20-minute tram ride from Melbourne's central business district. For many decades, St Kilda has served as a key site for contestations over sexual politics, space, and capital. During the 1970s and 1980s, amid a broader pattern of gentrification, St Kilda became synonymous in the media with sex work, illicit drug use, and youth culture. As police blitzes routinely dispersed sex workers from Fitzroy Street—where Pride March now takes place—one government official proclaimed 'transvestites, homosexuals ... [and] heroin addicts' as 'the worst types' frequenting the suburb (Rowe 2006, p. 8). The first Pride March took place in the wake of the introduction of new penalties for street sex work offences under the 1994 *Prostitution Control Act*, which saw increasing numbers of sex workers serving short periods of imprisonment for first and repeated offenses (Rowe 2006, p. 10). While local resident lobby groups have frequently campaigned for the council to clean up the streets (Rowe 2006), the social diversity of St Kilda (including artists, performers, sex workers, drug users, and queer and trans people) has long been a selling point for real estate agents, council members, and business owners who market the municipality as a place of 'difference' and 'tolerance' (Kerkin 2003). Playing host to the annual Pride March undoubtedly helps with this marketable image of 'diversity'.

In their research on LGBT pride festival spaces in Australia, cultural geographers Kevin Markwell and Gordon Waitt (2009) analyse how discourses of pride have been negotiated and adapted in different ways between the cities of Melbourne, Brisbane, Adelaide, and Perth. They argue that each pride event is historically contingent, contested, ambivalent, and continually evolving (Markwell & Waitt 2009). Like festival spaces in general, spaces of pride are characterised by ambiguity and plurality (Ammaturo 2016). Since space is 'the product of interrelations' on multiple different scales and therefore always open or 'under construction' (Massey 2005, p. 9), individual and collective responses in spaces of pride are contingent and complex, leaving open the possibility of a multiplicity of narratives or trajectories in any one festival space (Baird 2018; Markwell & Waitt 2009). The same pride festival can therefore be perceived in very different ways by organisers, performers, spectators, sponsors, and participants, just as perceptions may differ before, during, and after a festival event (Markwell & Waitt 2009). However, as the chapter's opening accounts demonstrate, not all narratives circulate equally. Some accounts and interpretations of LGBT pride are viewed with more legitimacy and authority than others, as the following chapter will explore further. Ultimately, LGBT pride spaces cannot be conceptualised as single, closed, or bounded entities. They are multi-scalar and connected to ideas, finance, and political movements that stretch far beyond the particular time and space in which they take place.

The call to 'gay pride' has been a part of the gay liberation repertoire since the movement's first days in Australia. On 1 December 1972, the gay liberation publication *Gay Rays* describes how 300 'dykes and poofters' congregated at City Square in Melbourne for 'Australia's largest ever homosexual demonstration' (Willett et al. 2011, p. 120). Demonstrators chanted, danced, handed out leaflets, flowers, and 'gay' apples to shoppers in Bourke Street mall, and held large cutout letters spelling 'GAY LIBERATION' (Joyce 1997, p. 2). Although two Gay Liberation members had been arrested during the week for putting up posters, the sense of fun at the demonstration generated no hostility from spectators and no arrests were made (Joyce 1997; Willett et al. 2011, p. 120). The following year, a national 'Gay Pride Week' was scheduled on 7–14 September, during which Melbourne Gay Liberation organised graffiti runs, talks at high schools, a dance, poetry and film, and a speak-out, culminating in a gay pride demonstration in City Square.[1] A picnic in the Botanic Gardens was attended by 150 people loudly singing and playing games, until a police officer threatened arrest after ludicrously declaring that 'games were not permitted in the park' (Ritale & Willett 2011, p. 88). A flyer for Gay Pride Week proclaimed: 'Being proud will also mean being angry at our oppressors and demanding that they change'.[2] This interpretation and activation of pride as an expression not simply of joy, but also of anger and resolve, shows how gay liberation activists effectively combined celebration and festivities with explicit protests against queer oppression. Protest and pride, then, are not necessarily mutually exclusive. The Melbourne Gay Liberation group published a newsletter in August 1973 that outlined the broader vision and goals of Gay Pride Week:

> We want to bring the idea of Gay Liberation, first of all, before as many gays as possible, and, second, confront the whole of society with our oppression and our demands for liberation … Gay Pride Week isn't just a homosexual party—if we lived in a liberated society perhaps it would be. But Gay Pride Week is going to be used to inform straight society … and it is going to involve attacks on the institutions that oppress us—for too long homosexuals have ignored the existence of anti-homosexual laws, police, shrinks, [m]edia etc., etc., and have concentrated on having big celebrations—well Gay Pride Week is going to do both![3]

The 1973 Gay Pride Week represented a distinctly confrontational approach to challenging 'straight society'. Gay Liberation named and rejected the powerful institutions perpetuating queer oppression, including police. It also argued for and enacted the need for defiance and protest alongside a 'homosexual party'.

In 1981, eight years after the first gay pride demonstration, 'Gay Day' was held in Melbourne as a celebration of homosexual law reform in Victoria (Joyce 1997). By 1989, the festival was named 'Midsumma', which has continued and evolved into 'Victoria's pre-eminent festival for the GLBTIQ communities and their friends, families and colleagues' (Midsumma Festival 2014). The first formal Victorian Pride March was organised as part of the 1996 Midsumma festival by Pride March Victoria Inc.[4] From the perspective of reporter Jodie Joyce (1997) writing for the publication *Brother/Sister* in 1997, earlier gay liberation actions in Melbourne evolved into the ongoing Midsumma festival, including Pride March, which is now promoted as an 'iconic march' that brings together 'parade, pride and party' to celebrate 'solidarity in gender and sexual diversity'.[5] However, this conventional narrative obscures many of the important differences between Midsumma and the gay liberation movement.

Since its inception, Midsumma was seen as a way to boost gay tourist economies in Victoria. Midsumma was initially proposed by the Melbourne Gay Business Association in 1988 and is the most 'professionalised' of Australia's gay pride festivals, with a fulltime festival coordinator employed in late 1989 (Markwell & Waitt 2009). In *Melbourne Star Observer* on 11 March 1988, Gill (1988, p. 1) described this alliance between pride and 'pink' capital as a 'new way of gaining increased national and international profile for the gay scene in Melbourne'. Although Midsumma may have links to earlier gay liberation protests, its conception was distinctly a commercial decision, with gay business people and venue owners playing a key role in the creation of the festival. This situates Midsumma firmly within 'pink dollar' economies—or the growth in markets directed at LGBT consumers, underpinned by the assumption that gay men and, to a lesser extent, lesbians have large disposable incomes. In promotion for the 2002 Pride March, for example, organisers attempted to exploit the concept of the 'pink dollar' as a way to align themselves with corporate interests and encourage sponsorship for the event:

> The benefits of targeted marketing to access the 'pink dollar' have been well publicised and Australia is home to more than 1.4 million gays and lesbians whose estimated total income is more than $2.4 billion per year. Pride March is a very positive event and we would welcome your support of this highly successful event.[6]

In addition to creating business opportunities, Midsumma has sought to build visibility for LGBT people as a way to challenge homophobia and inequality, especially through organising the Pride March. The first Victorian Pride March in 1996 was marketed as 'a public display of the courage, solidarity, pride and diversity' of LGBT people and supporters.[7] It attracted 11,000 people marching under 66 banners and drew a further 3,000 spectators; in the following year, it grew to 23,000 attendees (Joyce 1997).

By 1998, Pride March organisers promoted the event as a show of 'visibility, unity, and diversity', dropping the language of solidarity (and courage) from their promotional material.[8] According to the then president of Pride March Victoria, Inc., the organisation 'adopted a non-political stance in order to focus on sexuality and to avoid alienating the many groups which participate' (Bell 1998). In 1999, the following president of the organisation argued that Pride March was 'not a tits, arse and crotch spectacular', nor was it 'a recruitment drive' or 'a protest rally' (*Brother/Sister* 21 January 1999, p. 22). Rather, the event was promoted as 'a vehicle for every individual to express completeness, united in a common bond of pride. Pride March is our "one day of the year'" (*Brother/Sister* 21 January 1999, p. 22). Regardless of whether it is actually possible to distance sexuality from politics, in the late 1990s the annual Pride March in Melbourne was directed towards the goal of unity over and above the defiance and critique of heterosexual norms (Markwell & Waitt 2009). The above statements from Pride March presidents reveal that the call to 'unity' is premised on the regulation of queer expression to the exclusion of what is perceived as 'excessive', defiant, or threatening aspects of sexual 'otherness' (it's 'not a tits, arse and crotch spectacular', nor a 'recruitment drive' or a 'protest rally'). However, when the call to find a common point of connection relies upon the disavowal of sexualised queer bodies and radical politics, the content, positioning, and purpose of such a point of connection becomes unclear (Markwell & Waitt 2009). Theorists of homonormativity would suggest that this version of sexual politics—the 'unity' that brackets out some of the distinctiveness of queer cultures—reflects the privileging of 'a gay culture anchored in domesticity and consumption' and that seeks simply 'narrow, formal access to a few conservatizing institutions' (Duggan 2004, p. 50, 65).

Diane Richardson (2005) argues that since the 1990s, the dominant discourse of 'sexual politics' has come to be defined by seeking access into mainstream culture through demanding equal citizenship rights (see also Bell & Binnie 2000). As sexual and gender identity-based movements have professionalised and LGBT citizens have gained rapid visibility as consumers, the presence of marginal or overtly sexual populations at gay pride celebrations can become a cause of shame. David Halperin and Valerie Traub (2009, p. 9) argue that growing numbers of people have come to feel alienated from gay pride events and have had increasing difficulty finding a place for themselves among the 'contingents of gay policemen, business leaders, corporate employees, athletes and politicians'. Queer critics suggest that the emphasis on professional and respectable LGBT identities in campaigns for rights and visibility reflects a 'privatized, corporatized, and sanitized "gay agenda"' (Agathangelou et al. 2008, pp. 123–124). Scholars and activists have challenged the privileging of discourses of pride over and above notions of 'shame' that have long been associated with queer experience. Eve Sedgwick and Adam Frank's (Sedgwick 1993; Sedgwick & Frank 1995) ideas on the transformative capacities of shame suggest that shame should not be something we seek simply to overcome by turning to its dependent opposite: pride (Hemmings 2005). Shame itself has a resonance that extends beyond its homophobic generation, which may enable queer subjects to create community through empathy and shared experience (Halperin 2002; Probyn 2000). Reclaiming 'gay shame' may thereby foster alternative connections and collectivities that allow for greater recognition of the ways in which power works to produce sexual difference as unnatural and inferior (Halperin & Traub 2009; Nussbaum 2004). For instance in the USA, Halperin and Traub (2009) document how 'gay shame' movements have emerged as a refuge and site of solidarity for those queers whose identities or social markings make them feel out of place in gay pride's official ceremonies. The project of working with rather than against shame is thus a historical and political one that opens up new possibilities for queer collectives that do not involve a repudiation of the effects brought about by homophobia (Cvetkovich 2003).

Like many scholarly accounts of the shift towards professionalisation and normalisation in LGBT movements, the history of Midsumma and Pride March highlights how a local gay pride movement has been shaped more by professional and commercial interests striving to establish a non-confrontational LGBT consensus than by the grassroots protests that have historically inspired the idea of gay pride as a radical challenge to heteronormative society. While the Midsumma Pride March is a much smaller-scale event than the Sydney Mardi Gras and therefore draws less visibility, sponsorship, and tourism, Pride March organisers have tried to distance the event from the apparent commodification and hypersexualisation of the Sydney Mardi Gras (Markwell & Waitt 2009). Pride March organisers have also sought to distinguish the contemporary iteration of 'gay pride' from the confrontational approach of earlier gay liberationists and later queer activists, discussed further below. However, the professionalisation of the gay pride movement and the apparent shift from protest to pride is not totalising; nor is it a straightforward progression. Despite the explicit efforts of Pride March organisers to distance the gay pride movement from radical resistance (Thorne 2013), spaces of pride remain infused with protest. In an analysis of the Sydney Mardi Gras, Steven Kates (2003) suggests that both oppositional and mainstream cultural meanings are projected to its participants and spectators. Pride and protest continue to intermingle, intersect, and conflict, and they thereby create contradictions in LGBT politics.

'Our rightful place in society cannot be bought': queer anti-capitalist critique and action

My research into the history of Victorian Pride March documents a specific iteration of queer activism struggling with and against what they term 'inherently conservative individualist' politics within the Australian LGBT movement during the last decade of the 20th Century.[9] Although my coverage is not complete, it signals the existence of a mix of activist analyses of, and responses to, sexual and gender oppression. At the 2001 Midsumma Pride March the grassroots activist group Queers United to Eradicate Economic Rationalism (QUEER) mobilised an anti-capitalist critique to challenge and disrupt contingents of conservative Liberal Party members—with slogans such as 'Racist, Sexist, Anti-Queer, Liberals are not welcome here' (Pendleton 2001)—and (off-duty) lesbian and gay police officers (Carr 2001). Although the group was relatively short-lived—active principally between the period 1999–2002—the activist archive generated by QUEER and related groups provides an important window into the heterogeneous politics and internal conflicts that continue to shape the LGBT movement, and that manifest in locally and historically specific ways. The group linked queer oppression to capitalist exploitation in order to argue for a coalitional sexual politics and to develop a critique of what we might now term 'homonormativity'.

Along with its Brisbane counterpart Queers United Against Capitalist Exploitation (QuACE, pronounced 'quake'), QUEER formed to mobilise LGBT people for a mass demonstration and blockade against the World Economic Forum held in Melbourne from 11 to 13 September 2000. Just one year earlier, the successful mass demonstrations in Seattle in 1999 shut down a meeting of the World Trade Organization—an intervention which is typically credited with sparking a transnational anti- or 'alter-globalisation' movement that found powerful expression in Australia (Burgmann 2003). During the Melbourne protests known as 's11', 20,000 people including students, environmentalists, unionists, and others descended on the Crown Casino in an attempt to stop the meeting (Humphrys 2007, 2013; Pendleton 2001). The 'Queer Bloc' was made up of around 100 queer activists from across Australia and elsewhere, who sought to bring queer issues from the margins to the centre of a broader anti-capitalist/anti-globalisation movement, and to develop an analysis of homophobia under capitalism (Pendleton 2007). Mark Pendleton, QuACE activist and the National Union of Students Queer Officer during this period, writes that 'QUEER was originally formed out of cross-campus student queer groups, trade union queer groups and other community organizations' (Pendleton 2001, p. 1). After s11, QUEER continued to organise direct actions, including

> A speakout on HIV/AIDS exploitation on World AIDS Day (December 1) in 2000, actions around sex worker harassment in St Kilda, demonstrating against Archbishop George Pell and his renowned homophobia, and participating in the M1 demonstrations at the Melbourne Stock Exchange on 1 May 2001.
>
> (Pendleton 2001, pp. 1–2)

In 2001, QUEER and QuACE expanded their network to include Gays and Lesbians against Multinationals (GLAM) in Sydney, a brief predecessor to the ongoing organisation Community Action Against Homophobia (CAAH). These groups were connected by the belief that capitalism underpinned homophobia and that 'liberation could only be achieved by challenging that system at its core' (Humphrys 2007, p. 4). Elizabeth Humphrys, one of the organisers of the s11 protest and a member of QUEER throughout 2001, argues that the formation of these three queer anti-capitalist groups at this time in Australia can be attributed to two key political forces: 'the emergence of the alter-globalisation movement and growing dissatisfaction with identity politics, queer theory and the conservativeness of campaigns around equal rights recognition for same sex relationships' (Humphrys 2007, p. 3). As one QUEER activist argued, the core project of these groups 'really could only exist within the context of a larger anti-capitalist movement or a very vibrant ongoing anti-capitalist movement' (cited in Humphrys 2007, p. 4).

As the LGBT movement increasingly gained visibility in Australia, Humphrys (2007, p. 3) notes that its politics 'were pulled towards an almost exclusive focus on the celebration of a marketable identity'. By contrast, activists involved with QUEER, QuACE, and GLAM refused to accept 'the status quo in return for the "right" to a marginalised identity', recognising that 'sexual identity was inextricably linked to the broader structure of capitalist social relations' (Humphrys 2007, p. 3). In particular, the Melbourne-based group 'QUEER rejected the idea that an end to homophobia could be found solely in the autonomous organising of queers or the destabilisation of sexuality norms' (Humphrys 2007, p. 3). In contrast to what Pendleton (2001) named as the growing 'promotion of the "pink dollar"' and the identification of 'a growing middle and upper class in queer communities' as 'a prospective market by corporate interests', QUEER, QuACE, and GLAM were explicitly anti-corporate. For instance, QUEER members were involved in organising weekly pickets outside the Nike store in Melbourne as part of broader campaigns to eliminate sweatshops (Humphrys 2007, p. 4). These groups sought to challenge what they saw as the 'corporatisation of the gay community' as 'symptomatic of capitalism' (Humphrys 2007, p. 4). As one activist described:

> QUEER was reacting to identity politics, which saw … the gay and lesbian movement not really connecting homophobia to any other form of oppression in society and ultimately having middle class values. [The] struggle against homophobic oppression [at that time] was just about gay and lesbian identity and didn't really have anything to do with economics or capitalism … QUEER was a bit of a correction to that.
>
> (Cited in Humphrys 2007, p. 3)

These lesser-known histories of queer activism provide an important counternarrative to the 'liberal triumphalist narratives' that dominate in twenty-first-century LGBT politics in Australia (Baird 2018, p. 477). They further show that the push towards institutional inclusion and recognition was neither inevitable nor appealing for all members of the community.

QUEER, QuACE, and GLAM sought to challenge what they saw as 'assimilationist' tendencies in mainstream LGBT politics.[10] As Mark Pendleton (c. 2000) argued, the prevailing attitude among lesbian and gay activists seemed to be: 'If we are "normal" enough then we'll be accepted like everyone else, it's only the freaks that cause us problems'. In interview, Pendleton elaborated upon the predominant sexual politics to which groups such as QUEER were reacting:

> The late '90s, in many ways, was—I was going to say the peak of conservatism of the LGBT movement, but of course we have had a lot of stuff since then—but it was a period where it looked like you could actually have a kind of 'pink dollar' gay identity.

In Pendleton's (2001, p. 4) view, LGBT visibility increasingly represented 'a very narrow and sanitised version of the queer community', as 'images of free-spending, commodity-focussed, middle-class queer men [came to] dominate the media' (p. 6). This was influenced by the growth in circulation of commercialised lesbian and gay magazines in the 1990s that were reliant on corporate sponsorship and that in turn allowed advertisers direct access to an LGBT market (Calder 2016). In April 1994, a conference was held in Sydney with the remarkable title: 'Chasing the Pink Dollar'. The promotion read:

> Do you want to expand your customer base with a highly affluent, well informed and extremely loyal niche market? ... Gay couples are your classic DINKies (Double Income No Kids), thus are part of the biggest spenders in the community ... Marketers can no longer ignore this lucrative yet largely untapped market.
>
> (Flanagan 1994)

According to queer theorist Jasbir Puar (2012), all bodies in neoliberal capitalism are being evaluated in relation to their success or failure in terms of health, wealth, progressive productivity, upward mobility, and enhanced capacity. She argues that through modes of incorporation, certain queer bodies may be enabled temporarily to receive the 'measures of benevolence' that are afforded by liberal discourses of multicultural tolerance and diversity (Puar 2007, p. xii). Select bodies are included because they can be 'predictably productive under neoliberalism' and thus 'rewarded and trumpeted as evidence of an inclusive society' (Fritsch 2013, p. 142). Critical disabilities scholar Kelly Fritsch (2013, p. 142) contends that neoliberalism 'deems worthy' only those 'bodies that are profitable, that can be marketed to, can be enhanced, or incorporated into the labor force'. The emergent marketability of sexual identities during the 1990s in Australia, as reflected by the conference promotion above, shaped the branding of the Victorian Pride March (and other LGBT pride events, such as the Sydney Mardi Gras). As QUEER activist Alison Thorne argued in 2000, some lesbian and gay community leaders were attempting 'to silence or sideline queer radicals, while busily sucking up to corporate leaders for lucrative sponsorship deals' (Boyd & McKenzie 2000). Queer anti-capitalist groups sought to challenge the movement's emphasis upon upwardly mobile gay and lesbian identities in attempts to encourage sponsorship for events for the ways in which they ignored the reproduction of inequalities under capitalism. As another QUEER member put it: 'Gay liberation will not be brought about in this society because oppression is inherent to the (capitalist) system. We don't just want a piece of the pie. We want a whole new pie' (McKenzie 2000).

The shifting social, cultural, and financial conditions for sexual citizenship prompted queer activists to develop anti-capitalist and radical critiques of the ascendance of lesbian and gay liberalism. In interview, Mark Pendleton reflected that in the late 1990s the LGBT movement seemed 'so money-focused' and 'more interested in the privatisation of gay and lesbian life', in the sense of forcing it 'into the private realm'; whereas earlier iterations of radical sexual activism, such as gay liberation, 'had been much more interested in pushing [queer life] out into the public'. He added that since ACT UP in the early 1990s, the movement appeared uninterested in direct action tactics.[11] QUEER, QuACE, and GLAM viewed the emphasis of the LGBT movement on consumerism as a 'distraction' from collective struggle based on a critical analysis of capitalism. For instance, in a flyer distributed at Pride March in 2001, QUEER argued:

> The material conditions of queer people will never improve from the 'pink dollar' and consumer power alone. Our rightful place in society cannot be bought, and liberation from violence, discrimination and heterosexism will not come from consumption. Our struggle can never be left to multinational corporations, to politicians or major political parties. We are here because we believe in activism, and empowering individuals to work together at a grass roots level to fight for our rights and self-determination as queer people.[12]

By repurposing slogans such as 'Queer Liberation Not Gay Commodification', QUEER promoted radical and grassroots activism as an engine for social change and rejected the corporatisation of the gay pride movement.[13]

In addition to maintaining an anti-corporate stance, QUEER, QuACE, and GLAM 'challenged the police in militant and direct ways through events including s11, M1 (held on May Day 2001) as well as a general commitment to civil disobedience and direct action' (Pendleton 2001, p. 6). In particular, the police brutality against s11 demonstrators sharpened their critique of policing. Activists argued that police specifically targeted the 'Queer Bloc' at the s11 protests. Lesbian and gay newspaper *Melbourne Star Observer* (*MSO*) published one protester's account in an article titled 'Queer Bashings': 'Tuesday morning there was one particular blockade that the police broke through with a baton charge and walked horses over sitting protesters … that was actually the queer blockade' (Shaw 2000). Another protester stated that she 'was bashed up along with 200 protesters. They [the police] pushed through the line and they weren't just pushing, they were actually punching us. I got punched in the face' (Shaw 2000).[14]

When I interviewed Mark Pendleton in 2017, he described how QUEER and QuACE were 'well aware' of the 'tense relationship between the police and the community':

> For Melbourne people, the Tasty raid was still very much in living memory in 2000, it wasn't many years before[hand]. But also for many of us, I think s11 [was] the first time that we had witnessed direct police violence against peaceful protesters. The Queer Bloc was actually [holding] one of the main entrances [to the venue] that was broken open by the police. Quite a lot [of people] were injured and, you know, police horses and batons [were involved].

Witnessing and experiencing police violence at the s11 protests not only radicalised many young queer students, who according to Pendleton 'went back to [university] campuses and organised locally on a much more radical line'; it also generated hostility among QUEER activists to the participation of Gay and Lesbian Police Employees Network (GALPEN) members in Melbourne's Pride March the following year (Carr 2001). As QUEER member Alison Thorne (2013) writes, QUEER challenged Pride March organisers 'for uncritically involving Victoria Police in the march, pointing to the mass arrests at Sydney's first Mardi Gras, the 1994 raid and strip search of patrons at the Tasty nightclub, and the brutal attack by cops on anti-capitalist demonstrators who circled Crown Casino' during the s11 demonstrations. At the 2001 Pride March, QUEER activists heckled the contingent of (off-duty) members of GALPEN (Carr 2001). A statement released by QUEER recognised that although 'GALPEN members have challenged the homophobic and sexist institution for which they work', they nevertheless claim a police identity, and thereby became a target for activists' anger towards Victoria Police: 'Many of our contingent were at the s11 demonstration and saw, or were on the bloody end of, police savagery' (Carr 2001). QUEER used the visibility of Pride March to challenge the lack of police accountability for what they saw as anti-queer brutality, and to highlight the problem of police violence as institutional, and thus one that lesbian and gay police officers cannot ignore. QUEER's public intervention into what they identified as problematic LGBT alliances with corporate, political, and state institutions—including police at the 2001 Pride March—forms part of a continuing history of radical disruptions to the annual parade in Melbourne.

'How history could be reimagined in a different political environment': queer historical continuities

During the period 1999–2002, QUEER, QuACE, and GLAM consciously sought to locate themselves in 'a perceived tradition of largely continuous anti-capitalist queer activism', from Gay Liberation to HIV/AIDS activism and more (Pendleton 2007, p. 66). For instance, QUEER very explicitly drew on Melbourne ACT UP's early 1990s activism during the AIDS crisis. Alison Thorne (2013) writes that QUEER 'held a day of action against pharmaceutical company super profits and also marked the 10th anniversary of ACT UP's D Day'—the letter 'D' was used to symbolise 'death, drugs, delays and deadline'. As Mark Pendleton explained in interview, 'it was a dual thing: being historical, wanting to be aware of the queer history, present that history; but also, thinking about how that could be reimagined in a different political environment'.

Queer anti-capitalist activists drew on radical lineages of gay liberationist, feminist, and HIV/AIDS activism to highlight what they saw as a betrayal of earlier principles by an evolving 'mainstream' LGBT movement that appeared too ready to work within established political institutions for 'the crumbs of law reform and respectability' (Reynolds 2002, p. 161). Pendleton (2007, p. 70) suggests that 'by placing their actions and politics in a community history, ... the[se] groups were able to argue for the centrality of anti-capitalist politics to those communities, and critique commemorative processes that downplay the radical in favour of the commercial', such as those reflected in the historical development of the Sydney Mardi Gras and the Midsumma Pride March. In contrast to the economic rationalism and liberal politics advanced by Pride March organisers, QUEER's vision for the future is premised on societal transformation and might therefore be read as utopian. Their statements reflect, in the words of queer theorist José Munoz (2009, p. 20), 'expansive critiques of social asymmetries' and a 'field of utopian possibility' in which 'multiple forms of belonging in difference adhere to belonging in collectivity'. For example, a QUEER flyer argues for the importance of building solidarity across movements based on a conception of interlinked oppressions:

> As long as institutions continue to oppress womyn, the working class are exploited and devalued, Indigenous people are denied land rights, and so on, fighting to end homophobia alone has limited aspirations. The liberation of queers is intricately connected with the liberation of ALL people seeking a more just and equitable society.[15]

By highlighting the limitations of the 'single-issue' frameworks of many LGBT rights campaigns (Riggs 2006; Spade 2011), QUEER contributed to building a multi-issue and coalitional queer politics (Cohen 1997).

Conclusion

Queer anti-capitalist activists have sought to highlight the systemic and structural inequalities that are bracketed out of the politics of homonormativity. Through an analysis of homophobia within the context of capitalism, QUEER, QuACE, and GLAM developed critiques of the valorisation of privatised consumption and upward mobility in the LGBT movement for the ways in which it obscured the material inequalities and rights violations that are reproduced within global capitalism. They expanded political space to forge connections with other groups experiencing oppression and exploitation, and to build on alternative queer trajectories outside of homonormative paradigms. These marginalised perspectives highlight some of the fault lines and divergences within sexual and gender politics, and remind us that spaces of pride are more complex and contested than often assumed.

Many of the critiques these queer anti-capitalist groups articulated in the early 2000s continue to resonate today. For instance, when I interviewed Jane Green, a queer sex worker and representative of Vixen (Victoria's peer-only sex worker organisation), they raised a persistent 'tension over Pride March':

> Sex workers' ... have concerns about police presence and also about pink-washing; that there's a really high level of corporate presence [at Pride March] and a lot of those corporate entities haven't been kind to a variety of groups including sex workers, migrants, trans people and LGBT people more broadly.

The significant visibility of corporate and state institutions at LGBT pride events sits uneasily with many LGBT people, especially those that continue to experience surveillance, exploitation, and criminalisation by virtue of their work, precarious citizenship status, and/or gender non-conformity. 'Pink-washing' or 'rainbow-branding' (Russell 2018) practices by institutions that have a questionable or problematic track-record with LGBT rights understandably raises questions for queer communities about the potential for our identities and politics to be used superficially or as a cover for the advancement of capitalist projects and, in the case of police, 'strategies of pacification' (Neocleous 2011).

In the next chapter, I analyse the Chief Commissioner of Victoria Police's decision to participate in the Midsumma Pride March in 2002. Commenting on this decision, GALPEN member Luke Bryant argued that the Commissioner was supporting 'reasonable Gay and Lesbian citizens who lawfully wanted to get on with their lives' (Bryant 2012). This iteration of sexual citizenship is telling, as through the emphasis on reason and lawfulness, Bryant conjures practical and forward-looking lesbian and gay citizen-subjects who are suitable candidates for institutional recognition and police practices of community engagement. In contrast to QUEER's vision for the future based on 'a whole new pie', the 'good queer subject' constructed here is decidedly pragmatic—reflecting Munoz's (2009) conception of 'gay pragmatism' as that which erodes the gay and lesbian imagination and proceeds in opposition to queer idealism. By positing sexual citizens that desire simply to 'get on' with their lives 'lawfully', Bryant reimagines queer lives as having been untouched by criminalisation.

Notes

1 'Gay Pride Week' 1973, A6 poster, Melbourne, held at ALGA in the Pride Victoria ephemera file.
2 'Gay Pride: Homosexuals Come Out' 1973, Maxwell Printing Co. Pty Ltd, Waterloo, held at ALGA in the Pride Victoria ephemera file.
3 'Gay Pride Week', *Gay Lib News*, no. 10, July 1973, held at ALGA in the Pride Victoria ephemera file.
4 Pride March Victoria, Inc., 'Pride March 2002 Information Kit', held at ALGA in the Pride March Victoria, Inc. ephemera file.
5 Only Melbourne 2018, 'Midsumma Pride March 2019', viewed 2 December 2018, www.onlymelbourne.com.au/pride-march#.XANqXKloT-Y.
6 Held at ALGA in the Pride March Victoria Inc. ephemera file.
7 'Pride '96: February 4th 1996', information sheet/invitation to participate, held at ALGA in the Pride March Victoria, Inc. ephemera file.
8 Pride March Victoria, 'Pride '98 Information Kit', held at ALGA in Pride March Victoria, Inc. ephemera file.
9 Pendleton, M c. 2000, *A queer agenda: The futility of reformism*, Melbourne, QUEER, held at ALGA in the QUEER ephemera file.
10 QUEER c. 2000, 'Assimilation: A How-To Guide', *Queers bash back* (zine), Melbourne, held at ALGA in the QUEER ephemera file.
11 Following the establishment of ACT UP—the AIDS Coalition to Unleash Power—in Sydney, the Melbourne division formed on 28 May 1990 to organise direct actions to raise awareness about those living and dying with HIV/AIDS and campaign for free access to medical treatment in Australia (Hallett 2016).
12 QUEER flyer for Pride March 2001, 20 January, held at ALGA in the QUEER ephemera file.
13 QUEER c. 2000, as above at viii.
14 For a detailed account of the policing and surveillance of the s11 protests, see McCulloch 2001.
15 QUEER c. 2000, 'What is s11?' Melbourne, flyer held at ALGA in the QUEER ephemera file.

References

Agathangelou, AM, Bassichis, DM, & Spira, TL 2008, 'Intimate investments: Homonormativity, global lockdown, and the seductions of empire', *Radical History Review*, vol. 100, pp. 120–143.

Ammaturo, FR 2016, 'Spaces of pride: A visual ethnography of gay pride parades in Italy and the United Kingdom', *Social Movement Studies*, vol. 15, no. 1, pp. 19–40.

Baird, B 2018, 'Twenty-first century LGBTI activism in Australia: The limits of equality', *Australian Historical Studies*, vol. 49, no. 4, pp. 475–492.

Bell, R 1998, 'ALSO and VAC to Pride: Get a vision!' *Melbourne Star Observer*, 24 April, p. 3.

Bell, D & Binnie, J 2000, *The sexual citizen: Queer politics and beyond*, Polity Press, Cambridge.

Bernstein Sycamore, M 2008, *That's revolting! Queer strategies for resisting assimilation*, Soft Skull Press, Brooklyn.

Boyd, M & Mckenzie, J 2000, 'S11 fallout', *Brother/Sister*, vol. 220, 28 September, p. 3.

Bryant, L 2012, 'Times past: The gay and lesbian police employees network (Victoria, Australia)', *Prime Timers Worldwide*, 31 July, viewed 8 March 2015, www.primetimersww.com/index.php?option=com_k2&view=item&id=111:times-past&Itemid=590.

Burgmann, V 2003, *Power, profit and protest: Australian social movements and globalisation*, Allen & Unwin, Crows Nest.

Calder, B 2016, *Pink ink: The golden era for gay and lesbian magazines*, Cambridge Scholars Publishing, Newcastle upon Tyne.

Carbery, G 1995, *A history of the Sydney Gay and Lesbian Mardi Gras*, Australian Lesbian and Gay Archives, Parkville.

Carr, A 2001, 'Queer v police, liberals', *B News*, 15 February, p. 3.

Clark, M 2015, 'Are we queer? Reflections on "peopling the empty mirror" twenty years on', in D Hodge (ed.), *Colouring the rainbow: Blak queer and trans perspectives*, Wakefield Press, South Australia, pp. 238–252.

Clark, M 2016, 'Decolonising the queer movement in Australia: We need solidarity, not pink-washing', *NITV*, 3 March, viewed 26 February 2018, www.sbs.com.au/nitv/article/2016/03/03/decolonising-queer-movement-australia-we-need-solidarity-not-pink-washing.

Cohen, CJ 1997, 'Punks, bulldaggers, and welfare queens: The radical potential of queer politics?' *Gay and Lesbian Quarterly*, vol. 3, pp. 437–465.

Conrad, R 2014, *Against equality: Queer revolution, not mere inclusion*, AK Press, Oakland.

Cvetkovich, A 2003, *An archive of feelings: Trauma, sexuality, and lesbian public cultures*, Duke University Press, Durham.

Davis, K 2007, 'The "Bondi boys"—Un/Australian?', *Continuum*, vol. 21, no. 4, pp. 501–510.

Denike, M 2010, 'Homonormative collusions and the subject of rights: Reading terrorist assemblages', *Feminist Legal Studies*, vol. 18, pp. 85–100.

Duggan, L 2004, *The twilight of equality? Neoliberalism, cultural politics, and the attack on democracy*, Beacon Press, Boston.

Featherstone, L & Kaladelfos, A 2016, 'Chapter 7: The greatest menace', *Sex crimes in the fifties*, Melbourne University Press, Carlton.

Flanagan, T 1994, 'Chasing the gay and lesbian market' *Green Left Weekly*, no. 133, 2 March, viewed 5 August 2017, www.greenleft.org.au/content/chasing-gay-and-lesbian-market.

Fritsch, K 2013, 'The neoliberal circulation of affects: Happiness, accessibility and the capacitation of disability as wheelchair', *Health, Culture and Society*, vol. 5, no. 1, pp. 135–149.

Gill, C 1988, 'Gay festival for Melbourne?' *Melbourne Star Observer*, 11 March, p. 1.

Hallett, B 2016, 'ACT UP Melbourne', *Reason in Revolt*, 23 December, viewed 16 December 2018, www.reasoninrevolt.net.au/biogs/E000731b.htm.

Halperin, DM 2002, 'Homosexuality's closet', *Michigan Quarterly Review*, vol. 41, no. 1, pp. 21–54.

Halperin, DM & Traub, V 2009, *Gay shame*, University of Chicago Press, Chicago.

Hanhardt, CB 2013, *Safe space: Gay neighbourhood history and the politics of violence*, Duke University Press, Durham.

Haritaworn, J, Kuntsman, A, & Posocco, S 2013, 'Murderous inclusions', *International Feminist Journal of Politics*, vol. 15, no. 4, pp. 445–452.

Hemmings, C 2005, 'Invoking affect: Cultural theory and the ontological turn', *Cultural Studies*, vol. 19, no. 5, pp. 548–567.
Humphrys, E 2007, '"With their bodies on the line": Activist space and sexuality in the Australian alter-globalisation movement', paper presented at *Queer space: Centres and peripheries*, 20–21 February, University of Technology, Sydney, viewed 12 December 2018, https://anintegralstate.net/wp-content/blogs.dir/940/files/2014/08/globalisation_humphrys.pdf.
Humphrys, E 2013, 'Global justice organising in Australia: Crisis and realignment after 9/11', *Globalizations*, vol. 10, no. 3, pp. 451–464.
Joyce, J 1997, 'History of pride', *Brother/Sister*, 9 January, p. 2.
Kates, S 2003, 'Producing and consuming gendered representations: An interpretation of the Sydney Gay and Lesbian Mardi Gras', *Consumption, Markets and Culture*, vol. 6, no. 1, pp. 5–22.
Kerkin, K 2003, 'Re-placing difference: Planning and street sex work in a gentrifying area', *Urban Policy and Research*, vol. 21, no. 2, pp. 137–149.
Lamusse, T 2016, 'Politics at pride?', *New Zealand Sociology*, vol. 31, no. 6, pp. 49–70.
Manalansan, MF 1997, 'In the shadows of Stonewall: Examining gay transnational politics and the diasporic dilemma', in L Lowe & D Lloyd (eds), *The politics of culture in the shadow of capital*, Duke University Press, Durham, pp. 485–505.
Markwell, K 2002, 'Mardi Gras tourism and the construction of Sydney as an international gay and lesbian city', *GLQ: A Journal of Lesbian and Gay Studies*, vol. 8, no. 1–2, pp. 81–99.
Markwell, K & Waitt, G 2009, 'Festivals, space and sexuality: Gay pride in Australia', *Tourism Geographies: An International Journal of Tourism Space, Place and Environment*, vol. 11, no. 2, pp. 143–168.
Massey, D 2005, *For space*, Sage, London.
McCulloch, J 2001, 'Paramilitary surveillance: S11, globalisation, terrorists and counter-terrorists', *Current Issues in Criminal Justice*, vol. 13, no. 1, pp. 23–35.
McKenzie, J 2000, 'S11 queers demand new world', *Brother/Sister*, vol. 219, 21 September, p. 3.
Midsumma Festival 2014, 'Midsumma Festival 2014 annual report', Melbourne, viewed 30 March 2015, https://midsumma.org.au/annual-reports/197-annual-report-2014
Munoz, JE 2009, *Cruising utopia: The then and there of queer futurity*, New York University Press, New York.
Neocleous, M 2011, '"A brighter and nicer new life": Security as pacification', *Social & Legal Studies*, vol. 20, no. 2, pp. 191–208.
Nussbaum, M 2004, *Hiding from humanity: Disgust, shame and the law*, Princeton University Press, Princeton.
Pendleton, M 2001, 'Queers, anti-capitalism and war', *Word is Out online journal for gay, lesbian and queer liberation*, vol. 1, viewed 14 December 2018, http://pandora.nla.gov.au/pan/23857/20020430-0000/www.wordisout.info/back_issues.htm.
Pendleton, M 2007, 'Looking back to look forward: The past in Australian queer anti-capitalism, 1999–2002', *Melbourne Historical Journal*, vol. 35, pp. 51–71.
Probyn, E 2000, 'Shaming bodies: Dynamics of shame and pride', *Body and Society*, vol. 6, no. 1, pp. 13–28.
Puar, JK 2007, *Terrorist assemblages: Homonationalism in queer times*, Duke University Press, Durham.

Puar, JK 2012, 'Coda: The cost of getting better: Suicide, sensation, switchpoints', *GLQ*, vol. 18, no. 1, pp. 149–158.
'Put your feet on the street' 1999, *Brother/Sister*, 21 January, p. 22.
Queering the Air & The Abolition Collective 2012, *No pride in a police state*, pamphlet, 3CR Community Radio, Melbourne, viewed 17 December 2018, www.3cr.org.au/files/NO%20PRIDE%20IN%20A%20POLICE%20STATE.pdf.
Reynolds, R 2002, *From camp to queer: Remaking the Australian homosexual*, Melbourne University Press, Carlton.
Richardson, D 2005, 'Desiring sameness? The rise of a neoliberal politics of normalisation', *Antipode*, vol. 37, no. 3, pp. 515–535.
Riggs, DW 2006, *Priscilla, (white) queen of the desert: Queer rights/race privilege*, Peter Lang Publishing, New York.
Ritale, J & Willett, G 2011, 'Rennie Ellis at Gay Pride Week, September 1973', *The La Trobe Journal*, vol. 1, no. 87, pp. 86–93.
Rowe, J 2006, *Street walking blues: Sex work, St Kilda and the street*, RMIT Publishing, Melbourne.
Russell, EK 2017, 'A "fair cop": Queer histories, affect and police image work in Pride March', *Crime Media Culture*, vol. 13, no. 3, pp. 277–293.
Russell, EK 2018, 'Carceral pride: The fusion of police imagery with LGBTI rights', *Feminist Legal Studies*, vol. 26, no. 3, pp. 331–350.
Sedgwick, EK 1993, 'Queer performativity: Henry James's *The art of the novel*', *GLQ*, vol. 1, no. 1, pp. 1–16.
Sedgwick, EK & Frank, A 1995, *Shame and its sisters: A Silvan Tomkins reader*, Duke University Press, Durham.
Shaw, A 2000, 'Queer bashings', *Melbourne Star Observer*, 15 September, p. 3.
Spade, D 2011, *Normal life: Administrative violence, critical trans politics, and the limits of law*, South End Press, Brooklyn.
Stanley, EA 2011, 'Fugitive flesh: Gender self-determination, queer abolition and trans resistance', in EA Stanley & N Smith (eds), *Captive genders: Trans embodiment and the prison industrial complex*, AK Press, Oakland, pp. 1–11.
Thorne, A 2013, 'Queer liberation and the feminist connection', *The Organiser*, 16 November, viewed 5 August 2017, www.socialism.com/drupal-6.8/organiser-articles/queer-liberation-and-feminist-connection.
Victoria Police 2011, *Prejudice motivated crime*, media release, 8 July, viewed 19 November 2014, www.police.vic.gov.au/content.asp?document_id=32278.
Warner, M 1999, *The trouble with normal: Sex, politics and the ethics of queer life*, Harvard University Press, Cambridge, MA.
Willett, G, Murdoch, W, & Marshall, D 2011, *Secret histories of queer Melbourne*, Australian Lesbian and Gay Archives, Parkville.

Chapter 5

A new 'feeling force'

The police commissioner goes to Pride March

Introduction

On 20 January 2002, Victoria Police Chief Commissioner Christine Nixon became the first police commissioner in Australia to march in a public gay pride event. Upon request from the Gay and Lesbian Police Employees Network (GALPEN), Nixon agreed not only to allow police members to march in Melbourne's Pride March on-duty and in uniform, but also to march alongside her (Nixon & Chandler 2011). In the lead-up, Pride March promotion called for LGBT people to 'be a part of history' by marching alongside the Chief Commissioner (Pride March Committee 2001). During the event, all reports suggest that the police contingent received loud and 'tumultuous applause' from the crowd, and that the Chief Commissioner had inspired other marchers to dress up in drag as 'Christine Nixons', wearing mock police uniforms comprised of miniskirts, high heels, and handcuffs (Jackson 2002; Jacobs 2002; de Kretser 2002). The participation of police commissioners in the annual Midsumma Pride March has continued intermittently since 2002. Nixon herself returned to Pride in 2009 upon her succession as police commissioner by Simon Overland (Firkin 2010; Gough 2014). In the last few years, police chiefs in other Australian and international cities such as Philadelphia and Tampa in the USA (Philly Pride 2015; Silvestrini 2015), and Liverpool in the UK (Thomas 2016) have made appearances at LGBT Pride parades. These appearances form part of a larger trend that I noted at the beginning of this book: of ceremonious police performances of 'official anti-homophobia', particularly at LGBT Pride events. A quick Google image search for 'police pride' brings up hundreds of photographs fusing police and LGBT rights imagery: various combinations of rainbow flags, police uniforms, Pride parades, and revamped cop cars. In numerous Western liberal jurisdictions, police organisations are directing resources to pro-LGBT 'make-overs' of the police image (Russell 2018).

Chief Commissioner Nixon's participation in Pride March in 2002 is an exemplary case of police image work. Image work refers to the various activities police forces engage in to project meanings of policing, which variously work for and against legitimate policing (Mawby 2002, 2014). It is also a case that raises questions not yet dealt with by policing scholars. As long-term queer community advocate Sally Goldner described it when I interviewed her in 2017, Nixon's leadership at Pride March 'was a very good piece of emotionally intelligent communication'. Indeed, themes of *affect* and emotion permeate textual representations of this event. How might insights developed by feminist and queer writings on the politics of emotion, such as those of Sara Ahmed and Heather Love, help us understand how proactive police image work contends with the politics of queer history? Or more specifically, how does this image work engage with and respond to ongoing histories of state violence and queer resistance? As the analysis that I develop in this chapter will show, histories of homophobic police violence can be used strategically to fortify a positive police image, buttressed by notions of recognition, tolerance, and progress (Russell 2017). A positive police image at Pride March is achieved by recalling and rewriting the meaning of homophobic police violence in the past to enhance the legitimacy of policing in the present. Police participation in Pride March is positioned in opposition to past practices and constructs a new image of police as modern, adaptive, and tolerant—however precariously—as police violence continues to resurface in some of the most visible spaces of LGBT pride. The construction of police or 'carceral pride'—the fusion of police and LGBT rights imagery (Russell 2018)—can provide a mask for the escalation of police powers and violence mapped in the previous chapters. Notably, Chief Commissioner Nixon accepted the invitation to Pride March only one year after Victoria Police officers brutalised queer protesters at the S11 protests. Constructed as a 'fair cop', Nixon engendered a new 'feeling' face of policing that encompassed the entwined politics of respectability and responsibilisation: 'good sexual citizens' align with police to advance (a carceral vision of) queer safety and security. Yet this affective circuitry distracts us from the violence that is inherent to the structural work of policing.

Strategic police image work at Pride March appropriates and re-signifies histories of state violence with implications not only for police legitimacy—both contesting and fortifying it—but also for the politics of queer history. While some authoritative voices and teleological narratives are widely circulated and reproduced (such as the idea that police participation in Pride signals progress), others (such as disorderly histories of queer anti-capitalist activism) fade into the background. The discourse of 'Policing with Pride' may subsume radical queer histories into a police public relations project.

'Our cops go girlie': masculinity and police authority

Since the establishment of the Victorian Pride March in 1996, Victoria Police had banned its officers from official participation in the parade. This changed in 2002, when Christine Nixon reversed this decision early in her term as Chief Commissioner by allowing officers to 'wear their uniforms, and march on police time' (Nixon & Chandler 2011, p. 132). Around this time, Nixon was seen as a popular Chief Commissioner and a role model for women police officers (Chulov 2002). Participating in Pride March resonated with her broader objective to reinforce an image of Victoria Police as aligned with community concerns and values, as she stated: 'I talk about us being the people's police and I think that's what we are' (News24 2002). Her decision appealed to community members: one letter published in the *Age* characterised Nixon as 'gutsy' and her participation in Pride March as 'one of the most important of her many and varied police force reforms' (Condon 2002). However, it also alienated and upset conservative politicians, media commentators, and police members. Politicians declared that it was 'inappropriate for Victoria Police to align itself with a minority cause' (Crawford 2003), and that 'the Chief Commissioner should be above these sorts of activities' (Donovan 2002). Nixon recounts in her biography, *Fair Cop*, that she received 'letters and emails from police officers apoplectic with rage', who thought it was 'appalling' and 'an assault to the image of Victoria Police' (Nixon & Chandler 2011, p. 132).

The shock and criticism directed towards Chief Commissioner Nixon's decision to participate in Pride March occurred in the context of the Police Association's general scepticism of Nixon's 'soft' approach to policing, which was underpinned by sexist attitudes. Because Nixon was the first woman to serve as Chief Commissioner of any police force in Australia, conservative responses to Nixon's Pride March decision were driven at least in part by hostility towards the femininity that Nixon represented, constituting a threat to a traditionally hyper-masculine organisation (Donovan 2002; Nixon & Chandler 2011). For example, in a *Herald Sun* opinion piece titled 'Our cops go girlie' published on 11 November 2006, renowned ultra-conservative commentator Andrew Bolt (2006) labelled Nixon's approach to policing 'passive': a new 'back-off' style resulting in a 'feminised' and 'non-authoritarian' force. Bolt suggested that police marching 'in gay pride and women's events' weakened police power. When Nixon retired amid controversy in 2011,[1] Police Association secretary Greg Davies asserted that Nixon 'destroyed' her own reputation by 'emasculating' the police force, 'trying to turn it into something that she thought would have been lovely for everyone' (Levy 2011).

In contrast to these assertions that community policing approaches undermine police authority; many critical policing scholars argue that community policing strategies actually complement more aggressive and paramilitary styles of policing. This is because community policing can legitimise more overtly forceful and coercive policing, while enabling the 'government to expand the applicable targets of control and to draw openly on a much larger array of tactics' (Kappeler & Kraska 1998, p. 306). Far from constraining police and state power, Nixon's focus on 'community engagement' in her role as Chief Commissioner is more likely to have increased policing capacities and strengthened the legitimacy of law enforcement through realigning the institution with prevailing moral norms (Tyler 2006). The liberal democratic state needs to take on some of the values of those it polices in order to gain the consent of those policed. The enforcement of social order is therefore not a simple strategy of 'command and control'; policing also seeks to 'persuade and align' (Garland 2001, p. 126). As Criminologist Victoria Sentas (2014, pp. 31–32) argues, police power is continually negotiated; and while garnering consent depends on constant repositioning and reworking of the police identity, those who are policed must always retain 'flexibility to adapt to the needs and wishes of the police'. The appearance of consent is only part of the equation for police power, however, and it is important not to obscure its foundation on domination and the unique ability of police to use force with legitimacy (Hall et al. 1978).

Police authority and legitimacy are actively cultivated through strategies of 'impression management', or the ways in which the organisation and individuals within it are marketed and presented to observers (Mawby 2002, 2010). While subject to the ebbs and flows of trends in policing, the presentation of a professionalised image of police can be traced back to the earliest days of policing in Victoria, when the first police magistrate for the Port Phillip district, Captain William Lonsdale, introduced the original police uniform in the late 1830s. The uniform was heavily militaristic in style and intended to let the constables 'be at once known as such, but also to ensure some respectability in their appearance' (Haldane 1995, p. 12). In other words, police uniforms were developed to construct a visible 'law and order' presence during a volatile context of rapidly expanding settler colonialism. The public presentation of police is important because most people today gain their knowledge of the criminal justice system through the media, rather than personal experience or interaction (Marsh & Melville 2009). Indeed, evidence suggests that citizens who have the greatest satisfaction with the police are those who have no direct contact with them (Bradford et al. 2009). Accordingly, police-controlled 'image work' is tasked with the promotion of a professionalised institutional identity, designed to influence audience perceptions and behaviour (Manning 1992). This is what Aiello (2014) refers to as a police 'self-portrait', constructed through various mediums: 'ceremonies, visible daily activities, props and symbols, and special knowledge and techniques constitute resources by which police can mark, claim, display, defend, and reaffirm their mandate' and identity (Manning 1992, p. 144). Criminologist Andrew Goldsmith (2010, p. 915) argues that the appearance of police professionalism can be pursued by 'ensuring visibility of positive acts and achievements and equally by concealing negative instances'.

While the visibility of positive acts is certainly important to the police image, this chapter illustrates how negative examples of policing do not necessarily have to be concealed for a desirable police image to be achieved. Instead, examples of negative police–citizen encounters may be revised, retold, and legitimised by strategic police image work in the present. Chief Commissioner Nixon's participation in Melbourne's Pride March in 2002 presented a 'new' image of police—what I describe as a 'feeling' force—premised on a moving retelling of queer and police history. This institutional narrative effectively mobilised emotional rhetoric to centre the personal journey of a police leader, tethering the force, however tenuously, to liberal notions of teleological progress that underpin LGBT rights and the politics of recognition.

'The best Pride March ever!': the affective circuitry of police pride

In contrast to the anger and apprehension of Police Association members and conservative politicians, others including Pride March organisers, LGBT organisations and individuals, and GALPEN expressed excitement, optimism, elation, and gratitude in response to Chief Commissioner Nixon's decision. Both the mainstream and the lesbian and gay press represented Nixon's participation in the 2002 Pride March as an overwhelmingly positive and historically significant event. In the lesbian and gay press coverage, Pride March president Penny McDonald described it as 'the best Pride March ever!' (Jacobs 2002), while GALPEN member Luke Bryant (2012) portrayed it online as 'the day that changed Melbourne's Pride March for ever'. VGLRL (2001) labelled Nixon's decision to participate in Pride March as a 'turning point' for LGBT–police relations. Themes of institutional change and progress resonated in the mainstream press. An article in the *Herald Sun* described how cries of 'Good on ya, Christine!' and 'Go coppers!' were heard from 'hundreds of people more accustomed to avoiding authority than cheering it' (de Kretser 2002). Nixon herself stated: 'I think people of the community really hope that we have overcome some of the prejudices that used to be there' (de Kretser 2002). Indeed, a letter published in the *Age* argued that it was 'refreshing' to see 'our own Victoria Police making a strong statement, starting at the very top for open-mindedness and acceptance of the gay community' (Condon 2002). In interview, long-time gay activist and lobbyist Jamie Gardiner described Nixon's participation in Pride March as 'fabulous and she got fabulous applause'. He added that 'whether there was anyone "booing", I don't know. I don't think I heard about it'. Another of my LGBT informants, who elected to remain anonymous, stated in an interview:

> The police themselves said that they thought they would be 'booed'. They really hadn't thought through the degree to which the community was absolutely thrilled to see that level of support from an organisation that they have experienced as hostile … We understood the significance of that, both as a symbolic gesture, but with the hope that that was the sign of a transformation over time from the top right down to police on the ground.

By almost all accounts, Nixon's participation in Pride March is a clear example of impactful and 'emotionally intelligent communication' on the part of police.

Following Sara Ahmed (2004), my reading of these textual representations of the Chief Commissioner's participation in Pride March is anchored by a particular concern for 'emotional metonymy and metaphor', or how such texts might generate and reflect *affect* and its expression through emotion (Russell 2017). These processes might also be captured by more everyday terms like 'sentiment' and 'feelings' (Gould 2009; Jackson & Meiners 2011). In this chapter, affect or emotions are not analysed as being 'in' these texts. Rather, by tracking 'words for feeling, and objects of feeling' (Ahmed 2004, pp. 13–14), we can begin to assess their social and political significance for social movements and for institutions, such as police. Placing emphasis on affective metaphors or figures of speech thus enables us to explore the 'emotionality of texts' (Ahmed 2004) or the way in which texts name or perform different emotions, how they construct historical narratives, and what the effects of these practices may be. The significance of emotional rhetoric is apparent before, during, and after Nixon's contribution to the 2002 Pride March.

In the lead-up to the march, Pride March President Penny McDonald promoted the event by emphasising the unprecedented nature of Nixon's decision to participate. Her comments were printed in an article in the lesbian and gay newspaper *Melbourne Community Voice* (*MCV*) on 7 December 2001 (p. 3):

> "Because of the Police Commissioner, Pride March is going to be big and exciting. It is making history—there has never been a commissioner march in a gay and lesbian event in Australia before, and it will have quite a bit of media attention," McDonald said. "It'll be great for people to say 'I marched in that' and 'I was on the sidelines and watching that'. I'd really love for lots of people to march along with Commissioner Nixon."

Here, McDonald positions the Chief Commissioner as the reason for excitement surrounding the parade—it is Nixon who enables it to 'make history', even in advance of the event itself. The possible effects of this discourse are reflected in the structure of narrative itself. As Ahmed (2010, p. 45) suggests, we can think of narrative as a 'form of conversion' whereby one feeling state is converted into another. This illustrates the importance of questioning 'who' or 'what' in the narrative gets seen as converting bad feeling into good feeling (and vice versa). Located within a broader discourse of 'history-making', the *MCV* constructs Nixon as the agent of conversion. It is she who propels the 2002 Pride March into the history books and converts bad feelings of queer oppression and exclusion into good feelings of LGBT recognition and acceptance. The Chief Commissioner is 'our conversion point' (Ahmed 2010, p. 45) in this narrative of progress. This construction reflects positively on police image. Since the Chief Commissioner is charged with directing and publicly representing the force, showing her in a positive light reflects well upon the force (and vice versa if she is portrayed in a negative light) and is thus a priority for police media units (Lee & McGovern 2014). Yet it also serves Nixon as an individual. Nixon cultivated an image as a courageous, progressive, and 'successful woman leader', particularly in her biography *Fair Cop* (Nixon & Chandler 2011), and she has gone on to establish herself as a consultant and public speaker on the topics of leadership, cultural change, and women in business (ICMI Speakers & Entertainers 2015; Nixon 2015).[2]

The positive image of police that circulated at Pride March in 2002 resonated beyond the event itself, and organisers continued to promote policing as a social good. For example, an image of Chief Commissioner Nixon was featured on a promotional postcard for Pride March the following year. She appeared alongside a photograph of a placard that read 'Equity & Diversity' and the phrase 'Peace through Pride' was printed on the reverse side of the postcard.[3] This textual reproduction of police in Pride March might be productively read as part of rebranding the police as 'gay-friendly' (Russell 2018). Pride March promotion thereby becomes a tool that augments the police public image. Popular understandings of policing may be refined and reworked by virtue of association with liberal values of equality, diversity, and peace, even though policing is more often associated with inequality, dominant masculine culture, and war such as the 'war on crime' or 'war on drugs'. As Nixon's successor Simon Overland suggested, police participation in Pride March sends 'a message to the broader community about tolerance and inclusivity' (Firkin 2010). This performative participation thereby assigns and communicates new meanings to the public about policing and the institutional valorisation of difference. Since administrative power has to 'affirm difference to demonstrate institutional protocols and progress' (Ferguson 2008, p. 163), the presentation of police in Pride March enables policing to approach the ideals of modernity and adaptability. As I outlined in the previous chapter, gay pride events are often criticised for their depoliticised and commercialised nature. This sanitised and marketable version of queer culture also appears to provide police with a platform to promote their organisation as inclusive and tolerant.

At the beginning of 2017, I interviewed Sally Goldner—the Executive Director of Transgender Victoria, key member of Bisexual Alliance Victoria, and long-time presenter of the local queer radio show 'Out of the Pan'. She described marching with uniformed police for the first time in 2002 as 'a landmark' event. As Goldner explained, for her:

> It was a very good piece of symbolic and practical communication. I tend a little at times to be a bit more on the practical side, but I've come

> to realise you need both. And that did both. It was just a brilliant piece of creative leadership and I think that she made a huge difference. She said she would march and had no hesitation. I remember her saying she had to brush up on her marching skills because she hadn't done any for a while, but good on her. I suppose she's willing to put her hand in, so to speak, and I think that was a good thing at the time, it began to really shift things. It was just so visible.

As Goldner's analysis indicates, 'looks' and aesthetics played an important role in the construction of a proud police image at this event. In *Fair Cop*, Nixon recalls how the police marching group had 'drilled their routine thoroughly and put on a nice display' (Nixon & Chandler 2011, pp. 133–134). Pride March President McDonald argued that 'the presence of the Police went beyond the expectations of everyone'; they 'just looked so good' (Jacobs 2002). A member of an outer eastern-suburbs lesbian social group stated: 'they looked as proud to be there as we were to have them' (Jackson 2002). The aesthetics of police pride also resonated strongly in mainstream media reporting, which described a 'smiley' and 'beaming Ms. Nixon' marching 'in her neatly pressed uniform alongside more casually dressed participants sporting items such as … leather vests and metallic shorts' (Jackson 2002; de Kretser 2002). Photographs of the Chief Commissioner at Pride March in 2002 that circulated in both the lesbian and gay and the mainstream press present a style of approach that is warm, smiling, and at ease (Jacobs 2002). Simultaneously, the sharp and neat police uniforms combine with a disciplined marching routine to affirm police authority through military symbolism. Indeed, from my observations of the Victoria Police contingents in Midsumma Pride March in 2011, 2012, 2014, and 2019, police appear in the parade as an ordered marching formation that is more muted than celebratory and certainly militaristic in style: neatly uniformed police march in straight rows, staring straight ahead. At the conclusion of the march, however, police stand around more casually in the gardens, often posing for photographs.

The pairing of a friendly, personable, and 'open-minded' Chief Commissioner with a traditional and disciplinarian representation of police officers in Pride March reflects policing scholar Robert Reiner's (2003, p. 259) observation that the positive representation of the police to the public 'involves the continuous reconstruction and reinterpretation of the nature of policing'. In this case, symbols of authority are paired with representations of progress, modernity, and adaptability to produce a dynamic image of policing that appeals simultaneously to notions of tradition and order, and social and institutional change. Yet, while Nixon's participation in Pride March is frequently constructed as both a product and sign of institutional progress, a closer examination of relevant texts reveals it as a site of significant complexity and contestation among both police and LGBT people. Jamie Gardiner noted in interview that it 'caused grand anxiety within the police force, demonstrating that they weren't across the line yet'. Senior Constable Melinda Edwards (2004) recounted in a 2004 conference presentation:

> I still receive homophobic threats whenever I do the call for [Pride March] participants from [police] members … I have to admit one of the most concerning ones was, 'I fear God more than I fear the Equal Opportunity Act'.

The circulation of threats highlights the persistent and 'entrenched culture of homophobia' within the force, as the Victorian Gay and Lesbian Rights Lobby (VGLRL) (2001) described it. While the image of the Chief Commissioner in Pride March communicates institutional progress, it also highlights and draws out conservatism and explicit reactions of homophobia from police members.

LGBT people did not uniformly welcome the news of the Chief Commissioner marching in Pride. The 'significant progress' or 'turning point' that Nixon's participation in Pride March represents for many LGBT people and organisations, such as VGLRL (2001), also sits uneasily alongside noted patterns of institutional, interpersonal, and structural violence. This awareness creates a sense of ambivalence in relation to the event. For example, when I asked former GLRC Vice President and later QUEER activist Alison Thorne about the significance of uniformed police marching in Pride, she reasoned that in some ways it was 'a step forward', because it is 'really important for gay men and lesbians in the police force to be able to be open' about their sexual identity. However, she pointed out that it also represents 'an attempt to normalise the police as an institution of the state'. Thorne elaborated on the limitations of the Chief Commissioner's symbolic gesture:

> Taking a more multi-issue perspective of the queer community, [that accounts for the experiences of] indigenous queers, homeless queers, queers with mental illnesses, people out on the streets and whatever, today the police might be the friend of the well-to-do gay male stockbroker, but for the homeless Aboriginal Sistergirl living in a park, the fact that Christine Nixon is marching in Pride doesn't make any difference.[4]

Thorne highlights the material inequalities between and among LGBT people—often accorded along lines of Aboriginality, class, race, and gender—that mediate subjective and affective relations to policing and the state (Boon-Kuo et al. 2018). While Nixon's very public demonstration of anti-homophobia at Pride March may affirm 'progress' for LGBT identities that are now less likely to experience negative encounters with police, queers who are members of communities that continue to be both over- and under-policed may have more reason to be cynical about (or simply have different insights into) the degree to which marching in Pride reorients everyday policing practices and cultures.

'It seemed that we had come to love Big Brother': co-option and competing queer temporalities

Chief Commissioner Nixon's participation in the 2002 Pride March gave rise to debate around the possible risks and benefits of police presence in queer spaces. *MCV* published a letter written by Gregory Doran on 18 January 2002 (one week before the 2002 Pride March), which questioned the broader acceptance and celebration of police in gay pride events. Taking a critical stance on the promotion of police in Pride March media, and reflecting Thorne's reasoning above, Doran (2002) argued that 'whether gay men and lesbians are police officers is a matter for individual choice, but that it should be the occasion of communal joy and pride, well that's another matter entirely'. In so doing, he made a distinction between individual employees' right to participate in Pride March as LGBT people, and the promotion and legitimisation of policing itself. Doran posed the question to *MCV* readers:

> Have we forgotten that police forces, historically, have been at the forefront of the oppression of gay men? Realising this fact, it baffled me that a squad of uniformed police received such a rapturous reception at the 2001 Mardi Gras parade. It had an almost Orwellian chill to it. Like Winston Smith in *Nineteen Eighty-four*, it seemed that we had come to love Big Brother.
>
> (Doran 2002)

Doran queries the 'affective attachments' (Ahmed 2004)—the 'rapturous reception' and 'love' for police—that contribute to, in Thorne's words, the normalisation of police as 'an institution of the state'. In doing so, he evokes Lauren Berlant's (2011, p. 13) notion of 'cruel optimism': a situation whereby individuals or groups become emotionally invested or attached to the 'continuity, progress and development' of a harmful institution—in this case, one that has historically targeted them and that, perhaps still, constitutes a barrier to the flourishing of queer life and culture.

The following week, Sally Goldner responded to Doran's letter in *MCV* and provided a contrasting perspective. As she wrote:

> I welcome the unilateral strong initiative (leadership defined, perhaps) of Chief Commissioner Nixon. She is at least trying to move things on from the past. No one suggests forgetting, as someone who has been on the direct receiving end of police discrimination I understand that only too well. However, here is a chance to turn things for the better and I'm willing to work with the police where possible.
>
> (Goldner 2002)

These two perspectives highlight some of the contradictions and compromises LGBT people encountered in the context of this event, producing conflicting responses to the Chief Commissioner's participation in Pride March. Both of these letters draw on a history defined by violence and exclusion; yet it is a history that is unevenly shared. As Chapter 2 illustrated, some LGBT people are more likely to be erased in historical accounts and those excluded are 'variously and often simultaneously black, female, queer' (Freeman 2005, p. 57). Doran's depiction of histories of police violence inaccurately implies only 'gay men' were the recipients, whereas Goldner reflects on her personal experience without making broader claims as to who was or was not targeted by police historically. Doran expresses wariness towards the potential for the co-option of gay pride by police. By suggesting that LGBT people are welcoming their oppressor, Doran reflects on the way that an institution known to harm 'gay men' through criminalisation and harassment is now being celebrated and promoted. The implication is that LGBT people are no longer resisting police interventions into queer spaces, but inviting them in. For Doran, this is dangerous because of the violent track record of police among LGBT people, whereas Goldner emphasises the possibility of genuine reform, perhaps including the disappearance of police homophobia, which for her seems to outweigh any risks the scenario might pose.

The optimism placed in a potential future outcome in Goldner's letter suggests that in this instance, Nixon functions as a 'promise' (Agathangelou et al. 2008; Ahmed 2010). The promise comes to rest upon the possibility of Nixon's leadership overcoming the (past) injury of queer oppression, much like the 'conversion point' analogy used above. In this formulation, an over-attachment to police homophobia—represented here as a memory of unresolved pain for LGBT people—threatens to hinder the possibilities of developing positive relationships with police. While 'forgetting' might be too much to ask, Goldner attempts to lead by example, putting these violent histories behind us so that we can move forward.[5] 'Moving on' from the painful past thereby becomes a 'moral task' (Ahmed 2010, p. 143), because it seems to offers 'a chance to turn things for the better' (Goldner 2002). Queer theorist Heather Love (2007, p. 163) argues that because of the 'scene of destruction at our backs, queers feel compelled to keep moving on toward a brighter future'. In contrast to the positive affects commonly associated with virtue and futurity, negative affects such as shame, disidentification, and trauma can be pathologised and cast as backward. Although 'bad feelings have been central to the history of queer experience and queer feeling', Love (2007, p. 27) argues that 'there is little room for them in the contemporary climate'. Yet at the same time, the history of queer experience has made a sustained positive orientation to the future difficult—as both of these letters illustrate. As Love (2007, p. 162, emphasis in original) points out and as both Doran and Goldner imply, 'queers are intimately familiar with the *costs* of being queer'.

From Love's (2007) perspective, intimate familiarity with oppression cannot simply be disavowed, because it's what makes us queer as much as anything—as Goldner (2002) puts it, 'no one suggests forgetting'. Similarly, Ahmed (2004, p. 172) argues that a politics that is critical cannot simply 'overcome' through detachment the affects of histories of violence, injustice, and inequality. Indeed, negative affect or 'backward feelings', experienced or expressed collectively, may serve an important political function (Halperin & Traub 2009). Backward feelings can 'serve as an index to the ruined state of the social world; they indicate continuities between the bad gay past and the present; and they show up the inadequacy of queer narratives of progress' (Love 2007, p. 27). Much like QUEER's approach outlined in the previous chapter, Ahmed (2004) suggests that these 'negative' affects can be used to structure and inform demands or hopes for social transformation as we orient ourselves towards the future. The radical potential of negative affect suggests that 'bad feeling' need not be backwardly oriented, and thus positioned as inferior to the more pragmatic approach of working 'with the police where possible', because the Chief Commissioner is 'at least trying to move things on from the past' (Goldner 2002). The popular representation of Nixon as a bold and progressive leader aligns closely with the narrative constructed in her biography *Fair Cop*, which attempts to recraft queer and police history.

'I rejoiced at every single step': the *Fair Cop* narrative of progress

In *Fair Cop*, Christine Nixon makes a considerable effort to explain and justify her decision to break Victoria Police tradition by marching alongside LGBT police officers as Chief Commissioner at a gay pride event. The biography links the driving force behind this decision to one of Nixon's early experiences as a police officer, when she witnessed the aftermath of the gay solidarity demonstration, now referred to as the 'first Mardi Gras', in Sydney in June 1978, which 'turned into a violent clash with police' (Nixon & Chandler 2011, p. 52). Alternative accounts testify in more detail to the nature and extent of this violence, including police not wearing badges and bashing queer protesters, as well as protesters resisting police by pulling friends out of paddy wagons and throwing garbage cans (Carbery 1995; Duncan 1998). Nixon recalls how she turned up to work to find the Darlinghurst police station 'surrounded by a crowd of distraught, angry gay and lesbian protesters demanding the immediate release of friends being held—and beaten, they claimed—in the cells' (Nixon & Chandler 2011, p. 52). In the *Fair Cop* narrative, Nixon represents herself as 'profoundly' impacted and moved by the protests in her role as a junior police officer. Her response is depicted in emotional terms:

> I was deeply distressed at the schism I observed that day between the police force and members of the community it served. The scene had a profound effect on me. I'd become increasingly preoccupied with questions around the role of police in a changing society. What I saw that day

> represented, to me, the worst of policing—the clash of a kind of occupying force with its own citizens. It was symptomatic of the gap between narrow police culture and the diversity of the broader community. I felt ashamed as I picked my way across Taylor Square and through the barricade in my police uniform.
>
> (Nixon & Chandler 2011, p. 53)

In this specific historical context of police violence, what role does Nixon play as she bears witness and recognises shame? And how does naming these feelings function as a vehicle for recovering institutional pride and repairing police image later on? To gain insight into the relationship between bearing witness and recovering pride, Ahmed (2004) investigates how 'national shame' can function as a mechanism for 'self-reconciliation'. She argues that an acknowledgement of the 'wrong' committed in the past provides the grounds for claiming a proud national identity in the present.[6] In the moment of recognition national pride is threatened, but then is immediately regained in the capacity to bear witness and feel shame (Ahmed 2004). By witnessing what is shameful about the past, 'the nation can "live up to" the ideals that secure its identity or being in the present', since the identification of personal or institutional shame means that 'we mean well' and can work to reproduce national ideals (Ahmed 2004, p. 109). Nixon's depiction of shame thus conveys that she is 'well meaning', cognisant of the 'diversity of the broader community', and committed to changing 'narrow police culture'. Nixon's account is embodied—she feels distressed, preoccupied, and ashamed. Her introspective and personal journey is at the centre of the historical narrative; her pain displaces and obscures queer pain. Once again, Nixon is the conversion point in the narrative. Her feelings and her foresight propel LGBT rights and recognition forward. Through witnessing and recalling past wrongs, the Chief Commissioner, and by extension, the police force, can take on the imagined values of tolerance and recognition that contribute to the production of a positive police image in the present. The exposure of past injustice is therefore only temporary, and becomes the ground for a narrative of institutional recovery that is embodied by a powerful white femininity (Ahmed 2004).

Fair Cop presents Nixon's emotive response to the 1978 gay protest as one that deeply shaped her overall approach to the role of Chief Commissioner. As outlined earlier, her focus and vision for Victoria Police was directed towards community policing philosophies and techniques, for which she came to be renowned (Nixon & Chandler 2011). Nixon reconstructs this personal journey and identifies her memory of Sydney in 1978 as what informed her decision to join fellow police members in Melbourne's Pride March in 2002:

> The memory of that moment would echo through my career, eventually following me to Victoria, and propelling me down Fitzroy Street in

> St Kilda where I led a formation of gay and lesbian police participating in the gay pride march. It was one of my first public acts in the uniform of Victorian chief commissioner, and while it wasn't applauded universally, the reaction on the street was ecstatic. Remembering that very different, grim, long-ago morning in Darlinghurst, I rejoiced at every single step.
>
> (Nixon & Chandler 2011, p. 53)

This excerpt demonstrates an attribution of causality that works in part through affective metaphors: the shameful 'echo' of the first Mardi Gras 'propels' Nixon to join Pride March decades later. Importantly, it is because the police violence in Sydney in 1978 is positioned as 'very different, grim, long ago' that Nixon is able to rejoice 'at every single step' while in 'the uniform as Victorian chief commissioner'. The policing of the 1978 gay solidarity demonstration, labelled as 'the worst of policing—the clash of a kind of occupying force with its own citizens', maintains an important place in the evolution of policing gay pride. As a point of comparison that signals progress in the present, this narrative contributes to the legitimation of policing. *Fair Cop* thereby recasts contemporary policing as modern, adaptive, and inclusive not by forgetting past policing practices, but by remembering them (Russell 2017). The violent policing of LGBT people in the past is recalled in the present, but swiftly labelled as backwards, overly authoritarian, and ineffective, so that it may be ideologically disassociated from current institutional practices and priorities. In short, a violent and antagonistic past is conjured in order to reproduce the police anew as a 'feeling force', firmly on the 'right side' of struggles for sexual and gender equality.

The institutional progress narrative constructed in *Fair Cop* resonates in other accounts of police participation in Pride March. Typically, the story begins with prejudice and targeting, and ends with pride and inclusion. It is a tale that reflects and generates broader conceptual shifts and understandings regarding not only the relationship between police and LGBT people, but also the status of sexual and gender diversity in Australian society. For example, Richard Waterhouse (1995, p. 247), writing about the history of Australian popular culture, argues:

> During the 1950s homosexuals were condemned and treated as 'deviants,' as threats to society and the heterosexual family that underpinned it. The promotion of Mardi Gras in the 90s is a sign both of a more tolerant society and of widespread acceptance that the 'traditional' family is not a prerequisite for a stable and 'healthy' community.

While much may have changed for many race- and class-privileged lesbian and gay people who, for the most part, have escaped state surveillance and criminalisation with increased access to resources and cultural capital

(Moran 2012), pathologising scripts about LGBT people have not yet lost their currency (Raj 2015). Heteronormativity maintains a hold upon almost all facets of political and social life. It continues to shape the nature of policing, despite proactive police image work and community outreach efforts designed to govern the relationship between police and LGBT people, to counter negative perceptions of police (Dwyer & Tomsen 2016).

'We should always keep in mind our past and be ever-vigilant about our rights': the normalisation of policing in queer space

The multiple meanings assigned to the 1978 protests that now serve as the origin of the Sydney Mardi Gras continue to reverberate and circulate in Australian queer cultures and discourses. For instance, lesbian film-maker Digby Duncan (1998), one of the original 1978 protesters, states: 'I would hope we would never see police action like that again. But we should always keep in mind our past and be ever-vigilant about our rights'. In this statement, Duncan expresses tempered optimism about the future without erasing the past. Instead, she uses the past to call for LGBT vigilance in the present. Despite Duncan's hope for an end to violent police incursion into LGBT spaces, police brutality at the Sydney Mardi Gras made headlines in 2013, when police assaulted a white queer youth, 18-year-old Jamie Jackson Reed, and charged him with offensive language, resisting arrest, and assaulting police (Dwyer & Tomsen 2016). These three charges are commonly issued together for minor street-based offences—especially targeting Aboriginal and Torres Strait Islander people (Cunneen 2001)—and are colloquially known as 'the trifecta' (Boon-Kuo et al. 2018). Footage captured on a friend's phone showed police handcuffing Jackson Reed, then gripping his neck in a lock-hold, slamming his head against the ground, and stepping on his back. Jackson Reed is seen crying in the video, repeating that he 'didn't do anything wrong'. In an example of the changing circumstances of visibility for police as a product of widespread use of camera phones (Goldsmith 2010), the footage amassed more than one million views on YouTube in less than a week. It also sparked an internal police inquiry, a protest attended by at least 1,000 people, and a community forum focused on policing of Mardi Gras (Boon-Kuo et al. 2018; Dwyer & Tomsen 2016).[7]

Following the wide circulation of camera phone footage of Jackson Reed's brutal arrest, attendees at the protest and community forum expressed anger and frustration towards police for not only this explicit incident of abuse, but also the general problem of excessive securitisation during Mardi Gras, including sniffer dog operations, and police control and restriction of movements in public space (New Matilda 2015). As critical scholars have pointed out, the 2013 Mardi Gras complicates the notion that police violence against

LGBT people is a problem of the past, because 'traces of traditional policing' continue to re-emerge (Dwyer & Tomsen 2016) and 'shape *material* and *affective* modes of belonging' for queer youth (Boon-Kuo et al. 2018, p. 36, emphasis in original). The Jackson Reed case also raises questions about how and why particular incidents of police violence come to be viewed as worthy of recognition and redress, while others do not. In the weeks that followed Mardi Gras, hundreds of similar accounts of police hostility and aggression surfaced and circulated on social media (Dwyer & Tomsen 2016). Bryn Hutchinson, a gay activist who was also publicly assaulted and arrested by police at the 2013 Mardi Gras, argued that his case and that of Jackson Reed garnered media attention because they were white and middle class, whereas many Aboriginal and Torres Strait Islander people and migrants who regularly experience police violence rarely attain news headlines (Needham 2014). In Jackson Reed's case, a magistrate eventually withdrew all charges and awarded him AUD$39,000 in costs. Despite the critical mobilisation that followed this incident of police brutality and ongoing concerns surrounding the over-policing of what Fiona McGregor (2016) dubs 'Fortress Mardi Gras', Mardi Gras organisers proudly promoted the NSW Police contingent the following year and sought to strengthen their relationship with police (Akersten 2014 Australian Pride Network 2014). This highlights how police presence in queer space is now largely taken for granted, as LGBT people are left with limited options for negotiating and resisting state surveillance if we are to remain on the 'right side' of the criminalisation/protection line. In 2014, the spatial authority of police was reinforced, as NSW Police Superintendent Tony Crandell made it clear that there would be no 'special treatment' for parade-goers and no retreat in policing of the Mardi Gras: 'The community can expect to see sniffer dogs out there. There will also be CCTV cameras erected' (Gregoire 2014). Regardless of the significant dent in police legitimacy, police on duty at the 2014 Mardi Gras were, in Crandell's words, 'not going to be a soft touch' (Gregoire 2014).

Conclusion

The authoritative role of police in combination with the disproportionate application of police power across different sections of the population, including LGBT people, frequently generates public disdain and distrust towards police and their actions. At the Victorian Pride March in 2002, Chief Commissioner Nixon developed an opportunity to build the legitimacy of Victoria Police through image work and symbolic communication. Conventional representations of Nixon's participation in Pride March contributed to a rebranding and reimagining of contemporary policing as bold, modern, and adaptive. Ultimately this was done not by forgetting the violent policing of queer resistance in the past, but by selectively remembering it and prescribing new meaning to it. The affective circuitry that links past shame and regret with contemporary pride and joy risks glossing over the continuities of surveillance, securitisation, and violent assaults that undergird police power in the present. These 'public feelings' contribute to the production of new image of police as a 'feeling force' that reflects shifting social and cultural expectations of tolerance and inclusivity. The Chief Commissioner's participation in Pride March demonstrates how police can mobilise *negative* aspects of their organisational history to restore pride in policing and embrace a public identity of 'protector, patron, and sponsor of minorities' (Haritaworn 2010, p. 83).

My analysis of the 2002 Victorian Pride March confirms existing interpretations of police image and legitimacy as unstable, pluralised, and subject to ongoing contestation (Goldsmith 2010; Smith 2007) and validates the importance of symbolism to police power and authority (Lee & McGovern 2014; Mawby 2002; Reiner 2003). This case provides unique insights into how dominant conceptions of policing are challenged, reconstructed, and disseminated across time and space, and how they relate to marginal histories. By reading proactive police communications strategies alongside ongoing histories of state violence, the close and entwined relationship between inclusive and exclusive approaches to policing is more clearly revealed. The new professionalised and impartial image of police is destabilised by the heightened visibility of police brutality as a result of the rapid spread of camera phones and free online platforms for sharing footage. However, following the police assault of a queer youth at the Sydney Mardi Gras in 2013, police operations and surveillance were not curtailed. Instead, they were cemented even further by isolating the violence to individual officers and by constructing local police as a 'cultural authority' on queerness. This is indicative of the extent to which LGBT people are being brought into the fold of the state, despite the limited capacity of police to offer anything in return, as the next chapter will discuss.

Police appropriation and re-signification of histories of police violence against LGBT people has implications not only for police legitimacy, but also for the politics of queer history. Emerging historically out of grassroots protests focused on institutionalised homophobia, the new face of LGBT Pride that features police foremost among its celebrations raises important questions about police power—its ability to adapt and absorb critique—and the complex meanings attributed to queer visibility today (Russell 2018). Given that policing is far from a neutral or benign force, what role does it play in producing, striating, and constraining queer spaces? The normalisation of police presence at LGBT Pride events advances the processes of commodification, assimilation, and exclusion that gay liberationist and queer activists have long fought against. Read alongside the previous chapter's excavation of queer anti-capitalist activism occurring around the same time, and place, the swift embrace of policing in this case study highlights significant and simultaneous divergences within and between movements organised around sexual and gender identities in any given context. Indeed, the prominent place of police in pride marches has been subject to renewed challenge by queer and trans activists in recent years—most notoriously in Toronto and Auckland, where anti-racist interventions have successfully built pressure for formal bans on police marching in uniform (Lamusse 2016; Russell 2018).

As should be clear by now, LGBT movements have often cohered and splintered around issues of violence. Whether institutional, systemic, individual, or interpersonal, the nature of anti-queer violence—and how it should be addressed—has been a significant preoccupation of LGBT activists. Understandings of the causes and drivers of such violence directly shape the development of strategies to prevent and remedy it. During the period of time that the past three chapters have covered (roughly from the mid-1990s to the early 2000s), a new paradigm for understanding homophobic violence emerged: 'hate crime'. The LGBT take-up of this language has advanced the carceral investments of sexual and gender politics, since 'crime control' is of course the traditional mandate of police. The next chapter outlines how LGBT anti-violence campaigns have simultaneously advanced individualised conceptions of 'homophobic hate' and exposed the systemic failures of the state to 'protect' queer lives.

Notes

1 Nixon 'fell from grace' in the mainstream press when it emerged that she left the Integrated Emergency Co-ordination Centre to join friends for a pub meal at the height of the Black Saturday bushfire disaster, 7 February 2009, which left 173 people dead. She retired shortly after. Critical media commentators, as well as Nixon herself, pointed out that Nixon's harsh treatment by media and politicians such as former Victorian Premier Jeff Kennett was underpinned by fat discrimination and disdain for a woman in a leadership role (Sparrow 2010).

2 *Fair Cop* was written and published following Nixon's term as Chief Commissioner of Victoria Police; she is thus potentially much more open about her experiences in the force and critical of parts of police culture than she was during her tenure in the top role. While the biography is a personalised story of a female leader in a traditionally masculine institution, it nevertheless reflects positively on the professionalisation of policing more broadly.

3 'Pride March 2003: Sunday February 3rd', postcard held at ALGA in the Pride March Victoria, Inc. ephemera file.

4 Western nomenclature generally conceives of 'sistergirls' as transgender Aboriginal women. However, there is evidence that sistergirls lived within some Australian Aboriginal communities before colonisation and as such, a European understanding of this identity category cannot capture the complex cultural connections that shape it (Anwernekenhe Conference Committee 1994; Brown 2004).

5 In a chapter titled 'Melancholic Migrants', Ahmed (2010) addresses the idea that the repetition of the narrative of injury (racism, in this case) *causes* injury. She argues that the migrant is seen to preserve the power of racism through their attachment to it. The melancholic migrant's fixation with injury is read as an obstacle not only to their own happiness, 'but also to the happiness of the generation to come, and even to national happiness' (Ahmed 2010, p. 144).

6 Ahmed (2004) develops this argument through an analysis of the *Bringing Them Home* report tabled in Federal Parliament in 1997 that documents and condemns the past policy of forced removal of Aboriginal and Torres Strait Islander children, who are now known as the Australian Stolen Generations (Commonwealth of Australia 1997).

7 As many observers have argued, the diversification of communication technologies has exposed police to greater scrutiny. Advancing technologies and platforms for recording and broadcasting policing events are increasingly accessible to members of the public through the widespread use of cameras. This creates what Goldsmith (2010) terms 'policing's new visibility' in the context of police–citizen encounters. The new visibility complicates police efforts to manage organisational reputation and control policing news stories, because citizen cameras may capture an alternative 'version of events' than that provided by police, potentially creating increased scrutiny and pressure for accountability.

References

Agathangelou, AM, Bassichis, DM, & Spira, TL 2008, 'Intimate investments: Homonormativity, global lockdown, and the seductions of empire', *Radical History Review*, vol. 100, pp. 120–143.

Ahmed, S 2004, *The cultural politics of emotion*, Routledge, London.

Ahmed, S 2010, *The promise of happiness*, Duke University Press, Durham.

Aiello, M 2014, 'Policing the masculine frontier: Cultural criminological analysis of the gendered performance of policing', *Crime Media Culture*, vol. 10, no. 1, pp. 59–79.

Akersten, M 2014, 'Mardi gras welcomes new police accord', *Same Same*, viewed 25 November 2015, www.samesame.com.au/news/10574/Mardi-Gras-welcomes-new-police-accord.

Anwernekenhe Conference Committee 1994, *Report of 'Anwernekenhe': First national Aboriginal and Torres Strait Islander gay men and transgender sexual health conference*, Australian Federation of AIDS Organisations, Sydney.

Australian Pride Network 2014, '2015 Mardi Gras set to GLLO with police pride', 6 November, viewed 31 May 2017, http://australianpridenetwork.com.au/2015-mardi-gras-set-to-gllo-with-police-pride/.

Berlant, L 2011, *Cruel optimism*, Duke University Press Durham and London.

Bolt, A 2006, 'Our cops go girlie', *Herald Sun*, 22 November, p. 21.

Boon-Kuo, L, Meiners, ER, & Simpson, P 2018, 'Queer interruptions: Policing belonging in the carceral state', in P Aggleton, R Cover, D Leahy, D Marshall, & ML Rasmussen (eds), *Youth, sexuality and sexual citizenship*, Routledge, Oxon, pp. 34–49.

Bradford, B, Jackson, J, & Stanko, EA 2009, 'Contact and confidence: Revisiting the impact of public encounters with the police', *Policing and Society*, vol. 19, no. 1, pp. 20–46.

Brown, K 2004, 'Sistergirls: Stories from Indigenous Australian transgender people', *Aboriginal and Islander Health Worker Journal*, vol. 28, no. 6, pp. 25–26.

Bryant, L 2012, 'Times past: The gay and lesbian police employees network' (Victoria, Australia', *Prime Timers Worldwide*, 31 July 2012, viewed 10 February 2014, www.primetimersww.com/index.php?option=com_k2&view=item&id=111:times-past&Itemid=590.

Carbery, G 1995, *A history of the Sydney Gay and Lesbian Mardi Gras*, Australian Lesbian and Gay Archives, Parkville.
Chulov, M 2002, 'The force is with her: The rise and rise of Australia's first female police chief', *The Weekend Australian Magazine*, 29 September, pp. 13–15.
Commonwealth of Australia 1997, *Bringing them home: Report of the National Inquiry into the Separation of Aboriginal and Torres Strait Islander Children from their Families*, Commonwealth of Australia, Canberra.
Condon, R 2002, 'Power to the force', *Age*, 22 January, p. 10.
Crawford, C 2003, 'Police gay payday – pay for officers who attend gay parade, whether on duty or not', *Herald Sun*, 28 December, p. 5.
Cunneen, C 2001, *Conflict, politics and crime: Aboriginal communities and the police*, Allen & Unwin, Sydney.
De Kretser, L 2002, 'Pride of force a hit at gay march', *Herald Sun*, 21 January 2002, p. 5.
Donovan, B 2002, 'The Nixon years', *Australian Story*, 22 April, television transcript, viewed 16 March 2015, www.abc.net.au/austory/transcripts/s533773.htm.
Doran, G 2002, 'Big brother marches?' *Melbourne Community Voice*, 18 January, p. 5.
Duncan, K 1998, 'Get your laws off our bodies', *Lesbians on the Loose*, February iss., pp. 18–20.
Dwyer, A & Tomsen, S 2016, 'The past is the past? The impossibility of erasure of historical LGBTIQ policing', in A Dwyer, M Ball, & T Crofts (eds), *Queering criminology*, Palgrave Macmillan, London, pp. 36–53.
Edwards, M 2004, 'Victoria Police', Australian GLBTIQ Multicultural Council, viewed 20 March 2015, www.agmc.org.au/wp-content/MediaReleases/2004 ConferenceTranscripts/Melinda%20Edwards.doc.
Ferguson, RA 2008, 'Administering sexuality; or, the will to institutionality', *Radical History Review*, vol. 100, pp. 158–169.
Firkin, K 2010, 'Top cop Simon Overland stars in gay day of pride', *Herald Sun*, 15 February, viewed 4 December 2013, www.heraldsun.com.au/news/top-cop-simon-overland-stars-in-gay-day-of-pride/story-e6frf7jo-1225827620805.
Freeman, E 2005, 'Time binds, or, erotohistoriography', *Social Text*, vol. 23, no. 3–4 (84–85), pp. 57–68.
Garland, D 2001, *Culture of control: Crime and social order in contemporary society*, Oxford University Press, Oxford.
Goldner, S 2002, 'Issues of trust', *Melbourne Community Voice*, 25 January, p. 5.
Goldsmith, AJ 2010, 'Policing's new visibility', *British Journal of Criminology*, vol. 50, pp. 914–934.
Gough, D 2014, 'Homophobic police stuck in time warp, says chief commissioner Ken Lay', *Age*, 3 February, viewed 27 August 2015, www.theage.com.au/victoria/homophobic-police-stuck-in-a-time-warp-says-chief-commissioner-ken-lay-20140203-31wsj.html.
Gould, DB 2009, *Moving politics: Emotion and ACT UP's fight against AIDS*, The University of Chicago Press, Chicago.
Gregoire, P 2014, '"I need to fix some things": Police chief', 27 February, viewed Day Month, www.altmedia.net.au/89989/89989.
Haldane, R 1995, *The people's force: A history of the Victoria Police*, Melbourne University Press, Carlton South.
Hall, S, Critcher, C, Jefferson, T, Clarke, J, & Roberts, B 1978, *Policing the crisis: Mugging, the state, and law and order*, Macmillan, London.

Halperin, DM & Traub, V 2009, *Gay shame*, University of Chicago Press, Chicago.
Haritaworn, J 2010, 'Queer injuries: The racial politics of "homophobic hate crime" in Germany', *Social Justice*, vol. 37, no. 1, pp. 69–91.
ICMI Speakers & Entertainers 2015, *Christine Nixon APM*, viewed 1 November 2015, www.icmi.com.au/christine-nixon.
Jackson, A 2002, 'Nixon the pride of a purple day out', *Age*, 21 January, p. 3.
Jackson, JL & Meiners, ER 2011, 'Fear and loathing: Public feelings in antiprison work', *Women's Studies Quarterly*, vol. 39, no. 1/2, pp. 270–291.
Jacobs, R 2002, 'Cop that!', *Melbourne Community Voice*, 25 January, p. 1.
Kappeler, V & Kraska, P 1998, 'A textual critique of community policing: Police adaption to high modernity', *Policing: An International Journal of Police Strategies and Management*, vol. 21, no. 2, pp. 293–313.
Lamusse, T 2016, 'Politics at pride?' *New Zealand Sociology*, vol. 31, no. 6, pp. 49–70.
Lee, M & McGovern, A 2014, *Policing and media: Public relations, simulations and communications*, Routledge, Oxon.
Levy, M 2011, 'Nixon authored own demise, police association says', *Age*, 28 July, viewed 27 October 2015, www.theage.com.au/victoria/nixon-authored-own-demise-police-association-says-20110728-1i146.html.
Love, H 2007, *Feeling backward: Loss and the politics of queer history*, Harvard University Press, Cambridge, MA.
Manning, PK 1992, *Organizational communication*, Aldine De Gruyter, New York.
Marsh, I & Melville, G 2009, *Crime, justice and the media*, Routledge, London.
Mawby, RC 2002, *Policing images: Policing, communication and legitimacy*, Willan, Cullompton.
Mawby, RC 2010, 'Police corporate communications, crime reporting and the shaping of policing news', *Policing and Society*, vol. 20, no. 1, pp. 124–139.
Mawby, RC 2014, 'The presentation of police in everyday life: Police-press relations, impression management and the Leveson Inquiry', *Crime Media Culture*, vol. 10, no. 3, pp. 239–257.
McGregor, F 2016, 'Fortress Mardi Gras', *Overland Literary Journal*, 30 March, viewed 26 February 2018, https://overland.org.au/2016/03/fortress-mardi-gras/.
Moran, LJ 2012, 'The changing landscape of policing male sexualities: A minor revolution', in P Johnson & D Dalton (eds), *Policing sex*, Routledge, London, pp. 11–22.
Needham, K 2014, 'Police powers, not violence, cast a cloud over Mardi Gras', *The Sydney Morning Herald*, 9 February, viewed 30 July 2015, www.smh.com.au/comment/police-powers-not-violence-cast-a-cloud-over-mardi-gras-20140208-328fb.html.
New Matilda 2015, *Ever seen a drug dog at the opera? The Mardi Gras is a whole other story*, posted 5 March, viewed 25 November 2015, https://newmatilda.com/2015/03/05/ever-seen-drug-dog-opera-mardi-gras-whole-other-story/.
News24 2002, *Chief cop in gay pride march*, posted 20 January, viewed 1 March 2014, www.news24.com/xArchive/Archive/Chief-cop-in-gay-pride-march-20020120.
Nixon, C 2015, *Consulting*, Christine Nixon, viewed 1 November 2015, http://christinenixon.com.au/consulting.
Nixon, C & Chandler, J 2011, *Fair cop*, Melbourne University Publishing, Melbourne.
Philly Pride 2015, 'Officials', *Philly Pride Presents*, viewed 27 August 2015, www.phillygaypride.org/events/philly-pride-parade-and-festival/officials/.

Pride March Committee 2001, 'Pride March: Sunday 20th January', *Footsteps*, newsletter, October.

Raj, S 2015, 'Disturbing disgust: Gesturing to the abject in queer cases', in A Dwyer, M Ball, & T Crofts (eds), *Queering criminology*, Palgrave Macmillan, Basingstoke, pp. 83–101.

Reiner, R 2003, 'Policing and the media', in T Newburn (ed.), *Handbook of policing*, Willan, Cullompton, pp. 259–281.

Russell, EK 2017, 'A "fair cop": Queer histories, affect and police image work in Pride March', *Crime Media Culture*, vol. 13, no. 3, pp. 277–293.

Russell, EK 2018, 'Carceral pride: The fusion of police imagery with LGBTI rights', *Feminist Legal Studies*, vol. 26, no. 3, pp. 331–350.

Sentas, V 2014, *Traces of terror: Counter-terrorism law, policing, and race*, Oxford University Press, Oxford.

Silvestrini, E 2015, 'Police chief headlines Tampa's first gay pride parade in 14 years', *The Tampa Tribune*, 28 March, viewed 27 August 2015, www.tbo.com/events-tampa-bay/police-chief-headlines-tampas-first-gay-pride-parade-in-14-years-20150328/.

Smith, DJ 2007, 'New challenges to police legitimacy', in A Henry & DJ Smith (eds), *Transformations of policing*, Ashgate, Aldershot, pp. 273–306.

Sparrow, J 2010, 'The bizarre case against Christine Nixon', *ABC News*, 29 September, viewed 27 October 2015, www.abc.net.au/news/2010-04-20/33730.

Thomas, M 2016, 'Merseyside chief constable first to join Liverpool Pride March', *Echo*, 25 July, viewed 5 December 2017, www.liverpoolecho.co.uk/news/liverpool-news/merseyside-chief-constable-first-join-11661627.

Tyler, TR 2006, *Why people obey the law*, Princeton University Press, Princeton.

Victorian Gay and Lesbian Rights Lobby 2001, *Annual report 2001—corners turned, paths ahead made clear*, Victorian Gay and Lesbian Rights Lobby (VGLRL), viewed 30 March 2015, www.vglrl.org.au/about/history/2001-overview.

Waterhouse, R 1995, *Private pleasures, public leisures: A history of Australian popular culture since 1788*, Longman, Melbourne.

Chapter 6

Arresting 'hate'

Queer penalities and the take-up of a crime paradigm

Introduction

In September 2018, the Human Rights Law Centre (HRLC) published a report titled *End the hate: Responding to prejudice motivated speech and violence against the LGBTI community*. In the report, the HRLC called on the Victorian government to 'introduce a Hate Crimes Act to ensure all people are equally protected from hate crime, hate speech and hate conduct, including LGBTI Victorians' (Human Rights Law Centre 2018, p. 1). The HRLC began to establish its case for a new act by drawing readers' attention to two recent events that highlight how sexual and gender minorities are being targeted by 'hate': the 'horrific hate crime' of a mass shooting at the Pulse nightclub in Orlando, Florida in the USA in 2016, and 'the drastic spike in incidents of hate conduct during the marriage equality postal survey in Australia in 2017' (Human Rights Law Centre 2018, p. 1). The call for the introduction of a specific Hate Crimes Act through an appeal to LGBT safety is a significant political development in the local context. By lobbying to widen the net of criminalisation and strengthen the state's power to punish, this development reflects an intensification of what Lamble (2013) terms 'queer investments in punishment': the emotional and material commitments that LGBT people make to affirming, enhancing, and extending the operations of carceral systems of policing and punishment. The demand for a Hate Crimes Act by LGBT advocates is not surprising, nor is it unprecedented.

Over the past two to three decades, the language of 'crime', 'criminal justice', and 'victims' rights'—traditionally conservative rhetoric—has been taken up by LGBT campaigners focused on ending homophobic and transphobic violence in various North American and Western European contexts (Hanhardt 2013; Moran & Skeggs 2004). In particular, campaigns for hate crime laws have achieved significant success, and Australian and New Zealand activists have gradually followed suit with this approach (Asquith 2014; Russell 2017b). In part this is because the media mobilises so effectively around social issues when they are framed as problems of 'crime' and social disorder (Aharonson 2010). The government also appears more receptive to calls for increasing criminalisation because crime has become such a significant electoral issue. For example, during the lead-up to the 2010 state election, the Victorian Labor government passed a motion to amend the *Sentencing Act 1991* to enable harsher sentences for offences motivated by hate or prejudice (Russell 2017a). This particular election was dubbed the 'law-and-order' election, as the conservative Liberal-National Coalition won on a platform of expanding police powers and tougher sentencing for 'street violence' (Tubex et al. 2015). The enactment of hate crime legislation firmly resonates with the traditional ideologies and logics of policing and punishment, such as denunciation, deterrence, and retribution, despite the progressive reputation of these laws as a means towards achieving greater social equality for groups targeted by prejudicial violence.

Growing concerns surrounding particular forms of homophobic and transphobic violence—namely, those that can be classed as 'hate crime'[1]—among politicians, police, media, and other governmental agencies reflect the political strength and organisation of LGBT movements in Australia (Tomsen 1996). LGBT activists, advocates, and researchers have played an important role in creating political pressure for the enactment of hate crime legislation in the local context. The amendment to subsection 5(2) of the Victorian *Sentencing Act 1991* came into effect on 2 December 2009, making a crime motivated (wholly or partly) by hate or prejudice an aggravating factor at sentencing, which would allow for harsher sentences to be imposed for such offences. The HRLC (2018, p. 2) points out that this legislation has rarely been used, for reasons such as 'under-reporting, failure to identify and record crimes as hate crimes by police, difficulties locating perpetrators, reluctance by prosecutors to raise the provision and the high threshold of proving prejudice motivation in court'. Yet, at the time that it was announced, hate crime legislation was publicly welcomed by mainstream LGBT organisations, including the ALSO Foundation, Victorian AIDS Council, Gay and Lesbian Health Victoria, Rainbow Families Council, Victorian Gay and Lesbian Rights Lobby (VGLRL), and the Anti-Violence Project of Victoria. LGBT news source *Star Observer* (2009a) reported that Victorian Attorney-General Rob Hulls 'had already been in lengthy discussions with the gay and lesbian community' before proposing the change. When recommending the amendment to the Sentencing Act, the Sentencing Advisory Council (2009) used a fictional example of an assault on a lesbian at a train station, indicating that narratives of lesbian and gay victimisation were influential at the policy level.

While mainstream criminology has in many ways excluded queer concerns and constructed stigmatising notions of sexual 'deviance' and pathology (Woods 2014), criminology has also provided LGBT anti-violence movements with tools and frameworks to highlight the problems of homophobic and transphobic violence as 'hate crimes' and 'hidden crimes'. Once seen as simply a 'gay issue', homophobic violence—and to a lesser extent, transphobic violence—now figures into government debates and can lend weight to the case for increased punishment, even as some LGBT advocates continue to express concerns about a possible use of increasingly punitive sanctions. This chapter explores how a crime paradigm has influenced sexual and gender politics through an examination of anti-violence research and lobbying in Victoria focused on homophobic and transphobic hate crime. It tracks how the LGBT anti-violence movement has utilised criminal–legal theories, methodologies, and approaches to explain and attempt to remedy patterns of individual violence in the lives of LGBT people.[2] A paradigm is a kind of 'world view' (Kuhn 1970). My use of the term 'crime paradigm' broadly encompasses the key concepts, theories, and methods of an administrative criminology that inform not only criminal–legal policies and practices, but also more general understandings of 'crime' and social disorder propagated through the media and political discourse. Administrative or 'state-defined criminology' proceeds from the assumption that the concept of 'crime' is a given (rather than a social and political construction) (Hillyard et al. 2004b, p. 382). Its central task is the quantitative measurement and definitive explanation of 'crime', generally utilising individual and psychological frameworks (Scraton 2002). Barbara Hudson (2000, p. 177) argues that this version of criminology, being the dominant one, 'has the most dangerous relationship to power' because it constructs 'the categories and classifications, the labels and diagnoses and the images of the "criminal"' that are both stigmatising and pejorative. Accordingly, the crime paradigm that is reflected in the strategies and tactics of the LGBT anti-violence movement raises cause for concern, provoking questions about the exclusive effects of sexual citizenship claims.

I conceptualise the process whereby LGBT anti-violence campaigning has contributed to shaping the social, political, and cultural meaning of terms such as 'crime' and 'victimization' as productive of what I term 'queer penalities' (Russell 2017b). The term 'penality' denotes 'the broad field of institutions, practices, discourses, and social relations which surround the ideas and practices of punishment' (Baldry et al. 2011, p. 26). The chapter examines a series of reports on homophobic and transphobic violence and LGBT media coverage of the 2009 hate crime law reform in Victoria.[3] It considers three interconnected examples in which criminal–legal logics permeated into LGBT anti-violence campaigning: (1) the victimisation survey method, (2) the focus on police reform, and (3) elements of a punitive public discourse surrounding homophobic and transphobic 'hate crime'. These examples reflect queer 'desires for law' (Moran 2001; Pendleton & Serisier 2009) that are nevertheless complicated by the persistence of state violence and the lack of support and protection for LGBT lives. As Moran (2001) argues, LGBT victimisation surveys may tell us more about institutional practices (and failures) than the distribution of 'hate crime' itself. The turn towards law therefore occupies an ambiguous place in LGBT politics: both promoting and challenging criminal–legal 'solutions' to violence and social inequality.

Classifying 'homophobic hate': crime as a queer issue

In Australia, violence against LGBT people captured little public attention outside of queer communities up until the 1990s, when the first major research on 'homophobic hate crime' was conducted by activists and academics, often in collaboration with police (Baird et al. 1994; Cox 1990; Gays & Lesbians Against Discrimination 1994; Mason 1993; Sandroussi & Thompson 1995). Much of the rhetoric and symbolism used to draw attention to homophobic (and later, transphobic) violence in Australia has been borrowed from American campaigns and policy approaches (Tomsen 2006), as the recourse to a crime paradigm gradually became a common characteristic of sexual and gender politics centred on violence and safety (Hanhardt 2013; Stanko & Curry 1997). Scholars have linked the growth in hate crime legislation in the USA to the rise of anti-violence projects and victim-rights groups (Jenness & Grattet 2001). As 'law-and-order' issues garner increasing media attention, the hate crime framework has served as a particularly effective tool for identity-based social movements to lobby state agencies for recognition and resources (Jenness & Broad 1997; Tomsen 2006; Tomsen & Mason 2001).

The emphasis on 'crime' within these movements reflects broader social and political trends towards 'governance through crime' (Simon 2007). Jonathan Simon (2007) argues that in the USA, criminalisation and imprisonment have been used increasingly as a tool of social policy (see also Wacquant 2009). This focus has been coupled with an emphasis on reducing the risk of crime, largely through extending modes of surveillance. The alignment between anti-violence movements and a wider 'culture of control' (Garland 2001) has contributed to producing what Aharonson (2010) terms 'a trend in "pro-minority" criminalisation', through which criminalisation is redefined as a tool to minimise (rather than exacerbate) social inequalities (see also Mason 2009). Given that hate crime legislation has emerged in a political context of 'hyper-incarceration' (Cunneen et al. 2013; Wacquant 2010), critics argue that it bolsters a culture of positivism that extends and legitimises the carceral state, which may ultimately entrench and institutionalise hate, rather than alleviate it (Lamble 2013; Moran 2004; Spade & Willse 2000). The recourse to a crime paradigm further risks fortifying social divisions between 'good queer citizens' and those unable to escape the stigma of criminality (Haritaworn 2015). As select LGBT people transition from one side of the 'criminalisation/protection' line to the other through appeals to a minority victim status, the uneven process of criminalisation itself can be left unchallenged (Haritaworn 2010; Lamble 2013).

Advocating for criminal–legal responses to targeted violence is of course not unique to LGBT anti-violence campaigning. The evolution of feminist campaigns against sexual and family violence has been challenged for their evocation of 'law-and-order' tenets of victimisation, prompting critics to suggest that this movement has been subject to 'neoliberal appropriation' (Bumiller 2008; INCITE! Women of Color Against Violence 2006). Kristin Bumiller (2008) argues that institutional responses to rape and domestic violence promote problematic state control over the disrupted lives of victims. She connects this to a narrow focus on 'individualistic forms of problem solving' rather than seeking a more comprehensive understanding of the phenomenon of gendered violence, or 'counteracting other forms of domination in women's private and public lives' (Bumiller 2008, p. xiv). Similarly to feminist responses to violence against women, LGBT anti-violence campaigns now often evoke 'law-and-order' tenets of victimisation and 'get tough on crime' (Harris 2011).

The discursive manoeuvres that recast *some* LGBT people as potential victims, rather than inherent criminals, reflect an important historical shift in how sexual minorities are positioned in relation to processes of criminalisation: potentially moving from its objects to its subjects (Moran & Skeggs 2004). Though LGBT people were previously targeted by the criminal–legal system as sexual and gender 'outlaws', many LGBT anti-violence campaigns now call upon that same system to criminalise 'others' on our behalf—a difficult transition that may be 'fraught with unexpected outcomes' (Tomsen 1993, p. 209). When a resolution for social 'hurt' is sought from the law, political theorist Wendy Brown (1995) argues that political ground is ceded to moral and juridical ground—and both of these spheres are particularly difficult and tenuous for queers. When social problems are articulated in criminal–legal terms, they become individualistic and static, and can obscure the collective and political grounds for social change. The moralisation of queer victimhood has particularly troubling consequences, as Chapter 3 explored, which include erasing and 'casting out' the aspects of queerness that are deemed excessive or deviant in the quest for respectability and palatability in a heteronormative context. The language of crime and victimisation also ties LGBT politics to the dominant discourses of the criminal–legal system. As Barbara Baird (1997, p. 128), a key member of the South Australian group Lesbian and Gay Community Action (LGCA) in the 1990s, argues:

> Through adherence to a model that maintained gay and lesbian people as a victimised minority group, our identity was generally constituted on territory where the police, individually and institutionally, set the defining terms ... we were rarely in a position to speak from within our own discourse [or question] the positioning of the police force as a neutral, apolitical and asexual (read heterosexual) institution.

Through a moral and legal framework of minority victimhood, LGCA had little power to speak from within their 'own [queer] discourse'. Instead, activists became constrained by a crime paradigm that fortifies police legitimacy. That is, individual victims who fall within the remit of state protection are constructed in opposition to individual offenders who require punishment. Working from within this framework, police are implicitly positioned as a 'neutral' institution that can objectively advance queer safety, rather than an institution thoroughly implicated in the politics and practices that sustain social ideologies of queer inferiority. In this context, LGCA's ability to promote discussion that questioned police complicity in gender and sexual oppression was significantly limited, because there is little room for alternative viewpoints or analyses of violence and power when appealing to the state for protection. As Brown (1995, p. 27) argues in *States of Injury*, efforts to 'establish racism, sexism and homophobia as morally heinous in the law, and to prosecute its individual perpetrators there' cast the 'law in particular and the state more generally as neutral arbiters of injury rather than as themselves invested with the power to injure'. Advocating from the position of victimised minority has political costs, as Baird highlights, since activists are forced to cede collective power to institutional ground in the hope of becoming the beneficiaries of police operations.

As Chapter 3 argued, moves towards recognition as ideal or 'good' victims of homophobic violence often rely upon a differentiation from those whose queerness is stereotypically and excessively visible, particularly through gender non-conformity, and from those frequently cast as irresponsible, risky, and criminal, such as drug- or beat-users, or sex workers. For instance, when I interviewed Jane Green from Vixen Collective, they suggested that there is a misconception that sex workers are 'all straight cis women', when in reality many sex workers identify as queer or LGBT. I asked Green if the framework of 'homophobic violence' used by LGBT anti-violence campaigns resonated with queer sex workers' experiences of violence and they responded:

> The issue that we struggle with is public perceptions that we're somehow deserving of violence or that it should be expected. And that's incredibly problematic: that violence in the context of sex work is viewed as an occupational hazard; that we should expect [it]. And we have incredibly limited avenues to access police assistance and access justice [when it occurs].

Green's account indicates that while homophobic (and to a lesser extent, transphobic) violence is now more widely condemned and recognised within criminal–legal frameworks, queer sex workers do not neatly fit the ideal of 'good queer victims' that is frequently the prerequisite for such recognition (Hanhardt 2013; Haritaworn 2015). Instead, the continued stigmatisation of sex work contributes to the normalisation of the violence that workers experience (Sanders 2016). The precarious legal status of sex work in Victoria (Renshaw et al. 2015) further jeopardises workers' safety and complicates their capacity to occupy a victim identity position, since such positions frequently rely upon a claim to 'innocence' (Wang 2012). According to Green, police perceptions of sex workers' inherent criminality are a direct product of the recent history of aggressive criminalisation of sex work, which reinforces the notion that the law contributes to producing the very subjects that it seeks to govern.

'Hidden pools': the crime paradigm in LGBT anti-violence campaigning

While the social sciences more broadly are without a convincing claim to 'value freedom' or 'neutrality', criminology has a particularly dubious relationship to administrative power and strategies of social control (Sim et al. 1987). Historically, criminology emerged around the institutions of punishment and control, which for the majority of the twentieth century were based in the ideas of correctionalism, such as individual positivism and penal welfarism (Garland 2001). In the 1980s and 1990s, this philosophy gave way to what Garland (2001) terms 'the crime control complex', whose emphasis on rational choice and situational crime prevention promotes retribution and incapacitation in prisons. Administrative criminology, reflecting the conditions of its emergence and the object of its study ('the criminal'), therefore has foundations rooted in personal and individual concerns, rather than structural issues such as settler colonialism or heteropatriarchy (Scraton 2002). Critical criminologists have critiqued the crime paradigm for its marginalisation and frequent exclusion of concerns surrounding processes of harm and violence not captured by the legal category of 'crime', such as state crimes or corporate harm (Hillyard et al. 2004a), or what Dean Spade (2011) terms 'administrative violence'. Yet, as the opening discussion of recent calls for a Hate Crime Act in Victoria reflects, the power and appeal of a crime framework has endured for many anti-violence activists.

There are at least three overlapping areas in which a crime paradigm is discernible in LGBT anti-violence campaigning in Victoria: (1) the use of victimisation survey methodologies, (2) a focus on police reform in the translation of survey findings into policy recommendations, and (3) elements of a punitive public discourse surrounding homophobic and transphobic violence.

The victimisation survey method

Throughout the 1990s and 2000s, LGBT anti-violence lobbying efforts across national contexts such as the USA, the UK, and Australia largely focused on highlighting the need for different kinds of legislative, institutional, and social reforms through documenting homophobic and transphobic violence, often through the use of victimisation surveys (Jenness & Broad 1997; Moran & Skeggs 2004; Stanko & Curry 1997). In Victoria, this strategy culminated with a series of reports on the prevalence of homophobic (and, more recently, transphobic) violence and discrimination. These include *Not a Day Goes By*

(Gays & Lesbians Against Discrimination 1994), *Enough Is Enough* (Victorian Gay & Lesbian Rights Lobby 2000), *With Respect* (Gray et al. 2006), and *Coming Forward* (Leonard et al. 2008). These studies take their form and design from traditional crime surveys developed within criminology in the mid- to late 1960s in the USA, which were intended to measure and count unreported and unrecorded crime (Stanko & Curry 1997).[4]

The use of victimisation survey methodology has been subject to challenge within critical strands of criminology. Ben Bowling (1993) argues that the image of violence gleaned from victimisation surveys is partial and skewed because complex social processes are translated into a series of quantifiable 'moments' or events. Since they are static instruments, surveys may provide a 'decontextualised snapshot' (Bowling 1993) and fail to capture the low-level, persistent, and virtually unremarkable nature of oppression that enables it to shape the daily lives of those it affects (Leonard et al. 2008). Moreover, since research on homophobic and transphobic violence has generally not focused on LGBT people marginalised by race, class, or ability (Meyer 2014), the 'snapshot' of risk that they provide is more likely to be partial than representative or generalisable. Victimisation surveys have not been designed to garner more detailed qualitative information about the ways in which multiple forms of oppression intersect in the lives of LGBT people, producing different vulnerabilities to various forms of (interpersonal and institutional) violence (Chakraborti 2015).

The use of quantitative victimisation surveys plays an important role in the representation of homophobic and transphobic violence in and through a 'crime paradigm' (Moran & Skeggs 2004; Stanko & Curry 1997). Research tools focused on 'crime prevention'—such as surveys, audits, and evaluations—garner legitimacy as they are seen as 'pragmatic forms of positivist research', even as these methods can occlude the insights that may be garnered through more in-depth qualitative research (Scraton 2002, p. 33). Victimisation surveys are intended to highlight violence that has been previously hidden from official reports (Moran 2001). As Leslie Moran and Beverly Skeggs (2004, p. 16) point out, such surveys are often used to 'draw attention to state and legal failure to recognise this violence *as violence* and as an issue of law', a failure that manifests in 'an absence of police reports, lack of investigation, dearth of prosecutions and so forth'. Victimisation surveys therefore often represent violence in specific ways: as hidden violence and as unreported crimes, or as Anti-Violence Project of Victoria (AVP) convener Greg Adkins frames it, a 'hidden pool of hate and prejudice motivated crime' (Anti-Violence Project of Victoria 2009).

The notion of 'hidden violence' often precipitates calls for improving data collection and monitoring—generally by police through direct or third-party crime reporting. This is in order to understand the severity, pattern, and location of hate crime and identify 'target areas', 'potential victims', and 'likely perpetrators', within a risk-based logic of prevention (Gray et al. 2006;

Mason 1993). However, the practice of 'crime mapping' (Anti-Violence Project Victoria 2016; Flood & Hamilton 2008) and profiling of 'likely perpetrators' raises significant issues. Given the history of policing of homosexuality, if police are to target 'homophobic hot spots' (such as gay bars, beats, or even large-scale public events like the Sydney Mardi Gras), will more vulnerable LGBT people be harmed by an increased police presence? As previous chapters have explored, the increased policing of queer spaces, even in the name of protection, may heighten LGBT experiences of state intrusion and criminalisation (Spade & Willse 2000). From another perspective, if the 'typical perpetrators of violence towards gays and lesbians' are named by former AVP co-convener Fiona Kelly as 'males aged 15 to 25' (McKenzie 2000), are youths likely to be viewed with increased suspicion when accessing public space? The designation of young men (presumed to be heterosexual) as 'dangerous' or 'risky' to LGBT people may be an example of the stigmatising and pejorative labels that Hudson warns us about.

Ultimately, LGBT victimisation surveys may tell us more about institutional practices (and failures) than the distribution of 'homophobic hate crime' itself. A focus upon 'crime mapping' and the 'likely perpetrators' of homophobic violence threatens to obscure 'the failure of state institutions, especially criminal justice, to take certain types of violence seriously and the violence of those same institutions' (Moran 2001, p. 334). Crime maps and perpetrator profiles threaten to create an impression of escalating violence in particular areas and a lurking 'stranger danger' for LGBT people (Jacobs & Potter 1998; Mason 2005). But by and large this is not how victimisation surveys have been interpreted and promoted by many LGBT anti-violence advocates (Moran 2001). Victorian surveys consistently document low levels of confidence in the police, high expectations of indifference, and experiences and perceptions of institutionalised homophobia and transphobia (Gays & Lesbians Against Discrimination 1994; Leonard et al. 2008; Victorian Gay & Lesbian Rights Lobby 2000). They have also been used as evidence of the ways in which homophobic and transphobic violence and harassment is more ordinary than 'exceptional', largely because it is informed and reproduced by institutional discourses and practices (Leonard et al. 2008). This view challenges dominant representations of crime as isolated and individual occurrences (Valverde & Cirak 2003) and draws attention to the 'practices, memories and fears of routine homophobic violence within and through state institutions' (Moran 2001, p. 34).

Social surveys are often assumed to be a 'democratic' instrument because they garner a range of different or similar views from members of the public (Crawford et al. 1990). Yet, this is troubled by the role of the social analyst in the survey who interprets the data and 'gives weight' to the problems in policy terms (Walklate 1990). Survey results and their corresponding policy recommendations cannot be regarded as neutral or self-evident (Walklate 1990). Victimisation surveys are formulated and analysed in specific sociopolitical contexts and often with a particular agenda. Within the policy recommendations of the reports on homophobic and transphobic violence that I examined in the Victorian context, police reform emerged as a key theme. This interpretation and translation of survey findings reflects underlying ideas about the necessity and value of policing as an institution and its capacity to change and progress in the service of LGBT safety and security.

The focus on police reform

In light of the numerous institutional failures that can be gleaned from LGBT victimisation surveys, it is perhaps not surprising that the need for police reform serves as a significant focus of these reports.[5] As VGLRL (2000, p. 57) argues in *Enough Is Enough*, Victoria Police 'need to demonstrate they are serious about tackling the unacceptable levels of public violence inflicted on gay men, lesbian, bisexuals and transgender people in this state'. The emergence and growth of campaigns against hate crime further coincided with a broader push over the past three decades towards the professionalisation of policing—particularly in the realm of police image and community problem-solving initiatives (Moran 2007). In this context, police leaders have gradually responded to LGBT calls to establish partnerships, specialist units, and training programmes that integrate LGBT concerns and experiences into the force; but strictly on police terms.

Police reform serves as a focus for LGBT anti-violence advocates not only because of the obvious deficiencies in their operations, but because they are positioned as a necessary part of the response to a problem recently defined as one of 'crime'. The emphasis on improving police responses to the problems of homophobic and transphobic 'hate' lends support to the case for increased funding for policing. More broadly, it reproduces the notion that criminalisation can be used as a tool of social equality. Since the mid-1990s, Victorian reports on homophobic (and later, transphobic) violence and harassment have called upon the Minister for Police and the police force to develop new reporting mechanisms and education mechanisms to encourage and promote LGBT crime reporting; improve data collection and monitoring; establish, expand, and promote Gay and Lesbian Liaison Officers (GLLOs), including at LBGT community events; develop specialist LGBT-sensitivity training for all police personnel; and work in conjunction with LGBT organisations and others to initiate public awareness campaigns (Gays & Lesbians Against Discrimination 1994; Gray et al. 2006; Leonard et al. 2008; Victorian Gay & Lesbian Rights Lobby 2000).

In what may be seen as a series of successes for the LGBT anti-violence movement, all of the above recommendations have been taken up and implemented by Victoria Police in recent years, at least in some capacity. For example, official data collection on hate crime began in July 2011 as part of the force's Prejudice Motivated Crime Strategy (Dorrington 2013), the force has incorporated 'sexual and gender diversity' issues into its training programme (Grossman et al. 2013), and GLLOs (and sometimes police commissioners) participate in community events such as Pride March and the Midsumma carnival, as the previous chapter discussed. However, there are significant limitations associated with these responses. For example, despite repeated calls for improved data collection on hate crimes since at least 1994 (Gays & Lesbians Against Discrimination 1994), police have not made specific data on homophobic or transphobic hate crimes available, rendering existing police data collection practices virtually useless to LGBT anti-violence campaigners. Yet even if a breakdown of the type of hate crime were available, the overwhelming majority of anti-queer violence remains unreported to police (Leonard et al. 2008). As such, police records cannot provide a full or accurate picture of hate crime; there is always a gap, not just quantitatively due to lack of reporting, but also qualitatively in terms of the image of violence that such data produce (Mason 2005).

The emphasis on improving police training and increasing community engagement implies that police homophobia and transphobia are issues of individual ignorance or bad attitudes, rather than a systemic problem. As Brown (2006) argues, the assumption that greater acceptance and equality will come from increased awareness of 'difference' ignores the processes through which difference itself is produced and the power relations that make 'difference' matter. Policing is foremost among the institutions that have contributed to the production of sexuality and gender as categories of difference. Non-heteronormative lives and practices have been constructed as not only different (to the norm), but also inferior and variously criminal, pathological, and threatening (Willett 2008). From this perspective, sexual inequality is not simply a matter of biased or ignorant individuals; it is a product of institutional practices and the power relations that shape them. However, a structural analysis of inequality is much more difficult to translate into policy recommendations, because it requires broader social transformation premised on the redistribution of political and economic power and resources (Fraser 1997). In a political culture in which 'governing through crime' appears to overshadow alternative models of reconstructing and acting upon social problems (Simon 2007), Hillyard et al. (2004b) argue that policy recommendations that proceed from critical work tend to fall outside the increasingly narrowly defined terrain of legitimate political responses to the problem of 'crime'. Instead, the move towards 'short-term, expedient, evaluation research generates and reflects utilitarian trends in criminology', which are often informed by state- and market-driven research agendas (Hillyard et al. 2004b, p. 387). Reformist solutions are appealing because they seem achievable and therefore pragmatic, proceeding from a 'state-defined' discourse (Hillyard et al. 2004b). This discourse frames the questions that are asked and the answers that are reached in terms of their commensurability with existing approaches. Constructing homophobic and transphobic violence as a crime problem, rather than a social or institutional problem, impacts how solutions are envisaged (Hanhardt 2013; Stanko & Curry 1997). Hate crime laws do not target the institutional perpetrator, yet the dominance of heteronormativity means that 'the struggle against violence cannot be separated from, and ought not replace, an ongoing struggle against any legal repression of gays and lesbians' (Tomsen 1993, p. 214). An individual conception of crime causation encourages a punitive public discourse surrounding anti-queer violence. In part, this is countered by critical LGBT perspectives on punishment that focus on institutional harm as an area for change.

Punitive public discourse

The popularity of the hate crime framework implies an increasing concern with particular individualised forms of minority victimisation: that is, those forms of interpersonal violence through which individual bigots reaffirm racist, sexist, and heterosexist norms (Aharonson 2010). While this concern is not a problem per se, Ely Aharonson (2010) points out that simultaneously there appears to be less of an inclination to alleviate the structural economic and demographic conditions within which such patterns of victimisation thrive. Individualising and psychologising conceptions of homophobic and transphobic violence often invoke a 'rational actor' model of crime causation that draws from an economic or utilitarian philosophy of crime and is associated with 'classical' criminological thought (Akers 1990). This perspective is reflected in a 2009 news update on the AVP website, immediately following the news of hate crime legislation being introduced in Victoria:

> All [hate crimes] have been committed due to a bias or prejudice by the perpetrator against us because of our sexual orientation or gender identification. This means that perpetrators of hate-crime intentionally choose us as the targets of the crime because of who we are.
>
> (Anti-Violence Project of Victoria 2009)

This passage reflects a construction of LGBT vulnerability to violence that is produced through the actions of homophobic and transphobic individuals. This resonates with what Freeman (1995, p. 30) terms a 'perpetrator perspective', whereby the focus on individual intentionality positions homophobic and transphobic actions 'as outside of and apart from the social fabric and without historical continuity'. If homophobia and transphobia is viewed not as a social phenomenon, but as a result of the misguided conduct of atomistic individuals, it follows that the primary task of combating violence is to defuse the inappropriate conduct of individual perpetrators. This is often the point at which calls for punishment emerge. Indeed, and as AVP President Greg Adkins goes on to state, hate crime is seen to constitute 'higher-end crime' and to warrant the imposition of 'increased or additional penalties':

> Hate-crimes are criminal acts ... And if one gay man, one lesbian or one transgender individual is a victim of a hate-crime then the State has a responsibility to ensure that every crime is reported, that in each case the perpetrators are brought to justice and future hate-crime is prevented.
>
> (Anti-Violence Project of Victoria 2009)

Adkins' emotive statement reinforces a perpetrator perspective of LGBT victimisation—that it is a product of the behaviour of 'bad' individuals who must be 'brought to justice'. He extends this narrative by appealing to the notion that punishment aids in preventing 'future hate crime', gesturing towards the imagined deterrence effect of criminal law. Whether there is in fact a deterrent effect of judicial punishment is significantly contested (Fagan & Meares 2008).

LGBT discourses surrounding hate crime legislation strongly emphasise the expressive or symbolic functions of sentencing (Jacobs & Potter 1998; Russell 2017a). For example, the HRLC (2018, p. 21) argues that 'criminalising hate conduct is increasingly internationally accepted as a way to effectively deal with targeted violence', in part because hate crime laws 'send an important symbolic acknowledgment that hate crime is taken seriously' and 'increase public awareness'. The educative role of the law is also espoused by the former CEO of ALSO Foundation, Lyn Morgain, who states that the 2009 Victorian sentencing reform 'makes clear that any and all prejudice-motivated crime is unacceptable and criminal and will attract strong penalties' (*Star Observer* 2009a). In the absence of specific prosecutions, hate crime legislation itself is viewed as having an important symbolic role to play: it can send a message that sexual minorities 'matter', and make clear, by virtue of the moral dimensions of hate crime law (Mason 2014), that homophobic violence is unacceptable behaviour. However, as legal scholars such as William DeFord (2005) point out, the messages that punishment sends are never straightforward. They are often complex, contradictory, incomplete, and received in multiple, varying ways according to the audience. To be sure, hate crime legislation also has possible material effects, as its capacity to 'attract strong penalties' reminds us (even though this has largely not been borne out in the Victorian context to date). Following the release of (undifferentiated) hate crime figures by Victoria Police in 2013, the *Star Observer* announced that police 'will push for tougher sentencing on hate crimes, including those motivated by gender and sexuality', as VGLRL convener Anna Brown emphasised 'the need to tackle crime against LGBT people specifically' (Riley 2013).

Since 'crime' reflects a process concentrating on *individuals* (usually perpetrators and victims) (Valverde & Cirak 2003), the salience of hate crime campaigns may redirect public attention away from structural patterns of social marginalisation that cannot be effectively framed in individual terms: for example, those that cannot be attributed to the intentional activities of an individual perpetrator, or those that cannot be effectively policed or prosecuted (Hillyard & Tombs 2004). An emphasis on punishment and retribution largely derives from 'concern and anger with the brutality of assailants' and a 'belief in individual choice and responsibility in crime causation' (Tomsen 2009, p. 155). Yet the violence of heteronormativity is sustained and reproduced on many levels beyond the individual. Homophobic and transphobic cultures are evident in legal, political, medical, education, and media institutions throughout Australian society and history (Robinson 2008). In multiple explicit and implicit ways, these institutions have contributed to a cultural climate where same-sex behaviours and gender transgression have been outlawed and condemned, or rendered invisible or problematic (Tomsen 2009).

'Institutional violence': alternative analyses of anti-queer harm

In contrast to the recent HRLC report *End the Hate*, none of the reports published on homophobic and transphobic violence in Victoria between 2000 and 2010 recommended the creation of new criminal offences for hate crimes. For example, VGLRL (2000, p. 36) argues in *Enough Is Enough* that abuse 'cannot be easily stopped by introducing new laws and tougher penalties for offenders, given the circumstances of many incidents'. Similarly, the authors of *With Respect* suggested that existing criminal law provisions deal with violence and the focus should be on education and civil law responses (Gray et al. 2006). Despite the CEO's warning about the 'strong penalties' now associated with hate crime, an ALSO Foundation (2010) submission to the Australian Human Rights Commission did not support the imposition of additional criminal sanctions or the creation of separate hate provisions within existing Victorian legislation. News coverage of the introduction of hate crime legislation in Victoria by *Star Observer* (2009b) acknowledged that despite the overall 'welcome' response from LGBT organisations, there had 'been criticism the new laws may not hit at the causes of homophobic violence'. This stands in contrast to forms of LGBT activism—ones particularly visible in the USA (Hanhardt 2013; Spade & Willse 2000)—that demonstrate significant faith in criminal–legal solutions by seeking enhanced penalties for anti-queer violence.

With a view to the social and political foundations of homophobia and transphobia, the authors of *Coming Forward* foreground an analysis of institutional violence, arguing that the everyday harassment and vilification directed at LGBT people is 'supported by less visible but no less damaging forms of institutional violence' (Leonard et al. 2008, pp. 4–5). Institutional violence is defined as the ways in which the 'beliefs, policies and practices of particular organisations devalue and marginalise GLBT people' (Leonard et al. 2008, p. 4). While institutional violence is less likely to be captured in victimisation data because it cannot be whittled down to a discrete moment, the

Coming Forward authors suggest that it 'is part of the heterosexist machinery that sustains as it justifies harassment and abuse of GLBT people' (Leonard et al. 2008, p. 4). This contests the notion that homophobic or transphobic violence reflects a 'minority pathology' (Tomsen 2009) that can be addressed through either punishing individuals or reforming individual attitudes. Rather, homophobic and transphobic violence are revealed as '"legitimate" violence through which the social order is (re)produced' (Moran & Skeggs 2004, p. 27).

While there are elements of a punitive public discourse surrounding homophobic and transphobic hate crime, there is significant awareness among LGBT researchers and advocates of the limitations of punitive and individual responses. For instance, even as the HRLC (2018, p. 19) recommends the introduction of a new Hate Crimes Act, it acknowledges that 'individual-based remedies are ineffective at producing a broader systemic cultural change to prevent prejudice motivated conduct against LGBTI people'. Ultimately, the possibility of penalty enhancements and the creation of new criminal offences for hate crime in Victoria appear to be contentious within the LGBT anti-violence movement, although the recent call for a distinct law governing hate crimes suggests that this may well be shifting. Unsurprisingly, Victoria Police has used its non-transparent data on hate crime to promote the need for harsher penalties, but there is not necessarily a coherent or unified view among LGBT anti-violence campaigners about the role of criminalisation and punishment in efforts to address homophobic and transphobic violence. A review of local reports on the topic indicates a persistent scepticism of the criminal law's ability to offer protection or justice to LGBT people. Nevertheless, 'crime' remains a significant focus of LGBT politics, which reflects and reinforces a wider culture of governance through crime.

Queer penalities and their contradictions

Early in the 1990s, criminologist Stephen Tomsen (1993) warned that LGBT activists might uncritically reproduce 'law-and-order' rhetoric amid their attempts to build rapport with police leadership in strategies to counter anti-gay violence in Sydney. He argued that this could occur if 'important elements of the police and justice system regulation of gays' were overlooked (Tomsen 1993, p. 213). Numerous critical criminologists have made persuasive calls to move beyond the crime paradigm in favour of a 'social harm' approach, which might enable a more sustained engagement with forms of state violence and corporate harm (Hillyard et al. 2004a; Pemberton 2007). Yet, even though 'crime' is a constructed category—and debates over its definition are heavily conditioned by the uneven distribution of power between social groups—it maintains its power and appeal not only for ideological and emotional reasons, but also for material ones. Erica Meiners (2007) points out that often the use of the terminology of 'crime' does function to spotlight harm or a problem that needs addressing. Marginalised groups often utilise the language of crime and victimisation to lobby for access to state and other resources for legal means, social service provision, or research funding. The 'ontological reality' (or lived experience) of crime (Lasslett 2010) complicates attempts to challenge criminalisation agendas, because an uncritical rejection of criminal–legal responses to harm might reproduce the invisibilisation and minimisation of interpersonal violence against women or LGBT people. This highlights the importance of accounting for the broader social discourses and structural conditions that devalue and diminish feminine and queer subjectivities and remind us of the intrinsic connections between institutional and interpersonal violence. As critical legal scholar Angela P Harris (2006, p. 183) argues:

> Law is a powerful means by which to translate social demands into institutions and policies. Law by its nature is conservative, and when calls for change that threaten to destabilise existing distributions of material and symbolic power are made, change through law will occur in ways that preserve existing distributions to the greatest extent possible.

The problems with identity constructions based in victimhood or 'injury' are of course not new concerns for feminist and queer scholars and activists. Brown (1995) argues that the regulatory demands of the state encourage the formation of political identities that are not only founded on injury, but also invested in maintaining an injured status. The risk is that those 'injuries' may be recapitulated in the anti-violence strategies that subjects engage to oppose them (Bumiller 2008). This reflects the dangers of pursuing political goals of, for example, freedom from homophobic and transphobic violence within 'largely repressive, regulatory, and depoliticizing institutions' (Brown 1995 pp. ix–x), such as police who themselves carry elements of the regime whose subversion is being sought (see also Brown & Halley 2002; Kaplan 2008). In other words, queer investments in punitive solutions to social problems run the risk of entrenching and expanding the very systems of sexual and gender inequality they seek to undo.

If the overall goal is to end homophobic and transphobic violence, even if we maintain a relatively narrow focus on street-level violence or random individual attacks, positioning law and law enforcement as a key part of the solution has troubling implications. There are significant tensions in appealing to the police for protection against a socially condoned hatred. Police have administered and enabled homophobic and transphobic violence; they have also denied protection to LGBT people. Yet when the problem is defined as one of 'crime', police come to be regarded as a crucial part of the solution. Australian research documents police violence against LGBT people in the forms of coercion, harassment, intimidation, verbal abuse, and physical assault (Boon-Kuo et al. 2018; Couch et al. 2007; Dwyer 2015; Sitka 1997; Victorian

Gay & Lesbian Rights Lobby 2000). This is consistent with research in the USA (Amnesty International 2005; Mogul et al. 2011). In Victoria, in the early 1990s, GLAD (1994, pp. 15) argued that the 'most perturbing aspect' of the survey they conducted was 'the extent to which gay men and lesbians reported harassment, discrimination and violence at the hands of the police'. More recently, VGLRL expressed concerns that prejudice conditioned by the history of homosexual criminalisation informs current police treatment of 'people engaging in homosexual social and sexual activity' as 'suspicious' (Brown 2013). In light of this, it is relatively unsurprising that many LGBT people—and trans and gender-diverse people especially—remain reluctant to report incidents of violence and harassment to police (Human Rights Law Centre 2018; Leonard & Fileborn 2018; Victorian Gay & Lesbian Rights Lobby 2017). This is despite Victoria Police efforts to build trust and increase crime reporting among LGBT people through targeted communications initiatives, such as promotion for its prejudice-motivated crime strategy (Mason et al. 2016).

Police concern for its reputation among LGBT people is prescient, as accounts of police inaction and hostility in reports of anti-queer abuse continue to circulate in the media. In late 2016, national LGBT news source *Star Observer* reported on the dismal police response to a public assault upon three friends on a Friday night in Melbourne. Starlady, Canon, and Azja detailed how police failed to attend the scene after 30 minutes, forcing them to walk to the police station, and that the officers who separately interviewed each of the three friends refused to record the queer- and transphobic nature of the incident. Starlady, a white trans woman, outlined how the trio 'weren't even given a victim impact statement. I had to demand they give us each one' (Wade 2016). Canon, a white trans man, expressed the feeling that their experience was dismissed, as he stated: 'when you're a victim of crime you end up feeling like you're the criminal in terms of the way they engage with you. It's strange, a police officer trying to influence what you write about your own experience' (Wade 2016). Meanwhile, Azja, a queer-identifying migrant, said the incident has made her hesitant to reach out to the police in the future. She suggested: 'In future I don't even know if I'd go to the police again, we should be thinking about more community-based responses to this kind of violence' (Wade 2016).

Canon's comments are reminiscent of Barbara Baird's expression of frustration about the constraints and limitations of working within a discourse in which police set and control the defining criteria—in this case, whether something can be noted, recorded, and thereby validated as an experience of transphobic harm. When I discussed this case in interviews with several of my LGBT informants, they admitted that the report was deeply concerning, but also predicted the police viewpoint: for instance, that labelling something a prejudice-motivated crime would generate too much paperwork, or that there is not technically a specific offence of 'hate crime' with which police can charge someone. This prompts us to take account of the bureaucratic machinations of policing and criminal–legal systems, and their significant limitations in responding to harm. Notably, in the article, Azja gestures towards the possibilities of different ways of responding to harm, perhaps outside (or at least not firmly embedded in) dominant modes of criminalisation and punishment. Azja's comment alludes to an alternative discourse, albeit one not prescribed or at all elaborated here—perhaps what some have termed 'transformative justice' (Kim 2018)—and sparks questions about whether queer 'safety' could be envisioned differently.[6]

Conclusion

The LGBT anti-violence movement has focused significantly (though not exclusively) on documenting homophobic and transpohobic violence for the purposes of highlighting it as a social and political issue, and, increasingly, as a 'crime' and criminal–legal issue. This chapter has unpacked how these efforts reflect some of the methodologies, logics, and policy-oriented approaches found within the administrative criminological enterprise, which may have contributed to the infusion of LGBT social justice goals with punitive logics (Mason 2009). The reliance on victimisation surveys to promote awareness and increase understanding of homophobic and transphobic violence has contributed to its representation as a 'hidden crime' problem. This representation has led to calls for improved policing responses, by way of increasing resources dedicated to official data collection, officer training, and police-community outreach activities. It can also give rise to punitive sentiments that hinge on notions of individual crime causation and 'just deserts'. However, the Victorian example demonstrates significant scepticism among LGBT activists and advocates towards punitive 'solutions' to homophobic and transphobic violence. Awareness of the institutionalised nature of heterosexism points to an ambiguous and evolving relationship between queer politics, police, and law. The Victorian case study reveals that the LGBT anti-violence movement both affirms and contests the legitimacy of policing and punishment in different ways, and exposes the significant tensions and limitations associated with appeals to protection in a historical and ongoing context of institutional negligence and violence.

Through recourse to a crime paradigm, LGBT anti-violence campaigners inherit some of the limitations associated with administrative criminology. By constructing the problem of homophobic violence as 'hate crime', the ways in which processes of criminalisation can be violent and exclusive (for queers and others) may be neglected. My intention in this chapter has been to provide a critique not of the use of victimisation survey data per se, but of its interpretation, especially the promotion of responses to violent conditions that rely on strengthening and expanding 'crime control industries' (Christie 2000). Efforts to 'queer' criminology may represent an important intervention into the heteronormativity of the discipline. Yet, queer criminology risks being restricted by prevailing criminal–legal logics. Queer criminologists suggest that by incorporating queer perspectives and experiences into critical criminological research agendas, some of the oppressive effects of the discipline as a whole may be ameliorated (Ball et al. 2013). As a critical sub-discipline, it might have an important role to play in the development of alternative paradigms for interpreting social and political problems, including a broader conception of social harm. Yet queer criminology must also be attuned to the punitive currents in LGBT anti-violence movements and the risks inherent in 'law-and-order' trajectories. In efforts to realise queer safety through carceral protection, sexual and gender politics risk deeper entanglement in the institutional discourses and practices that continue to widen the net of criminalisation and punishment with damaging and uneven social consequences, including for LGBT people.

This chapter has focused on the take-up of a crime paradigm within LGBT movements in attempts to explain and remedy instances of individual victimisation that are largely represented as random, public offences perpetrated by strangers or those not intimately known to the victim (Human Rights Law Centre 2018).[7] The resultant discourse of homophobic and transphobic hate crime highlights how LGBT anti-violence activism produces new and locally situated knowledge about queer history, identity, and violence that comes to shape institutional and public understandings of LGBT lives and issues. However, there is another relevant iteration of queer injury that has been traced throughout the chapter and indeed the book, which is similarly situated within LGBT rights advocacy: namely, the harms perpetrated by state institutions, such as police. Thus, the queer penalities that I have sketched in this chapter are not the only threads of LGBT anti-violence activism that have powerful discursive and political effects. LGBT advocates have created pressure for other types of legislative reform—such as expungement bills for historical homosexual offences (Human Rights Law Centre 2014)—and discursive responses to historical violence, such as formal apologies. Unlike much anti-hate crime activism, the queer knowledge mobilisations that elicit formal apologies have been more successful in drawing attention to *systemic* harms perpetrated by powerful institutions of law, medicine, and policing, for example. Rather than the individual bigot that is the imagined target of anti-hate crime projects, the official apology (from government, or police—as discussed in the next chapter) foregrounds the identity of the institution. However, the discourse of queer apology is not necessarily more progressive than that of queer punitivism. Both iterations of LGBT rights discourse contribute to setting in train and encoding new institutional rituals and practices, from legislative reform and police data collection to the performance of apology and institutional renewal. Critical analysis of queer penalities alongside queer apologia lends significant insight into the ways in which sexual and gender politics might be brought into the fold of the state.

Notes

1 HRLC (2018, p. 1) defines 'hate crime' as 'unlawful actions which target marginalised and vulnerable members of our communities'.
2 In place of the more commonly used 'criminal justice system', I refer to the criminal–legal system, following Mogul et al. (2011, pp. xix–xx), to encompass public law enforcement agencies, including state and federal police, prosecutors, judges, prison officials, and parole boards. This reflects recognition of the significant *in*justices produced by this system throughout its history in Australia (as elsewhere), especially for Aboriginal and Torres Strait Islander people, poor and working-class people, many racialised migrant communities, and LGBT people.
3 The body of empirical material that I draw upon in this chapter includes six Victorian reports on LGBT victimisation published between 1994 and 2018, as well as LGBT media coverage of the Victorian hate crime legislative reform in 2009, hate crime data collection by Victoria Police, and critiques of policing that emerge in the context of LGBT reporting on anti-queer and anti-trans violence.
4 These surveys may also have been influenced by community health research design, for example surrounding women's health, gay men's health, and HIV.
5 Other recommendations appeal to state government and community leaders to publicly denounce statements that have the effect of vilifying or inciting violence against LGBT people, to pursue multiple legislative and policy avenues to address vilification and violence against LGBT people, and to fund and develop initiatives targeting LGBT communities that seek to increase their capacity to deal with the threat and effects of homophobic harassment. While I focus here on policy recommendations relating directly to policing, other recommendations target (and sometimes prioritise, as in *With Respect*) community education and civil law reforms.
6 Transformative justice refers to a philosophy and practice of preventing, responding to, and transforming harm and violence at the levels of individuals, communities, and society. As an approach, it seeks healing, justice, and accountability, while also transforming the ongoing social conditions (such as transphobia) that allow abuse and harm to occur. See Chen et al. 2011 and Generation Five 2017.
7 For a discussion and critique of the 'stranger danger' theme in hate crime discourses, see Mason 2005.

References

Aharonson, E 2010, ''Pro-minority' criminalization and the transformation of visions of citizenship in contemporary liberal democracies: A critique', *New Criminal Law Review*, vol. 13, no. 2, pp. 286–308.

Akers, RL 1990, 'Rational choice, deterrence, and social-learning theory in criminology—the path not taken', *Journal of Criminal Law & Criminology*, vol. 81, no. 3, pp. 653–676.

Also Foundation 2010, *Submission to the Australian Human Rights Commission regarding the possible inclusion of protections against discrimination and vilification on the basis of sexual orientation and sex and/or gender identity in Federal anti-discrimination law*, ALSO Foundation, Melbourne.

Amnesty International 2005, *USA: Stonewalled: Police abuse and misconduct against lesbian, gay, bisexual and transgender people in the U.S.*, Amnesty International, New York.

Anti-Violence Project of Victoria (AVP) 2009, *Hate-Crime in Victoria – next step announced*, media release, 9 December, viewed 19 January 2019, http://antiviolence.info/2009/12/hate-crime-in-victoria-next-step-announced/.

Anti-Violence Project of Victoria (AVP) 2016, *Violence & GLLOS*, viewed 15 July 2016, http://antiviolence.info/violence-map/.

Asquith, NL 2014, 'A governance of denial: Hate crime in Australia and New Zealand', in N Hall, A Corb, P Giannasi, & JGD Grieve (eds), *The Routledge international handbook on hate crime*, Routledge, Oxon, pp. 174–189.

Baird, B 1997, 'Putting police on notice: A South Australian case study', in G Mason & S Tomsen (eds), *Homophobic violence*, Hawkins Press, Leichhardt, pp. 118–131.

Baird, B, Mason, K, & Purcell, I 1994, *The police and you: A report of a survey of the experiences of lesbians and gay men in South Australia*, Adelaide Gay and Lesbian Community Action, Adelaide.

Baldry, E, Brown, D, Brown, M, Cunneen, C, Schwartz, M, & Steel, A 2011, 'Imprisoning rationalities', *Australian & New Zealand Journal of Criminology*, vol. 44, no. 1, pp. 24–40.

Ball, M, Buist, CL, & Woods, JB 2013, 'Introduction to the special issue on queer/ing criminology: New directions and frameworks', *Critical Criminology*, vol. 22, no. 1, pp. 1–4.

Boon-Kuo, L, Meiners, ER, & Simpson, P 2018, 'Queer interruptions: Policing belonging in the carceral state', in P Aggleton, R Cover, D Leahy, D Marshall, & ML Rasmussen (eds), *Youth, sexuality and sexual citizenship*, Routledge, Oxon, pp. 34–49.

Bowling, B 1993, 'Racial harassment and the process of victimization', *British Journal of Criminology*, vol. 33, no. 2, pp. 231–250.

Brown, A 2013, *VGLRL submission to Victoria Police community consultation*, Victorian Gay and Lesbian Rights Lobby (VGLRL), Melbourne, viewed 13 July 2016, www.vglrl.org.au/submissions/vglrl-submissions/item/vglrl-submission-victoria-police-community-consultation-2013.

Brown, W 1995, *States of injury: Power and freedom in late modernity*, Princeton University Press, Princeton.

Brown, W 2006, *Regulating aversion: Tolerance in the age of identity and empire*, Princeton University Press, Princeton.

Brown, W & Halley, J 2002, *Left legalism/left critique*, Duke University Press, Durham.

Bumiller, K 2008, *In an abusive state: How neoliberalism appropriated the feminist movement against sexual violence*, Duke University Press, Durham.

Chakraborti, N 2015, 'Re-thinking hate crime: Fresh challenges for policy and practice', *Journal of Interpersonal Violence*, vol. 30, no. 10, pp. 1738–1754.

Chen, C.-I, Dulani, J, & Piepzna-Samarasinha, LL 2011, *The revolution starts at home: Confronting intimate violence within activist communities*, South End Press, Brooklyn.

Christie, N 2000, *Crime control as industry: Towards gulags, Western style*, Routledge, Oxon.

Couch, M, Pitts, M, Mulcare, H, Croy, S, Mitchell, A, & Patel, S 2007, *Tranznation: A report on the health and wellbeing of transgender people in Australia and New Zealand*, Australian Research Centre in Sex, Health & Society (ARCSHS), Melbourne.

Cox, G 1990, *The streetwatch report: A study into violence against lesbians and gay men*, Sydney Gay and Lesbian Rights Lobby (NSW GLRL), Sydney.

Crawford, A, Jones, T, Woodhouse, T, & Young, J 1990, *Second Islington crime survey*, Middlesex Polytechnic: Center for Criminology, London.
Cunneen, C, Baldry, E, Brown, D, Brown, M, Schwartz, M, & Steel, A 2013, *Penal culture and hyperincarceration: The revival of the prison*, Ashgate, Surrey.
Deford, W 2005, 'The dilemma of expressive punishment', *Colorado Law Review*, vol. 76, pp. 843–864.
Dorrington, B 2013, 'Police ramp up hate crime training', *Star Observer*, 04 April, viewed 7 April 2015, www.starobserver.com.au/news/police-ramp-up-hate-crime-training/101824.
Dwyer, A 2015, 'Teaching young queers a lesson: How police teach lessons about non-heteronormativity in public spaces', *Sexuality and Culture*, vol. 19, no. 3, pp. 493–512.
Fagan, J & Meares, TL 2008, 'Punishment, deterrence and social control: The paradox of punishment in minority communities', *Ohio State Journal of Criminal Law*, vol. 6, pp. 173–229.
Flood, M & Hamilton, C 2008, 'Mapping homophobia in Australia', in S Robinson (ed.), *Homophobia: An Australian history*, The Federation Press, Sydney, pp. 16–38.
Fraser, N 1997, *Justice interruptus: Critical reflections on the 'postsocialist' condition*, Routledge, New York.
Freeman, AD 1995, 'Legitimizing racial discrimination through anti-discrimination law: A critical review of Supreme Court doctrine', in K Crenshaw, N Gotanda, G Peller, & K Thomas (eds), *Critical race studies: The key writings that formed the movement*, The New Press, New York, pp. 29–45.
Garland, D 2001, *Culture of control: Crime and social order in contemporary society*, Oxford University Press, Oxford.
Gays & Lesbians Against Discrimination 1994, *Not a day goes by: Report on the GLAD survey into discrimination and violence against lesbians and gay men in Victoria*, Gays and Lesbians Against Discrimination (GLAD), Melbourne.
Generation Five 2017, *Ending child sexual abuse: A transformative justice handbook*, Generation Five, Oakland.
Gray, B, Leonard, W, & Jack, M 2006, *With respect: A strategy for reducing homophobic harassment in Victoria: A discussion paper for the consideration of the Victorian Attorney General*. Joint Working Group of the Attorney-General's and Health Minister's Advisory Committees on GLBTI Issues, Melbourne.
Grossman, M, Bruck, D, Stephenson, P, Dwyer, R, & Roose, J 2013, *Learning to engage: A review of Victoria Police cross-cultural training practices*, Centre for Cultural Diversity and Wellbeing (CCDW), Victoria University, Melbourne.
Hanhardt, CB 2013, *Safe space: Gay neighborhood history and the politics of violence*, Duke University Press, Durham.
Haritaworn, J 2010, 'Queer injuries: The racial politics of 'homophobic hate crime' in Germany', *Social Justice*, vol. 37, no. 1, pp. 69–91.
Haritaworn, J 2015, *Queer lovers and hateful others: Regenerating violent times and places*, Pluto Press, London.
Harris, AP 2006, 'From Stonewall to the suburbs? Toward a political economy of sexuality', *William and Mary Bill of Rights Journal*, vol. 14, pp. 1539–1582.
Harris, AP 2011, 'Heteropatriarchy kills: Challenging gender violence in a prison nation', *Washington University Journal of Law & Policy*, vol. 37, no. 1, pp. 13–65.

Hillyard, P, Pantazis, C, Tombs, S, & Gordon, D 2004a, *Beyond criminology: Taking harm seriously*, Pluto Press, London.
Hillyard, P, Sim, J, Tombs, S, & Whyte, D 2004b, 'Leaving a 'stain upon the silence': Contemporary criminology and the politics of dissent', *British Journal of Criminology*, vol. 44, no. 3, pp. 369–390.
Hudson, B 2000, 'Critical reflection as research methodology', in V Jupp, P Davies, & P Francis (eds), *Doing criminological research*, Sage, London, pp. 328–344.
Human Rights Law Centre (HRLC) 2014, *Righting historical wrongs: Background paper for a legislative scheme to expunge convictions for historical consensual gay sex offences in Victoria*, HRLC, Melbourne.
Human Rights Law Centre (HRLC) 2018, *End the hate: Responding to prejudice motivated speech and violence against the LGBT community*, HRLC, Melbourne.
Incite! Women of Color against Violence 2006, *Color of violence: The Incite! anthology*, South End Press, Cambridge.
Jacobs, JB & Potter, K 1998, *Hate crimes: Criminal law and identity politics*, Oxford University Press, New York.
Jenness, V & Broad, K 1997, *Hate crimes: New social movements and the politics of violence*, Aldine de Gruyter, New York.
Jenness, V & Grattet, R 2001, *Making hate a crime: From social movement to law enforcement*, Russell Sage, New York.
Kaplan, MB 2008, 'Hate crime and the privatization of political responsibility: Protecting queer citizens in the United States?' *Liverpool Law Review*, vol. 29, pp. 37–50.
Kim, ME 2018, 'From carceral feminism to transformative justice: Women-of-color feminism and alternatives to incarceration', *Journal of Ethnic & Cultural Diversity in Social Work*, vol. 27, no. 3, pp. 219–233.
Kuhn, TS 1970, *The structure of scientific revolutions*, The University of Chicago Press, Chicago.
Lamble, S 2013, 'Queer necropolitics and the expanding carceral state: Interrogating sexual investments in punishment', *Law Critique*, vol. 24, no. 3, pp. 229–253.
Lasslett, K 2010, 'Crime or social harm? A dialectical perspective', *Crime, Law and Social Change*, vol. 54, no. 1, pp. 1–19.
Leonard, W & Fileborn, B 2018, *Policing for SSASGD young Victorians*, Gay and Lesbian Health Victoria (GLHV) and Australian Research Centre in Sex, Health and Society (ARCSHS), La Trobe University, Melbourne.
Leonard, W, Mitchell, A, Pitts, M, & Patel, S 2008, *Coming forward: The underreporting of heterosexist violence and same sex partner abuse in Victoria*, Australian Research Centre in Sex, Health and Society (ARCSHS), La Trobe University, Melbourne.
Mason, G 1993, *Violence against lesbians and gay men*, Australian Institute of Criminology (AIC), Canberra.
Mason, G 2005, 'Hate crime and the image of the stranger', *British Journal of Criminology*, vol. 45, no. 6, pp. 837–859.
Mason, G 2009, 'The penal politics of hatred', *The Australian and New Zealand Journal of Criminology*, vol. 42, no. 3, pp. 275–286.
Mason, G 2014, 'The symbolic purpose of hate crime law: Ideal victims and emotion', *Theoretical Criminology*, vol. 18, no. 1, pp. 75–92.

Mason, G, McCulloch, J, & Maher, J 2016, 'Policing hate crime: Markers for negotiating common ground in policy implementation', *Policing and Society*, vol. 26, no. 6, pp. 680–697.

McKenzie, J 2000, 'Anti-violence stand', *Star Observer*, 15 December, p. 7.

Meiners, ER 2007, *Right to be hostile: Schools, prisons, and the making of public enemies*, Routledge, New York.

Meyer, D 2014, 'Resisting hate crime discourse: Queer and intersectional challenges to neoliberal hate crime laws', *Critical Criminology*, vol. 22, no. 1, pp. 113–125.

Mogul, J, Ritchie, AJ, & Whitlock, K 2011, *Queer (in)justice: The criminalisation of LGBT people in the United States*, Beacon Press, Boston.

Moran, LJ 2001, 'Affairs of the heart: Hate crime and the politics of crime control', *Law and Critique*, vol. 12, pp. 331–334.

Moran, LJ 2004, 'The emotional dimensions of lesbian and gay demands for hate crime reform', *McGill Law Journal*, vol. 49, pp. 925–949.

Moran, LJ 2007, '"Invisible minorities": Challenging community and neighbourhood models of policing', *Journal of Criminology and Criminal Justice*, vol. 7, no. 4, pp. 417–441.

Moran, LJ & Skeggs, B 2004, *Sexuality and the politics of violence and safety*, Routledge, London.

Pemberton, S 2007, 'Social harm future(s): Exploring the potential of the social harm approach', *Crime Law, and Social Change*, vol. 48, no. 1, pp. 27–41.

Pendleton, M & Serisier, T 2009, Beyond the desire for law: Sex and crisis in Australian feminist and queer politics, *The Australian Feminist Law Journal*, vol. 31, pp. 77–98.

Renshaw, L, Kim, J, Fawkes, J, & Jeffreys, E 2015, 'Migrant sex workers in Australia', *Research and public policy series*, Australian Institute of Criminology, Canberra.

Riley, B 2013, 'Police call for tougher hate crime sentencing', *Star Observer*, 22 May, viewed 27 August 2014, www.starobserver.com.au/news/police-call-for-tougher-hate-crime-sentencing/104136.

Robinson, S 2008, *Homophobia: An Australian history*, The Federation Press, Sydney.

Russell, EK 2017a, 'Punishment in a 'tolerant society': Interrogating hate crime law reform discourse', *Griffith Law Review*, vol. 26, no. 3, pp. 315–333.

Russell, EK 2017b, 'Queer penalities: The criminal justice paradigm in lesbian and gay anti-violence politics', *Critical Criminology*, vol. 25, no. 1, pp. 21–35.

Sanders, T 2016, 'Inevitably violent? Dynamics of space, governance, and stigma in understanding violence against sex workers', *Law, Politics and Society*, vol. 71, pp. 93–114.

Sandroussi, J & Thompson, S 1995, *Out of the blue: A police survey of violence and harassment against gay men and lesbians*, NSW Police Service, Sydney.

Scraton, P 2002, 'Defining 'power' and challenging 'knowledge': Critical analysis as resistance in the UK', in K Carrington & R Hogg (eds), *Critical criminology: Issues, debates, challenges*, Willan Publishing, Cullompton, pp. 15–40.

Sentencing Advisory Council 2009, *Sentencing for offences motivated by hatred or prejudice*, State Government of Victoria, Melbourne.

Sim, J, Scraton, P, & Gordon, P 1987, 'Crime, the state and critical analysis', in P Scraton (ed.), *Law, order and the authoritarian state*, Open University Press, Milton Keynes, pp. 1–70.

Simon, J 2007, *Governing through crime: How the war on crime transformed American democracy and created a culture of fear*, Oxford University Press, New York.

Sitka, C 1997, *Violence against lesbians: A COAL research paper*, Coalition of Activist Lesbians (COAL), Waterloo.

Spade, D 2011, *Normal life: Administrative violence, critical trans politics, and the limits of law*, South End Press, Brooklyn.

Spade, D & Willse, C 2000, 'Confronting the limits of gay hate crimes activism: A radical critique', *Chicano-Latino Law Review*, vol. 21, pp. 38–52.

Stanko, EA & Curry, P 1997, 'Homophobic violence and the self 'at risk'', *Social and Legal Studies*, vol. 6, no. 4, pp. 513–532.

Star Observer 2009a, *Hate crime change pleases*, posted 10 June, viewed 19 January 2019, www.starobserver.com.au/news/national-news/victoria-news/hate-crime-change-pleases/36240.

Star Observer 2009b, *Hate-crime law review welcomed*, posted 16 December, viewed 20 January 2019, www.starobserver.com.au/news/national-news/victoria-news/hate-crime-law-review-welcomed-2/35623.

Tomsen, S 1993, 'The political contradictions of policing and countering anti-gay violence in New South Wales', *Current Issues in Criminal Justice*, vol. 5, no. 2, pp. 209–215.

Tomsen, S 1996, 'Gay homicides: Activism, victims and law and order', in C Sumner, M Israel, M O'Connell, & R Sarre (eds), *International victimology: Selected papers from the Eighth International Symposium on Victimology*, Australian Institute of Criminology (AIC), Canberra.

Tomsen, S 2006, 'Homophobic violence, cultural essentialism and shifting sexual identities', *Social and Legal Studies*, vol. 15, pp. 389–407.

Tomsen, S 2009, *Violence, prejudice and sexuality*, Routledge, New York.

Tomsen, S & Mason, G 2001, 'Engendering homophobia: Violence, sexuality and gender conformity', *Journal of Sociology*, vol. 37, no. 3, pp. 265–287.

Tubex, H, Brown, D, Freiberg, A, Gelb, K, & Sarre, R 2015, 'Penal diversity within Australia', *Punishment & Society*, vol. 17, no. 3, pp. 345–373.

Valverde, M & Cirak, M 2003, 'Governing bodies, creating gay spaces: Policing and security issues in 'gay' downtown Toronto', *British Journal of Criminology*, vol. 43, no. 1, pp. 102–121.

Victorian Gay & Lesbian Rights Lobby (VGLRL) 2000, *Enough is enough: A report on discrimination and abuse experienced by lesbians, gay men, bisexuals and transgender people in Victoria*, VGLRL, Melbourne.

Victorian Gay & Lesbian Rights Lobby (VGLRL) 2017, *Community survey 2017: Perceptions and experiences of Victoria Police*, VGLRL, Melbourne.

Wacquant, L 2009, *Punishing the poor: The neoliberal government of social insecurity*, Duke University Press, Durham.

Wacquant, L 2010, 'Class, race and hyperincarceration in revanchist America', *Daedalus*, vol. 140, no. 3, pp. 74–90.

Wade, M 2016, 'Three LGBT people assaulted in Melbourne', *Star Observer*, 7 November, viewed 14 February 2017, www.starobserver.com.au/news/national-news/victoria-news/lgbti-assault-melbourne-police/153761.

Walklate, S 1990, 'Researching victims of crime: Critical victimology', *Social Justice*, vol. 17, no. 3, pp. 25–42.

Wang, J 2012, 'Against innocence: Race, gender, and the politics of safety', *LIES: A Journal of Materialist Feminism*, vol. 1, pp. 145–172.

Willett, G 2008, 'From 'vice' to 'homosexuality': Policing perversion in the 1950s', in S Robinson (ed.), *Homophobia: An Australian history*, The Federation Press, Sydney, pp. 113–127.

Woods, JB 2014, "Queering criminology': Overview of the state of the field', in D Peterson & VR Panfil (eds), *Handbook of LGBT communities, crime, and justice*, Springer, New York, pp. 15–41.

Chapter 7

The fabrication of queer history

Narrating the police apology

Introduction

Two decades after Victoria Police conducted the raid and strip-searched hundreds of mostly queer patrons at the Tasty nightclub, the raid's effects persisted as a 'sticking point' in local LGBT–police relations. The Tasty raid's ongoing significance for police reputation was highlighted by the police decision to issue a formal apology to LGBT people, early in August 2014. The apology marked the 20th anniversary of the raid. It was broadcast on the official Victoria Police YouTube channel and reported on its *Cops and Bloggers* website. It was thus centrally located within the machinations of police strategic communications and public relations—both of which are now major vehicles for the promotion of police profile (Lee & McGovern 2014). Acting Chief Commissioner of Victoria Police Lucinda Nolan presented the apology on behalf of the force during a private press conference and meeting of Victoria Police's recently established LGBTI Portfolio Reference group in its new Priority Communities Division. The small event was held at the Victoria Police Museum. In the video 'Victoria Police issue Tasty nightclub apology' uploaded to YouTube, Nolan states:

> Today's event is an indication of Victoria Police's eagerness to build sustainable partnerships with the community to increase trust and confidence in our organisation. Thank you for your time and willingness to participate. Like the wider Victorian community—Victoria Police is changing. Sometimes change comes in response to painful experiences. Your presence here today is as a result of a very painful episode experienced by members of the LGBTI community at the Tasty nightclub in Melbourne on August 7 1994. Simply put—the events that took place that night caused distress to people who were in attendance and had a significant impact on the relationship between Victoria Police and the wider LGBTI community. It is therefore appropriate—as we near the 20th anniversary of this incident, that Victoria Police extends a sincere apology to the community members who were affected by events

> on that night. We also extend a general apology to the broader LGBTI community for the impact this event has had on our relationship over the past two decades. There is no doubt the Tasty nightclub incident was a low point in the relationship between the LGBTI community and Victoria Police. However, I think it is true to say that a great deal has changed in the last 20 years. Victoria Police has made great strides in regards to the recognition and celebration of diversity of gender and sexuality within our community.
>
> (Victoria Police 2014)

In Chapter 3, I argued that in the mid-1990s, police were ultimately unable to control media narratives of the Tasty raid. I outlined a number of ways in which Victoria Police attempted to navigate negative press and restore its legitimacy in the aftermath of the raid, including framing the raid as an 'isolated incident', denying homophobia, and making only partial and ambiguous admissions of wrongdoing. These efforts had limited success. For instance, an editorial published in the *Age* on 1 December 1994 (p. 19) describe the raid as 'overkill' and 'an event that could safely be described as a PR disaster for the force'. In light of the Tasty raid's historical 'bad press' and ongoing reverberations of fear and distrust of police within the LGBT community, the 2014 police apology took a new approach to managing its reputational damage. By issuing an apology, police performed the 'public feeling' of remorse and an acknowledgement of past wrongdoing. However, the acting Chief Commissioner's admission of error on behalf of the institution was markedly oblique: it skirted around and avoided ownership of police actions at the Tasty raid and qualified any reckoning with the past by over-emphasising institutional progress and change in the present. Perhaps most importantly, the official apology re-centred and elevated a proud police identity and policing agenda over and above queer injustice. In other words, the apology was less for the queer 'other' than the institution of policing itself.

This chapter extends Chapter 5's discussion of the public circulation of police discourses of individual and collective shame as a vehicle for recovering institutional pride. Once again, the pairing of shame and pride as the grounds upon which LGBT people might embrace inclusion in the policing project is noticeably embodied by white femininity, which comes to stand in—in these particular 'queer' contexts—for the 'new face' of policing: softer, more caring, more reflexive. This is no mere coincidence, as white femininity has long been seen in the settler colonial context of Australia as emblematic of purity and innocence (Moreton-Robinson 2000; Niccol 2000). Many forms of contemporary communicative work rely upon a particularly gendered mode of labour (Kanngieser 2012) and feminine voices are typically perceived as more pleasant, helpful, and supportive (Feiler 2010). Common examples of the use of feminine voices to direct and aid people now include GPS devices, artificial intelligence, and airport and train station announcements. These suggest that feminine voices are frequently heard as possessing the 'soft' skills critical to the evocation of a soothing and nurturing form of safety and security. In contrast, masculine voices are typically associated with a strong and dependable form of authority (Edworthy et al. 2003). While masculine voices transmit authoritative information, feminine voices convey care and emotion. As such, in instances where police leadership involves projecting (limited forms of) vulnerability and humility in order to evoke trust among sexual and gender minorities, the feminine voice evokes the appropriate amount of warmth, likeability, adaptability, and openness.

Instead of the colourful and joyous occasion of a public Pride parade examined in Chapter 5, this chapter considers how the more sombre performance of apology (Cels 2014) can transform shame into pride and fortify institutional and state legitimacy. Putting aside the possible impacts of the Tasty raid apology on Victoria Police policy and practice—while important, these are yet to be determined—I analyse the representational and discursive aspects of apology. This chapter considers how the apology represents 'the problematic period of the past' (Toth 2014, p. 555) and what it does for police as an institution. Far from being an exceptional utterance, the police apology reflects a broader pattern of attempts at institutional legitimation within 'the politics of regret' (Olick 2007).

'Righting historical wrongs': queer injuries and the politics of regret

Over the past two decades, the formal recognition of past injustices has become a seemingly ubiquitous speech act in a wide range of institutional settings (Mookherjee et al. 2009; Toth 2014). According to Jeffrey Olick (2007), the politics of regret has become the new grounds of legitimation for governments and other powerful institutions. Rather than glorifying past misdeeds, the apology crafts historical narratives of remorse in order to 'take some degree of responsibility for them' (Toth 2014, p. 553). It is therefore a rich site for interrogating the 'projected story and perceived character' (Bentley 2015, p. 4) of institutions as they morph and evolve in particular historical and geographical contexts in relation to specific marginalised groups that have been wronged in the past.

During this same time period in which the official apology has emerged as 'a novel form of self-legitimation and identification' (Toth 2014, p. 554), LGBT activists have vigorously campaigned to build awareness of the harms and inequalities experienced by sexual and gender minorities. LGBT researchers and advocates have produced and circulated knowledge of queer injuries—at the hands of both individual bigots, as the previous chapter outlined, and the state—that has gradually and unevenly been absorbed into the discourses of governments and other institutions. Though stilted and limited, the growing public awareness of homophobia has reshaped the political and cultural landscape within which state institutions operate. For instance, as police are being tasked with responding to homophobic attacks, the often-violent heteronormativity of the organisation comes under closer scrutiny (hence calls for more training, community outreach, and so forth). It is thus not surprising that, in 'the age of apology' (Gibney et al. 2008), LGBT people are now being called forth to bear the weight of forgiveness for the state's systematic wrongdoings.

Official apologies are becoming increasingly crucial 'textual, symbolic and ritualistic sites' (Bentley 2015, p. 4), where sexual citizenship is rearticulated, renegotiated, and reproduced. Fewer than two years after the Victoria Police apology for the Tasty raid, the NSW Parliament apologised for the arrests and beatings at the demonstration now known as 'the first Mardi Gras' in 1978 and the *Sydney Morning Herald* apologised for publishing the names, occupations, and addresses of arrestees (Power 2016a). Following a petition and calls from politicians, NSW Police followed suit, and Superintendent Tony Crandell expressed regret on 4 March 2016 for the way the force policed the renowned 1978 protest (Power 2016b).[1] During the years 2016–2018, the parliament of almost every Australian state and territory (except NSW and the Australian Capital Territory) issued a formal apology for historical laws targeting homosexuality (and, in the case of Tasmania, cross-dressing). This 'state of regret' is echoed internationally: British and Canadian parliaments have issued gay apologies, as have police forces in Toronto and New York for police actions during the famed bathhouse raids and Stonewall riots, respectively. It is thus not an exaggeration to assert that we are now witnessing a trend in gay apologies.

In this chapter, I am interested in exploring whether an official apology compels powerful institutions such as police and government to reckon with what they have done (and continue to do), or whether it merely allows them to congratulate themselves on reconciling LGBT people to the (heterosexual) nation state. As those in positions of political power have begun deeming particular past instances of queer injustice to be officially shameful, we need to ask: what does apology *do* for the apologiser? And what does it achieve 'for the injured on whom lies the onus of forgiving and forgetting'? (Mookherjee et al. 2009, p. 348). I suspect that the apology might do more to repair institutional identity than queer injustice. By exploring this dilemma, I do not intend to diminish the meanings that individuals attribute to the apology upon its reception, nor dismiss the apology as merely a farce or smokescreen. As feminist and queer theorist Sara Ahmed (2005) points out, shame is of course better than indifference to historical harm, or worse, pride in it. Indeed, the politics of regret are far from totalising; they often exist alongside and in contestation with other coping strategies, such as denial or silence (Cohen 2001). Potentially, an apology provides an opportunity to renegotiate an unequal relationship and change established ways of doing things. However, the terms of the official apology and any shifts that might emerge from it are not politically neutral, nor equally negotiated: police and government recognise the queer other from an unequal position and can choose which issues and events are worth feeling shame over. In other words, it is ultimately those in the more powerful position that determine 'what kinds of acts are, or are not, apologisable' (Mookherjee et al. 2009, p. 348). The official apology, then, must be viewed through a critical lens: one that allows us to read the speech act and the performance of apology as a claim to knowledge and a claim to power (Mookherjee et al. 2009, pp. 349–350).

'Making themselves look good': agency and power in the Tasty raid apology

The Victoria Police apology for the Tasty raid presents some glaring absences. There is no mention made of the issues of discrimination, the use of excessive force, or abusive treatment; nor is the Tasty raid placed in its wider historical context. This is despite the significance that LGBT people attributed to the raid as a symbol of institutionalised homophobia, which Chapter 3 discussed. Nolan conspicuously refrains from identifying what exactly caused such pain and distress to the LGBT community, instead referring vaguely to 'the events that took place that night'. These silences are important. Indeed, they might be just as crucial as what *is* said. As Michel Foucault (1972, p. 25) explains in *The Archaeology of Knowledge*, manifest discourse is 'really no more than the repressive presence of what it does not say; and this "not-said" is a hollow that undermines from within all that is said'. At no point is the Tasty raid confronted or described in the apology. Instead, it is obliquely referred to as 'a very painful episode experienced by members of the LGBT community'. The history that is narrated is thereby one that is devoid of agency. It is a story in which neither police repression nor queer resistance exists as driving forces—both are absent and erased. This distasteful 'episode' is presented passively, such that proactive police efforts to criminalise hundreds of queer nightclub patrons are not explained, let alone acknowledged. In the words of the apology, 'the events that took place that night caused distress to people in attendance', as if these events might be naturally caused phenomena, rather than a violent raid designed and enacted by individual police officers within larger institutional conditions that enabled and condoned it. Indeed, the term 'raid' is not even used. The apology instead opts for vague terms such as 'incident' and 'event'. By detaching the recognition of wrongdoing from individuals, the police apology projects injustice onto the past and depersonalises any reckoning with it in the present (Ahmed 2004). Indeed, the abstraction of wrongdoing and collectivisation of regret is, in this case, the precondition for the utterance of the apology. While the speech explicitly states that 'Victoria Police extends a sincere apology to the community members who were affected by events on that night', it remains unclear precisely what the police are apologising for. Responsibility is thus deferred and incomplete, as the Tasty raid is described passively (as experienced by; as having occurred), and therefore police actions are not scrutinised, admitted, or even noted. It articulates not simply a skewed historical narrative (as all of them are), but a markedly impoverished one, bereft of any detail or context.[2]

In *Empires of Remorse*, Tom Bentley (2015, p. 5) argues that 'apologies reflect an elite that have been forced to vie, negotiate and compromise with competing historical narratives so as to retain credible and plausible constructions of the past'. Through crafting a formal apology, powerful institutions 'impart particular perceptions of the … past and, in turn, employ such constructions in processes of state legitimation' (Bentley 2015, p. 4). The reconstruction of historical narrative is thus central to the discourse of apology and its legitimising effects. In the Tasty apology, police cast the raid as 'a low point in the relationship between the LGBT community and Victoria Police'. This 'low point' is not contextualised or explained for the listener, nor is it dwelled upon for long. The discourse of apology swiftly brings us back to the present, where it becomes clear that this 'low point' exists on a linear trajectory in a teleological narrative of progress, modernity, and institutional change. Nolan extends the apology insofar as she embraces and over-identifies with the institution and its public feelings—its regret, its eagerness to make amends. The performance of apology therefore begins and ends with allegiance to the institution and pride in representing it. LGBT people are told that 'Victoria Police has made great strides in regards to the recognition and celebration of diversity of gender and sexuality within our community'. As these 'strides' are recited for the audience in the form of a conventional list of police performances of the politics of recognition—participation in Pride March, flying the gay pride flag at central headquarters, and the promotion of GLLO programmes—the role played by LGBT activism in creating pressure for these and other changes remains unacknowledged and erased. Instead, a by-now-familiar story of bold and admirable police leadership and institutional evolution is narrated. As seen in Chapter 5, the construction and reception of this narrative is thoroughly steeped in and dependent upon police authority, which is recast as a force for good. Far from being relinquished or redistributed, this power is instead recalibrated and reconsolidated within and through this new emotional economy—of shame and pride, regret and resolve for a brighter future—which has ultimately served to rehabilitate the police image and fortify the institution. Thus, rather than challenging the conditions of queer injustice, the apology entrenches and reproduces them, by erasing queer agency and appropriating queer pain in the service of recovering institutional pride.

The absence of recognition of the extensive history of LGBT lobbying, education, and outreach work with police in the Tasty raid apology is a prime example of what Barbara Baird, Lesbian and Gay Community Action member in the 1990s, perceives as a lack of institutional memory. In interview, she relayed how South Australian police appropriate the past to construct a positive image of the institution that can be projected *outwards* to bolster legitimacy, rather than reform the organisation from within. She relayed an account which suggested:

> [Police leaders are] not interested in educating the police about a history of lesbian and gay activism and about how whatever change there is might have come about over the last 25 years. They are interested in making themselves look good to the GLBTIQ community.

Her comments support the idea that police discourses of LGBT recognition function as a form of public relations and corporate promotion, despite the narratives of internal reform that these official discourses frequently espouse. The Tasty raid apology (and the 'great strides' that it references) is therefore better understood as an exercise in what Erving Goffman (1959) terms 'impression management', rather than an attempt to fundamentally reckon with institutionalised homophobia and queer injustice. The public rehearsal of institutional regret functions foremost to re-establish the policing as a site for pride.

'I am very proud of this organisation': transforming shame into pride

As I argued in Chapter 5, emotions are not simply psychological and individual states, 'but social and cultural practices' and relations of power, especially when they are 'declared or named in public culture' (Ahmed 2005, p. 71). In my reading, the police apology is informed and bolstered by the kinds of emotional frameworks that, as Sara Ahmed (2004) argues, allow some individuals or groups to maintain dominance, while others risk further marginalisation, or simply fade into the background. Through the discourse of apology, police mobilise political emotions of shame and pride to craft a new historical narrative of institutional repair and renewal. The ceremony of apology represents a performance of self-reflexivity, without any individual or collective reckoning with the perpetration of historical injustice. For in the police version of events, the source of institutional shame is glossed over and elided. At most, it is the persistence of queer 'distress' that prompts the police apology, rather than any specific actions or errors on the part of police (since these are never acknowledged or explicated). Yet, the very utterance of apology, or the claim to *feel bad* about past events, allows police to reclaim a self-perception of *being good* (Ahmed 2004).

The evocation of shame in the discourse of apology has varying effects. Shame can be defined as a sense of negation and failure that is 'bound up with how the self feels about itself' (Ahmed 2004, p. 103). While it is self-oriented, shame is made all the more powerful because it is usually experienced before or in relation to another. It involves a form of exposure that often prompts an attempt at concealment, or self-protection. Shame can activate defensive modes of self-preservation, such as salvaging or preserving 'historical narratives that have, in recent years, been subject to severe duress' (Bentley 2015, p. 5). This highlights the ambiguous role of shame in any restorative project (Muldoon 2017), as Ahmed (2004, p. 102) points out:

> Despite its recognition of past wrongdoings, shame can still conceal how such wrongdoings shape lives in the present. The work of shame troubles and is troubling, exposing some wounds, at the same time as it conceals others.

The urge to hide or conceal the shameful aspects of identity can limit and prevent the self-reflexive and progressive potentials of shame, and, by extension, attempts at reconciliation. Despite common assumptions, the official apology may function as a conservatising gesture, shoring up pre-existing power relations and institutional arrangements, rather than reckoning with historical injustice. Perhaps most importantly, shame can function as a self-serving healing process by which we can, somewhat paradoxically, become good again by feeling bad (Ahmed 2004, 2005). As Paul Muldoon (2017, p. 214) argues in relation to the national apology to Australian Indigenous peoples,[3] 'to the extent that its primary objective is to alleviate the colonizer's sense of shame, reconciliation always betrays itself', as the desire to redeem the damaged institution undermines the ethical potential of attempts at atoning for the past.

Shame works to reconcile the institution to itself by 'coming to terms with' its own past in the expression of 'bad feeling' (Ahmed 2004, p. 103). As a 'salvaging mission' (Bentley 2015, p. 5), the official apology represents an effort to resolve these bad feelings through the recognition and promotion of ourselves as not bad cops or bad governments. Police are made good again by having made, in Nolan's words, 'great strides in regards to the recognition and celebration of diversity'. To flee this shameful identity, then, is to recover a new myth or identity that is, once more, good. As Ahmed (2005, p. 81) contends, 'the very claim to feel bad … also involve[s] a self-perception of "being good"'. Much like Nixon's constructed narrative in *Fair Cop*, the Tasty raid apology reflects how police leaders want to stop looking or even feeling bad, so take steps to discharge this historical guilt in a way that avoids reckoning with the nature of police power and impunity. In part, it is the recognition of a shameful past that allows police to affirm the inherent goodness of police: they can expunge bad elements (explicit and overt homophobia, violent and dramatic incursions into queer spaces, and so on) and claim that those are not part of the police's present identity. Police leaders essentially redeem the institution through acknowledging a shameful past—by feeling bad about the past, police become 'good' again.

Police pride is explicitly re-established and reasserted in the Tasty raid apology. When Nolan states, 'I am very proud of this organisation—but we can improve', we are directed away from the injustice of the past and back to the 'goodness' of the institution as it is made anew through its remorse in the present and its potential in the future. The progress to come suggests that it is not simply the shameful past that aids in the recovery of a proud police identity in the present; it is also the promising future of policing. This is an institutionalised future in which queers are being asked to invest.

'You're making a better police force': investments and promises

As a performance, the official apology is addressed outwards to the injured other. Yet despite its reliance on audience reception, the above discussion of the circular and self-oriented nature of shame suggests that the apology does more for the apologiser than those who have been wronged. The apology prioritises institutional redemption, seeking foremost to repair the damage to police reputation, rather than heal the pain wrought by past injustice and violence. As an act of cleansing, the apology works to free the institution of the guilt and shame associated with its history, and in doing so, it re-establishes police as worthy of respect, admiration, and investment.

In this particular instance of institutional recuperation, the apology shields police from responsibility and the audience from the past by sidestepping and eliding recognition of specific violent police practices. Instead, it places the onus on the queer other not only to forgive and forget, but also to invest in and guide police towards a stronger future. To an audience of LGBT advocates and activists, some of whom experienced the Tasty raid, Nolan proclaims: 'We can change and you can help show us the way. Thank you for investing time in this process—you're making Victoria Police a better police force'. Here, Nolan seeks an identification with the institution of policing from LGBT people that is not all that dissimilar to her own. The apology reiterates a call for LGBT labour and resources to mobilise in the service of advancing police proficiency and cultural knowledge that might—it is hoped—eventually translate into an offer of 'equal' treatment and protection to LGBT people.

The projection of an idealised police force to come reflects the structure of the 'promise', which was briefly discussed in Chapter 5. As developed by queer theorists interested in economies of affect, promises are investments in or orientations towards the future that are always tenuous but nevertheless persuasive, especially when offered by powerful institutions (Agathangelou et al. 2008). To promise is to 'make the future into an object': into something that can be declared in advance of its arrival (Puar 2012, p. 153). As a situation, the promise is an assurance, a positive declaration intended to give confidence and trust that an expectation will be met. The promise is also an expression of desire—for something to be promising is an indication of something favourable to come (Ahmed 2010). For example, many queer scholars argue that discourses of recognition, inclusion, diversity, and protection can generate optimistic investments in the potential rewards offered by the neoliberal state, even as the conditions of the promise may necessitate abandoning certain practices or excluding other subjects (Agathangelou et al. 2008; Ahmed 2010; Lamble 2013; Puar 2012), such as public sex or other 'criminal elements', as discussed in Chapter 3. A promise always lies ahead of us, 'at least if we do the right thing' (Ahmed 2010, p. 29). It is therefore conditional and precarious, with governing effects. A promise depends on certain conditions being in place that would allow the promise to be kept, such as active cooperation in police reform projects.

During the sombre yet ceremonious occasion, VGLRL representatives graciously receive the police apology, suggesting that it 'shone a light on a positive future' (Brown & Irlam 2014). Without casting doubt on the meanings that individual LGBT people attributed to the apology, I want to argue that both the text and the performance of the apology—delivered privately to a select group of LGBT representatives who are, predominantly, involved in the concrete work of advising and reforming police—significantly restricted the possibility of its own rejection (Muldoon 2017). That is, the potential that LGBT people might not accept the apology was all but eliminated by its very design and delivery. Formal LGBT responses to the apology proceeded from a position that was already committed to and invested in the 'continuity, progress and development' of the institution (Berlant 2011, p. 13).

Queer investments in policing are practices that are oriented towards a potential future outcome (Lamble 2013), such as 'a better police force'. Through the intimate affirmation of queer commitments to policing, the formal apology helps to bring the queer 'other' into the fold of the state. Queer theorist Roderick Ferguson argues that the dynamic of co-option is reproduced by a particular dilemma in the contemporary administration of institutional power. That is, while institutions have to 'affirm difference' in order to demonstrate progress, they must also 'restrict the collective, oppositional, and redistributive aims of difference' (Ferguson 2008, p. 163). In other words, sexual and gender difference must be evacuated of its radical and political potential before it can be incorporated. This form of containment can be highly effective for powerful institutions seeking to manage or quell the instability produced by categories of 'difference'. Beyond simply ideological or cultural appropriation, co-option is one of the mechanisms by which harmful systems can increase their legitimacy and thus their capacity to function efficiently. By viewing the official apology as an intimate mode of incorporation, the queer other can be confronted and neutralised by absorbing it into the dominant (heteronormative) order.

The apology makes clear that queer investments in policing are not simply emotional; they are also material. Material investments signal giving or devoting time and resources to something so that it might be sustained, strengthened, or expanded, with the intention of gaining something in return (Lamble 2013). The apology takes up the task of recruiting and sustaining LGBT involvement in the police project of 'fabricating social order', to borrow the words of policing scholar Mark Neocleous (2000). For instance, the police apology states:

> By developing a personalised approach with communities, by treating community members with fairness and respect, we will see a fall in crime as a result of active community cooperation. Not only will we reduce crime ... it is the right thing to do.

This is a misleading promise, as crime trends are notoriously complex social and political constructions, determined more by police and surveillance practices than actual rates of offending. Moreover, as the previous chapter argued, popular imaginaries of crime and disorder are anchored to conceptions and fears of individualised threats that fail to reckon with the institutionalised nature of heteronormativity that reproduces the stigmatisation and marginalisation that make queers the target of both interpersonal and systemic violence. Yet in the Tasty raid apology, proactive LGBT engagement in the police project is not simply a practical or utilitarian task that will elicit 'a fall in crime', but a moral one—'it is the right thing to do'. The idealised reimagining of policing as a benevolent or progressive project thus depends on LGBT labour and cooperation. The promise that is integral to the apology represents a deferral of responsibility for not repeating past mistakes, because it is constructed as *conditional* upon queer acquiescence and participation.

An 'ally in our journey for equality': LGBT responses and the legitimising functions of apology

The Tasty apology makes explicit its task of managing police image. For example, Nolan states: 'I want Victorians to look at police and see an organisation that both promotes and respects diversity'. The reworking of a public police identity—its revision and rebranding as a site of diversity, maturity, and progress—is a project that police are unlikely to achieve on their own. Instead, it involves willing audiences and collaborators. Goffman (1959) understood the process of impression management as a performance designed to influence those who observe it, to shape their perceptions. In other words, the audience must accept and reflect back the idealised image of the institutional self for the image project to be successful. Since shame frequently seeks to restore the damaged self in the eyes of the other, the performance of shame as enacted through the apology must be guided by the norms and goals of the specific social setting if it is to be accepted and affirmed by its audience (Bullock 2018). When managing public impressions, institutional actors present themselves based on the wider values and expectations associated with the character and qualities of the institution that they are aiming to portray. It follows, then, that 'a successful performance carries with it a moral claim; that is, a claim to the specific status which is conferred to, sanctioned and reinforced by the role being portrayed' (Bullock 2018, p. 2). The construction of an 'apologetic', self-reflexive, and caring police image, in this instance, is not monolithic, static, or necessarily consistent. The police image is rehearsed, refashioned, and reformed in accordance with specific situations and broader social contexts; it is also shaped by the reactions and assumptions of the audience to whom one is performing.

The responses of LGBT people in attendance at the police apology were exceedingly positive. When accepting and commenting on the apology, LGBT people overwhelmingly represented its significance through the use of *temporal* terms. Tasty patron Shaun Miller claimed the police apology as 'a wonderful milestone'; AVP Executive Director Greg Adkins stated that it marked 'a generational line in the sand'; and Tasty patron and lawyer Gary Singer labelled it 'the beginning of a new chapter' for police and the LGBT community (Victoria Police 2014). Long-time lesbian and gay advocate Jamie Gardiner suggested that the apology signalled 'a genuine time to move on, that there's a real regret and a real promise of a better future' (Riley 2014). In a speech following the apology, VGLRL's Anna Brown argued that the apology was a 'historical turning point', which demonstrates that Victoria Police 'has matured enough to face the darkness of the past' (Victoria Police 2014). She further stated that the LGBT community 'warmly welcomes this moment and this opportunity for transformation' (Victoria Police 2014).

If the formal apology is a claim to power and knowledge, it is affirmed and elevated in its reception, as LGBT representatives mark it as an event of profound historical significance. Here, LGBT recipients support and enact the cleansing aspect of apology as they wholeheartedly reflect back the idealised image of the institution. For example, in the article titled 'Tasty apology shines a light on a positive future', VGLRL co-conveners Anna Brown and Corey Irlam (2014) write that over the past 20 years:

> Victoria Police has worked hard to build our trust and confidence, developing a gay & lesbian liaison officer (GLLO) program, supporting diversity within the ranks of the police force, joining with us to say 'No To Homophobia' and joining with us to celebrate community events, such as marching in uniform at Pride March.

The article constructs a particular story about Victoria Police that is decidedly similar to the one narrated through the official apology. An organisation 'once viewed with fear and distrust', Victoria Police has now, according to Brown and Irlam (2014), become 'a key partner and ally in our journey for equality'. The developments they list are cast as evidence of institutional progress—again, credited to the goodwill and initiative of police leadership—and the impending arrival of a 'positive future' for LGBT people working in concert with the police. This conventional tale of progress—of moving from darkness to light—tidies up 'disorderly histories' as it reads 'a continuous narrative into one full of ruptures and contradictions' (Halberstam 2011, p. 15). Much like the discourse of apology, this neat account of the past romanticises policing as a site and tool for social justice. This simplified history of the present fails to account for not only the inconsistencies, contradictions, and 'backwards' steps in the policing of sexuality and gender, but also the LGBT activist labour involved in prompting and pressuring for such changes (Russell 2019)—the labour that is again being summoned to contribute to the 'brighter future' of policing.

Telling a story about the past is never a neutral exercise. History-telling is a highly political process, rife with subjective assumptions and selective inclusions. As Dan Stone (2003, p. 18, emphasis in original) argues, 'it is *how* we represent the past that determines how we feel its nearness, that is to say, how we make its absence into a presence'. History is constructed within discourse and is not pre-existing as a series of facts in and of itself. A normative concept of time—one that is segmented, measurable, regulatory, ordered, and coherent—is fundamental to the chronological narrative form. Yet, single and linear accounts of the past can have exclusionary effects, as 'transgressions from the official version of the past' are treated as 'taboo, which represses rational debate and ultimately favours the preservation of existing structures of power' (Toth 2014, p. 561). By interrogating the discourse of police apology (and LGBT responses to it), I am concerned with the ways in which histories are constructed, erased, normalised, and institutionalised. As Elisabeth Freeman (2005) argues, institutional and biopolitical power is exercised not only spatially—through borders, the designation and regulation of public and private zones, and various other forms of physical containment—but also temporally.

History is always partial and skewed, even if only because it is being constructed in the present. This does not mean that history is irrelevant or unimportant, nor that the biases in its construction render its use unethical or inherently misleading. Rather, engaging critically with history requires tuning into the power and knowledge relations that produce it. As Duncan Bell (2008, p. 149) argues:

> In attempting to grapple with ethical questions about the uses of the past it is vital to analyze the dynamics of popular historical consciousness and the ways in which particular 'collective memories' come to be formed and reproduced, the social and political roles they perform (whether intentionally or not), and the modes of inclusion and exclusion they sanction.

The story of institutional progress that emerges from this new ritual of apology—inclusive of the formal utterance itself and its acceptance—serves an important legitimising function for police. It helps to recast and rebrand police 'as protectors and defenders of gay liberties and homonormative life' (Russell 2018, p. 332) in order to encourage allegiance and cooperation with policing more broadly. In this instance, VGLRL mobilises queer labour, reputation, and resources in the service of police image, recuperating and aggrandising the reputation of the force through a teleological narrative of LGBT rights gains.

Although I am critical of both the police apology and immediate LGBT responses to it, this analysis requires some qualification. First, and as I mentioned earlier in the chapter, we cannot diminish or dismiss the symbolism of the apology for many individuals who experienced the violence of the raid. It is certainly possible that a formal apology (however conditional and limited) may provide a desired sense of closure and peace that is affirmed when the apology is accepted. Second, often when activists engage with mainstream and dominant media sources, they simplify more nuanced analyses in favour of more immediate tactical speech in order to persuade others of the importance of a particular issue or to achieve specific ends, such as more open communication and engagement from police leadership on LGBT issues and rights. In this instance, it is possible that LGBT responses to the apology used more simplistic terms of reference and established binaries ('from darkness to light' and so forth) to communicate directly and persuasively to police and, perhaps, to other LGBT people. Thus, we cannot attribute individual authorial intention to any one statement. We can, however, analyse the potential implications of such speech acts. As Mariana Valverde (2010) points out, tactical speech can create problems when these ideas and distinctions become 'elevated to the level of myth', which can have the effect of 'erasing all in-between possibilities', much like the tidy historical narrative I critique above.

Viewing LGBT responses to the apology as a form of tactical speech highlights the possibility that forgiveness may be less for 'unconditional purity' than for 'pragmatic, legal or political reasons, when a form of reconciliation is desired' (Mookherjee et al. 2009, p. 351). This pragmatism is evident in my interview with Sally Goldner, when we discussed the significance of the extensive volunteering she has done, training and educating police on LGBTI experiences, issues, and concerns:

> It's important, I suppose, if we are seeing this rise in anti-queerdom and the [broader political] shift to the right, that we do keep building the relationship with police, hopefully proactively, but if we can just get things onto a higher track. God, I'm sure we need to do everything [that we can] to prevent queerphobia, but if we can keep the police [on side, so that they are] there as a … bolster, so that if there is hate crime we've got somewhere safe to turn to, [through] which we can hopefully stamp it out. That's got to be happening too.
>
> …

ER: If this [LGBT–police] liaison work and this [police] training work stopped tomorrow, what's the risk then?

SG: Yikes! Oh, I shudder to think … I think the broader [political] context we're in at this time … we're now learning we can just never be complacent.

As a group historically targeted by police, LGBT activists in positions of relative and varying influence may seek inclusion, recognition, and protection from police in an attempt to mitigate against potential future violence and exclusion for their communities. There is a compromise though, whereby LGBT people must actively support

> the threat of force that lies on the other side of this tenuous promise [of inclusion, recognition, and protection], lest we slip (back) into the realm of the hated, the despised, the killable, and the disposable (that is, if we ever had a chance to leave).
>
> (Agathangelou et al. 2008, p. 129)

In other words, proactive LGBT support for policing emerges from a historical context of violent exclusion, which is not (and cannot ever be) firmly and strictly located solely in the past. As Angela Dwyer and Stephen Tomsen (2016) argue, the effort to delineate past from present is bound to be blurry and precarious, because the 'traces' of state violence cannot be erased or completely eradicated. These are the conditions in which LGBT people make political decisions and statements. This is not to imply that these choices are inevitable or predetermined, but to highlight the power imbalances and constraints that structure how LGBT people can and do engage with police in different arenas.

In other contexts, police efforts to cleanse themselves of a shameful past have been troubled by instances and circulations of negative affect among queer political formations, such as disappointment and refusal, in response to formal apologies. For instance, NSW Police Superintendent Tony Crandell issued a surprise apology in 2016 to six members of the 78ers committee (made up of activists from the 1978 protest now known as the first Mardi Gras) at a media conference 'for the way that the first Mardi Gras was policed back in 1978'. This gesture was labelled 'half an apology' by one of the 78ers, who argued that 'the Commissioner should have been the person to deliver it' (Power 2016b). Another committee member affirmed this view, stating 'we don't really accept [the apology] … we hoped the police would take the opportunity to apologise properly … the police needs [sic] to acknowledge how abusive and corrupt they were' (Power 2016b). In the same year, Toronto Police Chief Mark Saunders issued a formal apology for police raids on several gay bathhouses in 1981. The women's bathhouse committee rejected the apology, citing concerns about progress for some at the expense of others. As activist and committee member Chanelle Gallant (cited in Cecco 2016) argued:

> We didn't feel like it spoke to all of the issues that remain ... it leaves out the criminalization and violent targeting of racialized, indigenous and marginalized groups within and outside of LGBTQ communities. An apology is meaningless without concrete actions attached.

A 'climate of terror': queering official timelines

Thus far, I have argued that the ritual of formal apology is a practice of history-telling that has important power effects. While the police apology for the Tasty raid comprised a skewed and skeletal historical account, queer responses to it crafted and moulded the apology as a 'milestone' event in a teleological narrative of institutional progress in which the image of police was markedly detached from the social and historical role and function of policing. A critical examination of the use of temporal metaphors and tropes to attribute meaning within the discourse of formal apology highlights how power relations can be reproduced at multiple levels of history. Through the reconstruction of historical events and the circulation of linear narrative forms, queer histories and futures become bound up with—and risk being consumed by—institutional narratives of police progress. The temporal dimensions of the formal apology therefore have important implications not only for the institutional identity of police, but also for LGBT politics and, even more specifically, for the critical project of queer history-making. Does the utterance of an apology 'lead to an erasure of the past, a forgetting of the future? [And w]hat kinds of engagement or disengagement with the past(s) are necessary for forgiveness, apology and reconciliation?' (Mookherjee et al. 2009, p. 348).

One of the primary ways in which history is narrated, segmented, and ordered is through the construction and designation of *events* as discrete and impactful experiences that have the potential to disrupt and alter the established (political) order (Povinelli 2011, p. 71). Take, for instance, the idea that the apology 'marks the beginning of a new chapter', such that history can now be divided up as a result of this 'impactful event'. While events are often pronounced, *environments* are subtler in their influence, though no less important, for environments create 'the lenses through which actors view the world and the very categories of structure, action, and thought' (DiMaggio & Powell 1991, p. 13). Queer theorist Lauren Berlant (2011, p. 101) describes how an

> environment denotes a scene in which structural conditions are suffused through a variety of mediations, such as predictable repetitions and other spatial practices that might go under the radar or, in any case, not take up the form of event.

Contextualising events within environments reminds us that events are never isolated, but are products of specific historical conditions and forces.

This returns us to the production and determination of a historical event as worthy of apology (Mookherjee et al. 2009). How do we *define* what is shameful (or not) in the discourse of official apology? In this instance, police referred to a 'painful episode' that was seemingly inexplicable and without individual or collective agency—the 'events on that night' appeared to simply 'happen', rather than being designed, orchestrated, and carried out by police. The apology positioned the Tasty raid as a historical outlier, rather than an indicator or symptom of a deeply embedded culture of institutionalised homophobia. Yet, there were particular 'repetitions and other spatial practices' that went 'under the radar' and are thus harder to capture in the historical record.

Queer historical studies have taken up the task of showing that what has not entered the historical record is often encountered in other forms that are frequently relegated to non-rational or non-scientific realms, such as non-linear or circular narratives, embodied feelings, scars or ghosts (Cvetkovich 2003; Freeman 2007). In order to consider the subtler environment that preceded and surrounded the raid, I want to reflect upon an analysis that Jamie Gardiner developed in interview, when I asked him about the emergent trend in official apologies for LGBT people. He described the absence of reckoning with the 'climate of persecution', which does not take up the form of an event, but nevertheless powerfully shaped and mediated queer experiences. This environment appears unable to figure into the contemporary politics of recognition. Gardiner argues that it is this very background, mood, or fear that is not—or perhaps cannot be—captured in the state's attempts at closure:

> I guess the thing that we haven't adequately dealt with—generally, not just in this conversation—is the climate of persecution. One of the things I failed to get into the [historical homosexual convictions] expungement legislation was the specific acknowledgment of a climate of persecution, and that's also the thing that the police haven't quite acknowledged; like in the Tasty apology, for example … The climate of persecution was real and … the law was randomly [and] arbitrarily enforced, but it was a climate of terror. [It is] gradually lifting, but you know there are still people who are scared of the police—on this [basis]—lots of people are scared of the police on all sorts of grounds, but on this you feel the police are going to discriminate against [you] and be harsh and nasty, and probably there still are some [who do this]. But you don't need many instances of terror to make you terrified.[4]

Through this elaboration, Gardiner brings police agency back into the frame of queer history. He traces some of the continuities in police power and queer injustice. Rather than isolating state terror in the past, Gardiner highlights its lingering effects (and affects) that are felt in the present.

Human rights lawyer and LGBTI advocate Lee Carnie also provided a critical reading of the trend towards official apologies. In interview, Carnie reflected on the multiple levels of responsibility that an apology could and should involve, from the individual to the collective and the institutional:

> There's [an] institutional question as well about the role that the police force has played from a broader more societal level in terms of policing what is acceptable and what is unacceptable behaviour, and what is criminal behaviour and what is obscene behaviour, or what is offensive behaviour. And throughout history, LGBTI people's behaviour and their activism as well has been seen as breaching the peace, or causing a nuisance, or being offensive, or being immoral. And so, from an institutional level, I think that that's also really important.

Both Carnie's and Gardiner's comments are illustrative of the difficulties of capturing the subtler effects—and *affects*—of a punitive system of sexual and gender regulation that was not only proactively enforced by police, but reproduced by them. Gardiner condemns 'a climate of terror', while Carnie maps out the ways that system functioned to remake and uphold the boundaries of social and moral acceptability. Both analyses are reflective of not one *event* per se that is discrete and deemed apologisable, but an environment that is unbounded and pervasive. This affective environment is 'less visible and recognizable than legal statutes'; but it is nevertheless 'profoundly impactful in terms of differentially structuring LGBT subjectivities, experiences, and orientations to police, law, and society more broadly' (Russell 2019, p. 14).

Conclusion

In this chapter, I have argued for resisting the commonsensical urge to view official apologies as unambiguously good and socially progressive approaches to the past (Toth 2014). While the politics of regret might be morally and practically superior to the politics of denial or silence, 'political struggles and power games have an important part to play in the propagation of all of these strategies' (Toth 2014, p. 560). In other words, apologies are not morally pure or redemptive practices—they have important power effects. From the perspective of those systematically harmed or disadvantaged, an apology is not unequivocally good. Rather than being an altruistic gift or gesture towards the other, the formal apology foremost reflects and fortifies the identity of the powerful institution that issues it. Thus, it may do more to repair a damaged or outdated institutional image than it does to redress historical (and ongoing) injustice. Naming regret might simply make the institution feel better about itself, encouraging an over-identification with its inherent goodness.

I read Victoria Police's apology for the Tasty raid as a novel attempt to cleanse and redeem the institution of the negative image that resulted, in part, from the success of lesbian and gay club-goers in constructing an image of respectable citizenship and worthy victimhood following the raid. While the apology demonstrates a more reflexive and effective approach to securing a positive police image than strategies deployed by police in the 1990s, it does not necessarily repudiate homophobia, nor does it relinquish or lessen police power. In fact, it might actually strengthen institutional vitality and longevity. The 2014 apology reflects how police have refined their communications strategies and improved their public image, creating the conditions for not only a positive reception, but also the promotion of police as being 'on the side of equality' (Russell 2018). As a shameful past is transformed into a progressive present, queer pain is subsumed into the project of renovating the police image.

The recent spate of official apologies to LGBT people for past injustices supports the notion that the politics of regret have become the new grounds for legitimation (Olick 2007). They highlight how history—and our perception of it—powerfully shapes the present. History-telling coheres political identities and re-establishes material and *affective* citizenship structures—that is, a sense of belonging (Boon-Kuo et al. 2018). It can build allegiances and enact modes of inclusion, or it can recreate divisions and redraw lines of exclusion. When police and other state actors perform apologies, they revise and reconstruct queer histories in order to establish new 'norms' of conduct and discourse in relation to the past. The apology promotes a 'proper' orientation towards the past: one tinged with shame and regret, which paradoxically allows the state to reclaim moral capital and pride in the present. Queer apologia seeks to reconstruct the state as benevolently queer-inclusive through performances of 'closure' and the rhetoric of periodisation (namely, the end of a 'shameful' era). By firmly relegating and sealing queer injustice to the past, a progressive and 'modern' state emerges to claim a teleological narrative of progress that leads to a brighter future. While the future is promised, it is also tenuous and conditional, and thus has potential for governance: a brighter future awaits, at least if you do the right thing. The formal apology circulates a new historical narrative in which police and government leaders are cast as enlightened and humbled agents for progressive social change, yet queer resistance is absent. In this retelling of history, institutional change is inevitable, rather than the product of sustained social movement activity and initiative. Through the discourse of official apology, the shameful past becomes a source of pride in the power and superiority of the institution in the present.

Notes

1 In June 2018, Tony Crandell (now Assistant Commissioner of NSW Police) publicly reissued the apology on the 40th anniversary of the first Mardi Gras, when the 1978 protest was re-enacted in Sydney (Jones 2018).
2 Although the truth or 'reality' of what occurred in the past is often presumed to exist within the historical narrative form, narratives themselves cannot be simplistically regarded as factual or objective. Rather, they are a mode of explanation. History does not begin and end with facts; 'it must present a story' (Iggers & Wang 2008, p. 122).
3 After more than a decade of significant public pressure on the Australian government to formerly apologise for the past policy of forced removal of Aboriginal and Torres Strait Islander children, the newly elected Labor government headed by Prime Minister Kevin Rudd delivered the National Apology in 2008. It was self-consciously represented and received as a watershed moment, in which a 'great stain upon the nation's soul' was finally removed (Commonwealth of Australia 2008, p. 167).
4 Changes to the Victorian *Sentencing Act 1991* came into effect on 1 September 2015 that allow for the expungement (upon application) of historical convictions for homosexual activity that would not be a criminal offence today. The Department of Justice and Community Safety Victoria (2019) website states that eligible offences 'may include the type of criminal offences that were used to punish consensual homosexual sex between adults in the past, such as buggery, gross indecency with a male and loitering for homosexual purposes'. These changes were the result of significant campaigning by the Human Rights Law Centre and others affected by historical convictions. See Human Rights Law Centre (2014).

References

Agathangelou, AM, Bassichis, DM, & Spira, TL 2008, 'Intimate investments: Homonormativity, global lockdown, and the seductions of empire', *Radical History Review*, vol. 100, pp. 120–143.

Ahmed, S 2004, *The cultural politics of emotion*, Routledge, London.

Ahmed, S 2005, 'The politics of bad feelings', *Australian Critical Race and Whiteness Studies Association Journal*, vol. 1, pp. 72–85.

Ahmed, S 2010, *The promise of happiness*, Duke University Press, Durham. Bell, D 2008, 'Agonistic democracy and the politics of memory', *Constellations*, vol. 15, no. 1, pp. 148–166.

Bentley, T 2015, *Empires of remorse: Narrative, postcolonialism and apologies for colonial atrocity*, Routledge, Oxon.

Berlant, L 2011, *Cruel optimism*, Duke University Press, Durham and London.

Boon-Kuo, L, Meiners, ER, & Simpson, P 2018, 'Queer interruptions: Policing belonging in the carceral state', in P Aggleton, R Cover, D Leahy, D Marshall, & ML Rasmussen (eds), *Youth, sexuality and sexual citizenship*, Routledge, Oxon, pp. 34–49.

Brown, A & Irlam, C 2014, 'Tasty apology shines a light on a positive future', *Melbourne Community Voice*, 6 August, viewed 13 April 2015, http://gaynews-network.com.au/viewpoint/tasty-apology-shines-a-light-on-a-positive-future-14725.html.

Bullock, K 2018, '(Re)presenting "order" online: The construction of police presentational strategies on social media', *Policing and Society*, vol. 28, no. 3, pp. 345–359.

Cecco, L 2016, 'Activist on declining Toronto police apology for bathhouse raids', *Globe and Mail*, 24 June, viewed 17 September 2018, www.theglobeandmail.com/news/toronto/activist-on-declining-toronto-police-apology-for-1981-bathhouse-raids/article30615625/.

Cels, S 2014, 'Interpreting political apologies: The neglected role of performance', *Political Psychology*, vol. 36, no. 3, pp. 351–360.

Cohen, S 2001, *States of denial: Knowing about atrocities and suffering*, Polity Press, Cambridge.

Commonwealth of Australia, House of Representatives 2008, *Parliamentary Debates*, 13 February 2008, p. 167.

Cvetkovich, A 2003, *An archive of feelings: Trauma, sexuality, and lesbian public cultures*, Duke University Press, Durham.

Department of Justice and Community Safety Victoria 2019, 'Expungement scheme', *Justice System*, State of Victoria, 15 January 2019, viewed 19 February 2019, www.justice.vic.gov.au/justice-system/laws-and-regulation/criminal-law/expungement-scheme.

DiMaggio, PJ & Powell, WW 1991, 'Introduction', in WW Powell & PJ DiMaggio (eds), *The new institutionalism in organisational analysis*, University of Chicago Press, Chicago, pp. 1–38.

Dwyer, A & Tomsen, S 2016, 'The past is the past? The impossibility of erasure of historical LGBTIQ policing', in A Dwyer, M Ball, & T Crofts (eds), *Queering criminology*, Palgrave Macmillan, London, pp. 36–53.

Edworthy, J, Hellier, E, & Rivers, J 2003, 'The use of male or female voices in warnings systems: A question of acoustics', *Noise and Health*, vol. 6, no. 21, pp. 39–50.

Feiler, B 2010, 'Turn right, my love', *New York Times*, 10 June, viewed 9 March 2018, www.nytimes.com/2010/06/27/fashion/27FamilyMatters.html.

Ferguson, RA 2008, 'Administering sexuality; or, the will to institutionality', *Radical History Review*, vol. 100, pp. 158–169.

Foucault, M 1972, *The archaeology of knowledge*, trans. AMS Smith, Routledge, London.

Freeman, E 2005, 'Time binds, or, erotohistoriography', *Social Text*, vol. 23, no. 3–4 (84–85), pp. 57–68.

Freeman, E 2007, 'Introduction', *GLQ*, vol. 13, no. 2–3, pp. 159–176.

Gibney, M, Howard-Hassmann, RE, Coicaud, J.-M, & Steiner, N 2008, *The age of apology: Facing up to the past*, University of Pennsylvania Press, Philadelphia.

Goffman, E 1959, *The presentation of self in everyday life*, Doubleday, New York.

Halberstam, J 2011, *The queer art of failure*, Duke University Press, Durham.

Human Rights Law Centre (HRLC) 2014, 'Righting historical wrongs: Background paper for a legislative scheme to expunge convictions for historical consensual gay sex offences in Victoria', HRLC, Melbourne, viewed 8 May 2015, www.hrlc.org.au/reports/righting-historical-wrongs-background-paper-for-a-legislative-scheme-to-expunge-convictions-for-historical-consensual-gay-sex-offences-in-victoria.

Iggers, GG & Wang, QE 2008, *A global history of modern historiography*, Pearson Education Limited, Harlow.

Jones, J 2018, 'NSW police apologise to '78ers on Mardi Gras anniversary', *Star Observer*, 25 June, viewed 17 September 2018, www.starobserver.com.au/news/national-news/new-south-wales-news/nsw-police-apologise-lgbti-persecution/169836.

Kanngieser, A 2012, 'A sonic geography of voice: Towards an affective politics of voice', *Progress in Human Geography*, vol. 36, no. 3, pp. 336–353.

Lamble, S 2013, 'Queer necropolitics and the expanding carceral state: Interrogating sexual investments in punishment', *Law Critique*, vol. 24, no. 3, pp. 229–253.

Lee, M & McGovern, A 2014, *Policing and media: Public relations, simulations and communications*, Routledge, Oxon.

Mookherjee, N, Rapport, N, Josephides, L, Hage, G, Todd, LR, & Cowlishaw, G 2009, 'The ethics of apology: A set of commentaries', *Critique of Anthropology*, vol. 29, no. 3, pp. 345–366.

Moreton-Robinson, A 2000, *Talkin' up to the white woman: Indigenous women and feminism*, University of Queensland Press, St Lucia.

Muldoon, P 2017, 'A reconciliation most desirable: Shame, narcissism, justice and apology', *International Political Science Review*, vol. 38, no. 2, pp. 213–226.

Neocleous, M 2000, *The fabrication of social order: A critical theory of police power*, Pluto Press, London.

Niccol, F 2000, 'Indigenous sovereignty and the violence of perspective: A white woman's coming out story', *Australian Feminist Studies*, vol. 15, no. 33, pp. 369–386.

Olick, JK 2007, *The politics of regret: On collective memory and historical responsibility*, Routledge, New York.

Povinelli, EA 2011, *Economies of abandonment: Social belonging and endurance in late liberalism*, Duke University Press, Durham.

Power, S 2016a, 'Legacy of Mardi Gras founders the 78ers celebrated during NSW government apology', *Star Observer*, 25 February, viewed 17 September 2018, www.starobserver.com.au/news/national-news/new-south-wales-news/legacy-of-mardi-gras-founders-the-78ers-celebrated-during-nsw-government-apology/146445.

Power, S 2016b, 'NSW police apology for brutality in 1978 Mardi Gras not good enough: 78ers', *Star Observer*, 4 March, viewed 17 September 2018, www.starobserver.com.au/news/national-news/new-south-wales-news/nsw-police-apology-for-brutality-in-1978-mardi-gras-not-good-enough-78ers/147110.

Puar, JK 2012, 'Coda the cost of getting better: Suicide, sensation, switchpoints', *GLQ*, vol. 18, no. 1, pp. 149–158.

Riley, B 2014, 'We're sorry: Victoria police apologise for Tasty gay nightclub raid 20 years on', *Star Observer*, 5 August, viewed 7 October 2014, www.starobserver.com.au/news/local-news/victoria-news/were-sorry-victoria-police-apologise-for-tasty-gay-nightclub-raid-20-years-ago/126066.

Russell, EK 2018, 'Carceral pride: The fusion of police imagery with LGBTI rights', *Feminist Legal Studies*, vol. 26, no. 3, pp. 331–350.

Russell, EK 2019, 'Ambivalent investments: lessons from LGBTIQ efforts to reform policing', *Current Issues in Criminal Justice*, viewed 19 June 2019, www.tandfonline.com/doi/full/10.1080/10345329.2019.1623969

Stone, D 2003, *Constructing the Holocaust: A study in historiography*, Vallentine Mitchell, London.

Toth, M 2014, 'The myth of the politics of regret', *Millennium*, vol. 43, no. 2, pp. 551–566.
Valverde, M 2010, 'Practices of citizenship and scales of governance', *New Criminal Law Review*, vol. 13, no. 2, pp. 216–240.
Victoria Police 2014, *Victoria Police issue Tasty nightclub apology*, online video, 4 August, viewed 13 April 2015, www.youtube.com/watch?v=WvS0eFqiPE4.

Chapter 8

Afterword

Police power, queer resistance

I first presented on the drawbacks of using a narrative arc of progressive change to tell histories of policing queerness at an Australian Critical Criminology conference in 2012. I was only six months into my PhD research on LGBT–police relations in Victoria and I was new to academic conferences; I was also unsure of who would be in the room. After I and the other presenter in the session had finished delivering our papers, the first question from the audience came from a man in plain clothes who identified himself as a police officer. He explained to the room that there was a problem of competing meanings and agendas: when queer researchers and advocates use the term 'community policing', police think 'intelligence gathering'. It was a brazen admission of police interests in forming closer relationships with marginalised communities and one that, in my mind, confirmed some of the key limits of new reform initiatives in policing. LGBT and police 'partnerships' proceed from a fundamentally unequal basis, as police have significant power and the capacity to use invasive means and coercive force to curb and control any 'deviance' or resistance to the status quo. While the purpose of policing is to secure the existing social order, queers have typically sought to challenge it.

This book has explored the shifting contours of sexual citizenship as LGBT rights campaigns have challenged, altered, and buttressed systems of policing and law. I have shown how policing—as material practice, institution, and discourse—is reshaping sexual citizenship. Policing is not simply a top-down exercise that operates solely through repression and exclusion; it is deeply tied to modes of social production. In this sense, policing is no longer simply a site for the reproduction of queer deviancy, pathology, and criminality. Indeed, policing now also operates as a method for the reproduction of respectable and innocent sexual and gender identities that are seen as deserving of visibility, recognition, and protection. Policing and the criminal legal system more broadly are thus central to the conceptualisation and organisation of LGBT rights claims, as they are increasingly articulated and imagined through the logics of 'carceral protection' (Musto 2016). As the most respectable LGBT identities are brought into the fold of the state, 'our' lives are differentiated from those deemed unworthy or ineligible for state protection, those who threaten to bring the image of the law-abiding queer citizen into disrepute and return us to the realm of 'the despised … and the disposable' (Agathangelou et al. 2008, p. 129). In short, moves towards inclusion always require redrawing the boundaries of exclusion. The idea of escaping the historically embedded imaginaries of queer criminality, sickness, and perversion—and the punitive treatment that they elicit—is all the more desirable and powerful because of its impossibility. The past can never be entirely erased (Dwyer & Tomsen 2016).

While policing helps to mark the parameters of homonormative life, discourses of LGBT rights now also serve as a platform for the reimagining of police as a force for social justice. The story told through these chapters affirms that policing is a durable institution that can adapt and expand, absorb queer critiques, and repackage and retell violent histories as stories of social advancement and institutional maturity. The dynamism of policing as an institution therefore enables it to maintain power and legitimacy. New discourses and imagery of 'police pride' alter traditional views of police as a homophobic institution—not by forgetting antagonistic or shameful histories, but by revising them as a necessary part of an institutional progress narrative. The legitimacy that police gain through this process complicates the task of challenging injustice, because the powerful proclaim to be on the side of the weak while maintaining or building a position of dominance. Thus, paradoxically, LGBT rights discourses may bolster the power of an institution that has long functioned to shore up the 'proper' boundaries of normative sexuality and gender. For instance, in her research on young queer experiences with police in Australia, Dwyer (2015) describes how policing acts as a 'pedagogical' encounter for queer youth, insofar as policing 'teaches' them how to minimise the qualities, presentations, and mannerisms that are viewed as 'excessively queer' in order to avoid violent state incursions on their bodies or spaces. This highlights the capacity of policing to patrol and harden the borders of 'belonging' (Boon-Kuo et al. 2018) and reinforces the productive and regulatory aspects of police power.

Importantly, there is a growing international dialogue about the ways in which sexual and gender difference is being incorporated into hegemonic apparatuses (Haritaworn et al. 2014). Through a localised study, *Queer Histories and the Politics of Policing* contributes to these efforts to deepen understandings of sexual and gender politics as they evolve in increasingly punitive climates. For instance, the emergence of the hate crime paradigm has offered LGBT anti-violence campaigns unique opportunities for garnering institutional support and pressuring for policy and legal change within a broader context of rapid growth in policing and punishment industries. We live in a time of 'hyperincarceration' (Wacquant 2010), in which the prison looms large for the most marginalised and disadvantaged members of our communities: First Nations, those who are disabled, homeless, gender non-conforming, or otherwise negatively racialised (Cunneen et al. 2013). Although the analysis of the sexual and gender politics of policing in this book might seem somewhat removed from the 'pointy end' of the carceral state that the prison represents, such a view elides the ideologies and materialities of punishment that underpin policing and criminal law. As Chapter 2 established, police are far from a neutral or benign force. The challenge is to place both the 'celebratory' and 'somber' images of the new 'gay-friendly' police force, as captured in Chapters 5 and 7, within a continuum of state violence and strategies of 'pacification' (Linnemann 2017; Neocleous 2011). The task is to recognise the ways in which police power may have been reworked but not reduced in the period between the Tasty raid, for example, and the official police apology for it. While the former is constructed as the 'bad policing of the past' and the latter as 'a new era' of LGBT-police relations, in both instances police succeed in erasing collective queer resistance, recentring the institution of policing, and sidestepping accountability. Police narration of queer histories is typically self-serving; it impoverishes our understanding of the past and restricts the political possibilities that might flow from it in the present.

The renovated public image of police as 'gay-friendly' is a strategic approach to the maintenance of police legitimacy in the face of a legacy of lesbian and gay liberationist and radical queer and trans activism that has exposed the oppressive functions of policing. Yet, throughout this book, I have argued that institutional recognition is steeped in conditionality. As queers are now being called forth to forgive the state's errors and affirm its version of historical events, the promise of a brighter future rests upon our renewed commitments to the carceral logics of crime control, even as the practical capacities of police to provide or offer queer safety are minimal. Policing is ultimately a reactive, individualised, and punitive response to the complex social forces and issues that manifest interpersonal violence. Moreover, the promise of protection does not extend to all queers. Many LGBT people continue to experience criminalisation and LGBT experiences of policing differ along lines of gender, race, and ability. For example, a recent community survey conducted by the Victorian Gay and Lesbian Rights Lobby (2017) found that LGBT accounts of past experiences with police were 'evenly split' between positive and negative encounters, but that respondents who identified as trans or gender-diverse, non-white, and/or living with a disability were more likely to report a negative experience with police than a positive one. Evidently, the category 'LGBT' does not signify a homogenous or equivalent experience, and grouping these sexual and gender identities together risks glossing over the inequalities among us.

The concepts of homonormativity and homonationalism have been hotly debated within gender and sexuality studies, yet they have barely begun to be considered in queer criminology. *Queer Histories and the Politics of Policing* has examined some of the ways in which citizenship gains premised on homonormative performances of identity might come at the cost of 'seclusion' from 'those whose queerness appears excessive' (Harris 2006, p. 209) and those otherwise deemed 'undeserving' for reasons of poverty, gender non-conformity, and cultural difference. While the politics of respectability have enabled select lesbian and gay (and, less often, trans) subjects to gain recognition and legitimacy, this gradual and uneven move into the fold of the state appears to leave many behind—the queer sex workers and beat-users, the homeless, and criminalised queer and trans youth. As Gail Mason (2014, p. 79) argues in relation to hate crime laws, 'victims who are [viewed as] troublesome, distasteful, trivial or engaged in risky behavior are far less likely to be accorded legitimacy'. Although sexual and gender outlaws have historically attracted many of these labels and thus been located distinctly on the 'wrong' side of policing and punishment systems, we have witnessed a recalibration of the terms and criteria for belonging as sexual citizens. Without underestimating the power and pervasiveness of heteronormativity, these shifting criteria for belonging remind us that the imagined category of 'good queer citizenship' is ultimately unstable and far from simplistic. Privilege and oppression are not static or inherent to particular subject locations (McCall 2005). While historically and materially important, racial, gender, and sexual hierarchies are also socially produced and thus always negotiated, relative, and context-specific. The various discourses and representational practices that reproduce categories of identity must therefore be approached as embedded in specific local and historical contexts.

While this book highlights many of the risks, compromises, and problems associated with collaborating with and supporting the police project, it should not be taken to suggest that refusal to engage with the state is the only way to ensure ethical or inclusive activist practice. Since the emergence of a modern lesbian and gay movement in Australia, activists have been forced to strategically negotiate the contradictions of their representative practices and reform goals (Pendleton & Serisier 2009; Reynolds 2002). There are also historical examples of LGBT engagement with the state that have yielded positive and productive outcomes for many community members, in particular the negotiated public health efforts to prevent the spread of HIV/AIDS in the 1980s in Australia (Power 2011). I am not suggesting that the fold of the state is inherently dangerous for social justice movements. Rather, the point is to carefully weigh up the benefits and risks of particular activist strategies and framing devices by considering the lessons of history and how they inform power relations in the present. I also do not intend to cast doubt upon the intentions of activists and advocates to create positive change for LGBT people through the pursuit of criminal justice reform. As many have pointed out before me, intention does not equal effect, and there is a range of possible outcomes from any given campaign or strategy—many of them unexpected.

The decisions made in carrying out this research inevitably leave various lines of inquiry about queer history and policing unexplored. Theoretically, the central task of this book has been the development of frameworks through which to critique queer 'investments' in policing and law (Lamble 2013) by way of deepening understandings of the multifaceted and enduring nature of police power and of the normative pressures pressing upon LGBT lives, identities, and politics. However, this work also prompts questions about alternative possibilities and trajectories for reimagining queer safety and solidarity. Queer contestations, such as those documented in Chapter 4, remind us that the dominant liberal rights-based frameworks of sexual and gender identity-based movements are neither inevitable nor totalising. While there is a consistent 'push-pull' into the fold of the state, there continues to be organised queer resistance to this normative trajectory. Not all LGBT people view inclusion as inherently positive and desirable and police continue to confront considerable wariness, distrust, and unrest from queer quarters (Lamusse 2016). In light of the many failures and harms of punitive and carceral systems, LGBT people have explored and are exploring ways to decrease our reliance on them, rather than build them up (Chen et al. 2011). How might we imagine and pursue queer safety differently? What kind of demands for queer safety resist shoring up violent systems? How might we stake rights claims without reinforcing the ideas of respectability that have excluded and oppressed queers for so long and without further marginalising other experiences, identities, and ways of knowing sexuality and gender?

As a queer criminological text, this book issues a broader challenge to the discipline of criminology. It is a call to question the production of 'official time lines' and simplistic dichotomies for the exclusions that they engender and the complexities that they gloss over. Rather than tease out the 'good' police practices and strategies from the 'bad', a critical and historical queer optic allows us to appreciate the mutual constitution and interdependence of these categories, the slippages and continuities between them in practice, and the powerful forces that reproduce and circulate them. Rather than view the uneven and coercive effects of policing as products of the actions of biased, deficient, or ill-equipped individual officers, we should broaden our analytical framework to account for the historical genesis of policing as a heteronormative and settler colonial project. This reminds us of the importance of preventing (and pursuing accountability for) the immediate harms of policing and punishment—whether as activists or scholars—without getting swept up in the administration of these systems and therefore invested in their continuity. Instead, we might consider strategies to demilitarise and disempower police (McDowell & Fernandez 2018), as well as dedicating more resources towards exploring community-based responses to harm (Kim 2018). As an emerging field of study seeking to distinguish itself from 'mainstream' criminology, queer criminology has much to benefit from engagement with abolitionist and anti-carceral feminist thinking (Carlton & Russell 2018;

Stanley & Smith 2011; Thuma 2015). We must remain attuned to the violence that underpins the state's promise of protection. Rather than accepting it at face value that the incorporation of previously excluded groups signifies historical progress and positive change, this book has sought to illustrate the exclusive and regulatory effects of the politics of recognition.

My hope is that the narrative presented in this book sparks new questions about the relationship between sexual and gender politics and police power. The surface support for LGBT rights amongst police leaders might indicate success on some levels for LGBT activists who have long fought for queers to be seen as other than criminal and to have access to state protection when it is needed or desired. However, the adoption of LGBT rights language and symbols in by police public relations produces ambivalence and hostility towards police within LGBT movements (Russell 2019). Evolving LGBT-police relations prompt renewed discussion about the role and effects of policing in society, for queers and others. *Queer Histories and the Politics of Policing* has sought to make sense of contemporary strategies of governing sexuality and gender—the histories from which they emerge and the futures they foreclose—and the threads of resistance running through them.

References

Agathangelou, AM, Bassichis, DM, & Spira, TL 2008, 'Intimate investments: Homonormativity, global lockdown, and the seductions of empire', *Radical History Review*, vol. 100, pp. 120–143.

Boon-Kuo, L, Meiners, ER, & Simpson, P 2018, 'Queer interruptions: Policing belonging in the carceral state', in P Aggleton, R Cover, D Leahy, D Marshall, & ML Rasmussen (eds), *Youth, sexuality and sexual citizenship*, Routledge, Oxon, pp. 34–49.

Carlton, B & Russell, E 2018, *Resisting carceral violence: Women's imprisonment and the politics of abolition*, Palgrave, Switzerland.

Chen, C.-I, Dulani, J, & Piepzna-Samarasinha, LL 2011, *The revolution starts at home: Confronting intimate violence within activist communities*, South End Press, Brooklyn.

Cunneen, C, Baldry, E, Brown, D, Brown, M, Schwartz, M, & Steel, A 2013, *Penal culture and hyperincarceration: The revival of the prison*, Ashgate, Surrey.

Dwyer, A 2015, 'Teaching young queers a lesson: How police teach lessons about non-heteronormativity in public spaces', *Sexuality and Culture*, vol. 19, no. 3, pp. 493–512.

Dwyer, A & Tomsen, S 2016, 'The past is the past? The impossibility of erasure of historical LGBTIQ policing', in A Dwyer, M Ball, & T Crofts (eds), *Queering criminology*, Palgrave Macmillan, London, pp. 36–53.

Haritaworn, J, Kuntsman, A, & Posocco, S 2014, *Queer necropolitics*, Routledge, Oxfordshire.

Harris, AP 2006, 'From Stonewall to the suburbs? Toward a political economy of sexuality', *William and Mary Bill of Rights Journal*, vol. 14, pp. 1539–1582.

Kim, ME 2018, 'From carceral feminism to transformative justice: Women-of-color feminism and alternatives to incarceration', *Journal of Ethnic & Cultural Diversity in Social Work*, vol. 27, no. 3, pp. 219–233.

Lamble, S 2013, 'Queer necropolitics and the expanding carceral state: Interrogating sexual investments in punishment', *Law Critique*, vol. 24, no. 3, pp. 229–253.

Lamusse, T 2016, 'Politics at pride?', *New Zealand Sociology*, vol. 31, no. 6, pp. 49–70.

Linnemann, T 2017, 'In plain view: Violence and the police image', in M Brown & E Carrabine (eds), *International handbook of visual criminology*, Routledge, London, pp. 243–254.

Mason, G 2014, 'The symbolic purpose of hate crime law: Ideal victims and emotion', *Theoretical Criminology*, vol. 18, no. 1, pp. 75–92.

McCall, L 2005, 'The complexity of intersectionality', *Signs: Journal of Women in Culture and Society*, vol. 30, no. 3, pp. 1771–1800.

McDowell, MG & Fernandez, LA 2018, '"Disband, disempower, and disarm": Amplifying the theory and practice of police abolition', *Critical Criminology*, vol. 26, no. 3, pp. 373–391.

Musto, J 2016, *Control and protect: Collaboration, carceral protection, and domestic sex trafficking in the United States*, University of California Press, Oakland.

Neocleous, M 2011, '"A brighter and nicer new life": Security as pacification', *Social & Legal Studies*, vol. 20, no. 2, pp. 191–208.

Pendleton, M & Serisier, T 2009, 'Beyond the desire for law: Sex and crisis in Australian feminist and queer politics', *The Australian Feminist Law Journal*, vol. 31, pp. 77–98.

Power, J 2011, *Movement, knowledge, emotion: Gay activism and HIV/AIDS in Australia*, ANU E Press, Canberra.

Reynolds, R 2002, *From camp to queer: Remaking the Australian homosexual*, Melbourne University Press, Carlton.

Russell, EK 2019, 'Ambivalent investments: lessons from LGBTIQ efforts to reform policing', *Current Issues in Criminal Justice*, viewed 19 June 2019, www.tandfonline.com/doi/full/10.1080/10345329.2019.1623969

Stanley, EA & Smith, N 2011, *Captive genders: Trans embodiment and the prison industrial complex*, AK Press, Oakland.

Thuma, E 2019, *All our trials: Prisons, policing, and the feminist fight to end violence*, University of Illinois Press, Urbana.

Victorian Gay and Lesbian Rights Lobby (VGLRL) 2017, *Community survey 2017: Perceptions and experiences of Victoria Police*, Victorian Gay and Lesbian Rights Lobby (VGLRL), Melbourne.

Wacquant, L 2010, 'Class, race and hyperincarceration in revanchist America', *Daedalus*, vol. 140, no. 3, pp. 74–90.

Index

Note: Page numbers followed by "n" denote endnotes.

For Product Safety Concerns and Information please contact our EU representative GPSR@taylorandfrancis.com
Taylor & Francis Verlag GmbH, Kaufingerstraße 24, 80331 München, Germany

www.ingramcontent.com/pod-product-compliance
Ingram Content Group UK Ltd.
Pitfield, Milton Keynes, MK11 3LW, UK
UKHW011017180926
475701UK00004B/789
9780367784287